ASSESSING
STUDENT
PERFORMANCE

◆ ◆ ◆

Grant P. Wiggins

◆ ◆ ◆

ASSESSING STUDENT PERFORMANCE

Exploring the Purpose and Limits of Testing

Jossey-Bass Publishers • San Francisco

Portions of Chapter Eight are reprinted from Wiggins, Grant (February 1991), "Standards, Not Standardization: Evoking Quality Student Work," *Educational Leadership*, pp. 18–25, with permission of the Association for Supervision and Curriculum Development. Copyright 1991 by ASCD.

Substantial discounts on bulk quantities of Jossey-Bass books are available to corporations, professional associations, and other organizations. For details and discount information, contact the special sales department at Jossey-Bass Inc., Publishers. (415) 433-1740; Fax (415) 433-0499.

For international orders, please contact your local Paramount Publishing International office.

Manufactured in the United States of America. Nearly all Jossey-Bass books and jackets are printed on recycled paper that contains at least 50 percent recycled waste, including 10 percent postconsumer waste. Many of our materials are also printed with vegetable-based ink; during the printing process these inks emit fewer volatile organic compounds (VOCs) than petroleum-based inks. VOCs contribute to the formation of smog.

Library of Congress Cataloging-in-Publication Data

Wiggins, Grant P., date.
    Assessing student performance : exploring the purpose and limits of testing / Grant P. Wiggins.
       p.   cm.—(The Jossey-Bass education series)
    Includes bibliographical references (p.) and index.
    ISBN 1-55542-592-5
    1. Educational tests and measurements—United States. I. Title.
II. Series.
    LB3051.W494   1993
    371.2′64—dc20   93-29490
                                                   CIP

FIRST EDITION
HB Printing   10 9 8 7 6 5 4 3 2   *Code 9393*

◆ ◆ ◆

THE JOSSEY-BASS
EDUCATION SERIES

◆ ◆ ◆

Contents

♦ ♦ ♦

PREFACE

♦ ♦ ♦

This book has been five years, three different topics, and two different drafts in the making. In 1988, the drive to reform testing was just under way. The few of us who were describing the kinds of overhauls we thought necessary to make testing better serve learning were still whistling in the wind (though the laments and recommendations were as old as testing itself). The technical community was by and large treating us with polite indifference. Hard-boiled assistant superintendents were saying, "Nice ideas, but. . . ." In that climate, I was asked by Jossey-Bass Publishers to write a book justifying the development and use of "alternative" forms of testing— a book that would include emerging samples, feasible ideas, and design tips.

That was then; this is now. Alternative assessment rapidly became a prime topic of discussion at the national, state, and local levels. States such as California, Kentucky, and Vermont began to design and implement performance and portfolio requirements. Districts began to develop portfolios in K–12 language arts, in elementary science, and for high school graduation. And many teachers across America began dozens of experiments with performance-based forms of assessment.

The point of the original book became moot, in short. So for a long while the ideas lay fallow, and a topic for a book (at least one that I wanted to write) became less and less clear. Jossey-Bass, with my okay, assigned a developmental editor to the project. Two months later, a complete manuscript came to me from the editor, pasted together out of my old papers and articles. I was galvanized— because this was the sort of book I did *not* want to write, even though the manuscript was well done and reflected my earlier thinking.

On a warm July afternoon, I took a long walk around the village where I live, pondering what to do. By the downhill stretch toward home, I was suddenly clear about the book I wanted to write: a more "radical" book (in the sense of "going to the roots") concerning inchoate ideas about the very act of testing itself. Thanks to the patient support of Lesley Iura at Jossey-Bass, I started again— from scratch.

The purpose of this book, then, is to consider what testing should involve if the students' intellectual and moral interests are primary. In terms of the book's scope, I try to do the impossible here: talk about both the micro and macro worlds of educational testing and assessment—the individual classroom and the country as a whole. The book is written for teachers, school administrators with curriculum and testing responsibilities, professors of courses in curriculum and measurement, psychometricians and test developers at the state and national level, and policy makers—anyone with a stake in better testing. Ambitious? Yes. Necessary? Yes, because we are in the grip of too many unthinking and harmful habits related to testing of all kinds at all levels in education. This book is a very modest attempt at examining the unexamined. I leave it to the reader to judge the adequacy of the formulation of the problems and my efforts in addressing them.

The reader might well view this book as expounding a philosophy of student assessment. Why a "philosophy" of student assessment? Philosophy brings unthinking habits to the surface; it clarifies conceptual confusion in common practices and talk. And there are just too many unexamined habits and confused ideas about testing, whether we look at nationally given tests or teacher-designed tests.

The questions raised in this book are thus more moral and epistemological than technical and political. What do we mean by *mastery?* What justifications exist for how we grade the way we do? What is feedback? How can unrelenting secrecy in testing be justified? These and other questions are *logically prior* to the design and implementation of testing. The questions need to be asked because the student is at a moral disadvantage in all traditional testing and because the operant definition of *mastery*, which can be inferred from how and what we test, is impoverished.

It was Nietzsche who argued in *Beyond Good and Evil* that *all* philosophies are really unwitting autobiographies. My own educational biography bears witness to this. As impossible as it sounds, I cannot remember taking more than eight or nine multiple-choice tests of *any* kind, from kindergarten to graduate school. (Of the national kind, I have taken only the PSATs, the SATs [both aptitude and achievement tests], and the GREs, including a ludicrous one in philosophy: "Descartes's discussion of the wax in the *Meditations* proves a., b., c., d. . . .").

My unorthodox education is surely woven through many of these pages. It may help to know that I attended this assortment of schools: a one-room school in Mexico City called Edron Academy— named after Ed and Ron—where all our work was self-paced and project-oriented; the International School in Geneva, home of the International Baccalaureate; a fine Connecticut independent boarding school, where I *never once* in four years saw a multiple-choice test; a Great Books College (St. John's in Annapolis, Maryland), where we had only oral exams and papers that were meant to yield thoughtful analysis (as opposed to footnote-laden rehashes of the professor's ideas); and Harvard, where my graduate adviser always distributed exam questions in advance for study and discussion. In short, I had a wonderful and unusual education. I know from experience that simplistic testing is not necessary for and may well be harmful to a proper education. I also spent most of my graduate school years working on moral development and research issues with Carol Gilligan and writing my dissertation on "critical thinking." It stands to reason, then, that I would want to look at testing from an atypical critical vantage point and (thanks to my work with Gilligan) in a way that gives better "voice" to the student. (Carol also helped me find my voice as a writer.)

I also take from Nietzsche the unending desire to provoke thought in my writing. I am wont to consider and to ask others to consider the perpetually unexamined. This book should therefore be understood as primarily a provocation, not an exhaustive account of the issues.

Overview of the Contents

The book is an investigation of our long-standing habit in this country of testing students once and superficially, while failing to consider the value provided by and harm resulting from the practice. I assume two postulates: student assessment should improve performance, not just monitor or audit it, and testing should be only a small facet of assessment. With these postulates I present a series of arguments concerning the intellectual and moral harm of testing, if we follow the principle that the performer's needs are primary.

The first chapter lays out the issues: What is assessment and how does testing differ from it? What are the inherent limits of testing? How might we better "test our tests" beyond the technical standards that now apply? (These standards tell you how to test; they don't tell you when to test. They tell you how to design valid and reliable tests but not how to gauge the shortcomings of merely efficient tests.) I summarize the problems of the current official standards of testing and how little they protect students' interests, and why we can profit from a review of the legal challenges to test data, especially in adult testing, over the last thirty years.

The second chapter maps out the intellectual problem: Given any robust and meaningful definition of the aim of the liberal arts—a deep understanding of things—what follows for testing? Various dilemmas and postulates are laid out to show how compromise is inevitable but how it might be better negotiated to support the liberal arts. Particular emphasis is placed on the need for assessment that more closely examines a student's habit of mind, something not discernible from traditional items.

The third, fourth, and fifth chapters explore the more obvious moral issues that surround testing but are rarely discussed: secrecy, incentives/disincentives that are built into our common methods of testing, and the assessor's obligation to be tactful and responsive—neither of which is permitted by traditional test practices. The argument can be summarized as follows: the tester has a more substantial obligation than recognized or honored at present to minimize the use of practices that may make testing easier but make student performance and self-assessment more difficult.

The sixth chapter, on feedback, is the first of two chapters in which a discussion of validity, authenticity, and fairness are approached. If performance is improved by feedback, what obligations do testers have to provide more of it and to provide it during a test (since in real performance feedback is always available, causing us often to adjust performance while doing the task at hand)? Feedback is thus not merely a requirement to inform students of results and their meanings, but a contextual requirement of valid assessment of performance. (The student's use of feedback becomes part of the assessment).

The seventh chapter is the longest and the most technically complex: an analysis of traditional arguments about test validity, and why traditional validation methods are inadequate; what role "authenticity" should play in design, and why job analysis must be a part of test validation; and why traditional testing folks do not grasp that the problem is more than "face validity." The argument is made, citing a long history of research, that tests are rarely validated against adult performance challenges in context, rather, they are validated against other similar tests or college grades. Secondly, the chapter picks up the thread of Chapter Five to explain why context matters in using and demonstrating knowledge, and why, therefore, decontextualized testing is so problematic. Finally, the chapter reminds the reader that situational testing has a long history and that many distinguished psychometricians have been concerned about the limits of traditional validation through correlations with similar tests.

The eighth and last chapter is a discussion of why more testing, especially at state and national levels cannot, *in principle*, provide better accountability. Because accountability is dependent on school responsiveness to parent and student consumers, standardized testing reform has little to do with whether schools are more responsive to parent, student, alumni, or "institutional customer" concerns.

Acknowledgments

This book would not have been conceived or written if Ted Sizer had not seen fit to dump the "exhibition of mastery" problem in my lap when the Coalition of Essential Schools was still a small project based at Brown University and involved seven high schools. He and Holly Houston (then the executive director and now my partner in the professional and familial sense) had the confidence in me to say, in effect, Here: see what you can make of this idea. Ted gave me not merely the idea of diploma by exhibition but the gracious freedom to explore it in my own way. Our many walks and talks were instrumental in helping me grasp the importance of the role of assessment in instruction. I will always be grateful for his mentoring.

Art Powell, then a consultant to the Coalition, was crucial to the development of these ideas too. When asked to examine the idea and potential of "exhibitions" for graduation, he wrote some wonderful, clear, and generative working papers for us on the history of the idea. (He also alerted us to a book by Gerry Grant and Associates entitled *On Competence: A Critical Analysis of Competence-Based Reforms in Higher Education*, which has played an important role in furthering my thinking about all this.)

This book was also strongly influenced by many conversations held over the years. Thanks are due to Bev Andersen, Doug Archbald, Joan Baron, Sue Bennett, Ross Brewer, Dale Carlson, Mary Diez, Howard Gardner, Walt Haney, Bena Kalek, Paul LeMahieu, George Madaus, Deborah Meier, Ruth Mitchell, Fred Newmann, Tej Pandey, Rick Stiggins, and Dennie Wolf.

I especially appreciate the effort and time Gerry Bracey and Jay McTighe took to review the first draft of the book; they made many helpful suggestions. Kathy Reigstad did a wonderful job of copyediting. Her many suggestions for rephrasing, deleting, or amplifying ideas significantly improved the clarity of the text.

Too many wonderful practitioners to mention have been responsible for the dozens of sample tasks that I have been purveying around the country. Joe Accongio, James Allen, Elliot Asp, Bob Bedford, Leon Berkowitz, Diane Byers, Linda Calvin, Bob Cornell, Lorraine Costella, Joann Eresh, Dick Esner, Mike Goldman, Ralph

Gravelle, Steve Hess, Bil Johnson, Dewitt Jones, Kevin Kastner, Meg Keller-Cogan, Everett Kline, Judy Mayer, Jack McCabe, Glynn Meggison, Monte Moses, Bill and Ann O'Rourke, Terry Schwartz, Jean Slattery, Tim Westerberg, Deb White, and Sandi Williams, to name just a few, are some of the imaginative pioneers who have tried to make these ideas work with their students and faculty. They have helped me see what is possible.

Many of the ideas here go back to unending passionate talks with Chuck Burdick at Milton Academy and Bob Andrian and Jim "Grim" Wilson at Loomis Chaffee School. Grim in particular brought many of these ideas alive in his teaching, especially in his wonderful wilderness course in the seventies at Loomis—the most performance-based course I have ever seen, from which I derived the idea of "intellectual Outward Bound." Our conversations over the past twenty years have frequently centered on issues of assessment, often as we sat in the faculty locker room after practice discussing the parallels between teaching and coaching. (My experience as a coach has been formative, revealing to me what is possible when we work in an effective assessment system. The many analogies from athletics to academics may drive some readers crazy, but they are apt, I believe, if we concentrate on the feedback at work.) Grim also happily served as my "crap detector" (as Postman and Weingartner termed it)—the practitioner one always needs if idea(l)s are to become grounded and real. And, speaking of those early years, without the inspiration and support I received from Fred Torrey and John Ratté, I would probably be working in television or baseball instead of education. Ditto to Bob Anderson at St. John's.

Special thanks are due to Ron Thorpe and the Geraldine R. Dodge Foundation for their support of the work at CLASS on alternative assessment. Their generous support and Ron's thoughtful role as a critical friend in our work indirectly made the writing possible. And many thanks are also due to Heidi Quinlivan and Catherine Van Cook for their cheerful, tireless, and effective work for me at CLASS. Nothing would get done without them, and Catherine was extremely helpful in gathering research and assembling the final manuscript.

The most important sine quo non in all of this is my wife and partner at CLASS, Holly Houston. Without her wise counsel and ability to praise at just the time when praise is most needed, her patience, her tolerance of my energy level and my occasional need to write at four A.M., her unerring capacity to know when I need to talk and when I need to Just Do It, her willingness to hire me a decade ago, and her countless hours of editing and brainstorming— without her, there would be no book, only scattered thoughts. I am deeply grateful for and appreciative of her love and support.

August 1993   Grant P. Wiggins
Geneseo, New York

THE AUTHOR

◆ ◆ ◆

Grant P. Wiggins is the president and director of programs for the Center on Learning, Assessment, and School Structure (CLASS), a nonprofit educational organization in Geneseo, New York. He earned his B.A. degree (1972) from St. John's College in Annapolis and his Ed.D. degree (1987) from Harvard University. Wiggins was the first director of research for the Coalition of Essential Schools, the national high school reform project headed by Theodore Sizer. During his tenure from 1985 to 1988 at Brown University, Wiggins developed materials on "Student as Worker, Teacher as Coach" for teachers in the project, led workshops for Essential School faculties, and conducted a great deal of the preliminary research designed to further Sizer's idea of "diploma by exhibition of mastery."

Wiggins has been a consultant to some of the most closely watched state initiatives in assessment reform of recent years: he served as one of five team members who designed the blueprint for Kentucky's new performance-based student assessment system, consulted with Vermont concerning its portfolio system, and consulted with New York and California on their efforts to implement performance-based forms of testing. He has also consulted with many districts, large and small, across the country, including Bronxville, N.Y.; East Irondequoit, N.Y.; Louisville, Ky.; Littleton, Colo.; Pittsburgh, Pa.; New York City; Cherry Creek, Colo.; San Diego, Calif.; and Frederick County, Md. He has conducted numerous workshops on curriculum and assessment for the Association for Supervision and

Curriculum Development, National Council of Teachers of English, National Council of Teachers of Mathematics, American Federation of Teachers, and American Association of School Administrators, and other national educational organizations.

Wiggins's current work as a researcher and consultant on performance-based curricula and assessment is grounded in many years of teaching and coaching. His career spanned fourteen years and three different disciplines (English, social studies, and mathematics) at the secondary level. He is also known for his pioneering work in the teaching of philosophy at the secondary level. Wiggins has coached four interscholastic sports for boys and girls: soccer, cross-country, track, and baseball. He is married to Holly Houston; they have two young sons, Justin and Ian.

1 Introduction: Assessment and the Morality of Testing

People write the history of experiments on those born blind, on wolf-children, or those under hypnosis. But who will write the more general, more fluid, but also more determinant history of the "examination"—its rituals, its methods, its characters and their roles, its play of questions and answers, its systems of marking and classification? For in this slender technique are to be found a whole domain of knowledge, a whole type of power.

—Michel Foucault[1]

Consider, for a moment, one unorthodox "examination" strategy that now exists within our educational world. In this form of assessment, the challenges are not at all standardized; indeed, they are by design fully personalized, allowing each student free rein as to topic, format, and style. And although students are not subject to uniform tasks required of all, no one thinks this lack of uniformity is odd or "soft." Contrary to common practice, this test is never secret: the assessment is centered on students' intellectual interests and the thoughtfulness with which those ideas are pursued. Students are assessed on how well knowledge and interest are crafted into products and performances of their own design. No student must "earn" this right to create projects and works of one's choosing; this is an assumed right.

The setting for such assessment is mainstream, not "alternative." Nonetheless, the schedule in support of such assessment is out

1

of the ordinary, designed to suit the learner's, not the teacher's pace; each student is assessed only when ready. Instead of having an adversarial relationship, teacher and student are allies. The teacher is the student's guide through the challenges of the assessment, not an enemy to be "psyched out." The assessor is in fact *obligated* to understand the student's point of view in order to validly assess the student's grasp of things—a far cry from the typical "gotcha!" test.

Perhaps by now you have guessed the locale of such scenes: many kindergartens and graduate schools throughout our country. At both extremes of the school career, we deemphasize one-shot uniform testing in favor of a careful assessment, from different perspectives, of the student's own projects. We focus more on the student's ability to extend or play with ideas than on the correctness of answers to generic questions. Each piece of work, be it a drawing or a dissertation, is examined—often through dialogue—for what it reveals about the learner's habits of mind and ability to create meaning, not his or her "knowledge" of "facts." At the beginning and end of formal education, we understand that intellectual accomplishment is best judged through a "subjective" but rigorous interaction of mind and mind. Since performance based on one's own inquiry is being measured, test "security" is a moot issue. The essential aim behind this kind of tactful examining can be expressed as a question: Do the student's particular ideas, arguments, and products *work*—that is, do the work-products effectively and gracefully achieve the student's intention?

During the bulk of schooling, unfortunately, the story is far different. From first grade through at least the beginning (and often the end) of the undergraduate years in college, standardized and short-answer tests—and the mentality that they promote—are dominant. Students are tested not on the way they use, extend, or criticize "knowledge" but on their ability to generate a superficially correct response on cue. They are allowed one attempt at a test that they know nothing about until they begin taking it. For their efforts, they receive—and are judged by—a single numerical score that tells them little about their current level of progress and gives them no help in improving. The result is, as Lauren and Daniel Resnick, researchers and heads of the New Standards Project, have written, that American students are the "most tested but least examined" in the world.[2]

Better Assessment, Not Better Testing

But "read me well!" as Nietzsche asked of his readers in the preface to *Dawn*. This book is not a (predictable) critique of multiple-choice tests. On the contrary, *we have the tests we deserve,* including the tests that teachers design and give. The stubborn problems in assessment reform have to do with a pervasive thoughtlessness about testing and a failure to understand the relationship between assessment and learning. We have the tests we deserve because we are wont to reduce "assessment" to "testing" and to see testing as *separate* from learning—something you do expediently, once, after the teaching is over, to see how students did (usually for *other* people's benefit, not the performer's). Standardized multiple-choice tests thus represent an extreme version of an endemic problem: under these unspoken premises, it is inevitable that we come to rely on the most simple, efficient, and trivial tasks that can be reliably used. Saving time and labor becomes a paramount design virtue and causes every designer to rely on simple, quickly employed, and re-usable (hence "secure") items.

The willingness by faculties to machine-score a local test or refer student answers to a key devised for quick marking during a faculty meeting reveals that teachers too, not just professional test makers, think that human judgment is an unnecessary extravagance in sound assessment. "But we teach so many students! What else can we do?" Why not see it the other way around? Why have the band director, debate coach, science fair judge, play director, and volley-ball coach not succumbed to the same thoughtless or fatalistic expediency? Because they understand that the "test" of performance *is* the course, not something you do *after* it. Because they understand that both validity and reliability of judgment about complex performance depend upon many pieces of information gained over many performances. If our thoughtless assessment practices are going to change, we need to do more than simply replace traditional forms of "test" (multiple-choice) with new forms of "test" ("performance" or "portfolio"); we need to change the fundamental relationship between tester and student.

Let me put this more forcefully, as a proposition that provides a rationale for the book: *tests are intrinsically prone to sacrifice validity to achieve reliability and to sacrifice the student's interests for the test maker's.* All testing involves compromise. Tasks are simplified and decontextualized for the sake of precision in scoring. Limits are placed on the student's access to resources. Standardization establishes a distance between tester and student: the student can neither adapt the question to personal style nor question the questioner (a right, one would think, in a modern society, and something we would encourage in a more personal educational relationship). Many of the *inherently* questionable practices in our "slender technique" (such as excessive secrecy and the inability of the student to ask questions or use apt resources, discussed in Chapters Three, Four, and Five) are of such long standing in testing that we do not see their potential for harm.

What is educationally vital is inherently at odds with efficient, indirect testing and unambiguous test items. As senior Educational Testing Service (ETS) researcher Norman Frederiksen has put it, using more formal measurement terms, "Most of the important problems one faces in real life are ill structured, as are all the really important social, political, and scientific problems in the world today. But ill-structured problems are not found in standardized achievement tests. . . . We need a much broader conception of what a test is if we are to use test information in improving educational outcomes."[3] And by an overreliance on tools that reduce thoughtful discernment of achievement to adding or subtracting points, we have also unwittingly caused a progressive illiteracy about assessment that is visible everywhere in American education.[4]

Whatever the original intentions and benefits of efficient and reliable testing, we thus perpetually engage in self-deception about its impact. As Dennie Wolf, Janet Bixby, John Glen, and Howard Gardner of Project Zero at the Harvard University Graduate School of Education noted recently, in a comprehensive discussion of new forms of assessment, "The irony of social inventions is that one-time innovations turn to habit."[5] The self-deception consists in thinking that our habit of testing has no impact: the very word *instrument* as a synonym for *test* implies this illusory neutrality.[6] But a "test," no matter what the maker's intent, is not in fact a neutral instrument any more than tax tables are. When we assign value, we produce an impact: what gets measured gets noticed; what you test is what you get; what gets inspected gets respected. These and similar aphorisms point toward an inescapable cautionary lesson, particularly since tests inherently measure only what is easy to measure. (Wiser folks have called for the use of the most unobtrusive measures possible.[7])

The limits of all tests would be less of a problem if we were working sensibly and knowledgeably within those limits. John Dewey presciently warned us of the problem when standardized tests were first introduced: "The danger in the introduction of standardizing methods . . . is not in the tools themselves. It is in those who use them, lest they forget that it is only existing methods which can be measured."[8] What we must now face up to is that we have allowed a thoughtless proliferation of such tests in our educational world, without considering their limiting effects on pedagogy. As I will show, these ubiquitous "instruments" keep schools reliant on premodern psychological, moral, and epistemological assumptions about learners.

In our so-called culture of testing, "intelligence" is fixed. As a result, as Wolf and her colleagues have noted, "relative ranking matters more than accomplishment." The "easily quantifiable" is more significant than the "messy and complex." The "dominant image" of this culture is the "normal curve," in which the comparison of students against one another is viewed as more significant than the reporting of performance against standards.[9] In this testing culture, the use of one-shot events in June (instead of longitudinal assessment) is universal—despite the fact that the results are no longer useful to the performer (and that the reports from national tests are decipherable only by measurement experts).

Is it any wonder, then, that a fatalism pervades education? The tests we use result in a self-fulfilling prophecy about student ability—produced, in good measure, by the artifices of testing formats, schedules, and scoring mechanisms. Few educators really end up believing (no matter what a school mission statement says) that "all children can learn" to high standards, given that test results rarely show dramatic change. (And they *won't* show such change, because of their design and our current patterns of use.) To develop an educational system based on the premise that "all children *will* learn," we need assessment systems that treat each student with greater respect, assume greater promise about gains (and seek to measure them), and offer more worthy tasks and helpful feedback than are provided in our current culture of one-shot, "secure" testing.

The Morality of Testing

This book offers a philosophy of assessment based upon a basic and decidedly more modern and unfatalistic principle: because the *student* is the primary client of all assessment, assessment should be designed to *improve* performance, not just monitor it. Any modern testing (including testing used for accountability) must ensure that the primary client for the information is well served.

But any philosophy of student assessment depends upon more than a value statement as to what assessment "should" be. A philosophy should lay out a coherent and thorough position describing how the theory and practice of testing and assessment should be best understood. Any philosophy of assessment must therefore provide a set of justified principles to serve as criteria for "testing the test." Presenting these principles is a primary aim of this book. How would such criteria differ from technical standards (those already established by psychometricians, for example)? The simple answer is that the tester's standards can tell us only when tests are sound or unsound, not when we should and should not test. To answer the latter question, we need to raise questions normally not raised in such discussions: When is testing apt, and when is it not? What should happen when the interests of test makers, test users, and test takers diverge? How should schools and districts establish safeguards against the harm of excessive testing and inadequate assessment? These are questions crying out for consideration.

These questions are pressing not merely because we are in the midst of unparalleled debate about testing and schooling. A logically prior question has never been adequately considered in the testing debates: Are the primary client's interests served by testing?

As I hope to show, a preponderance of testing (as opposed to assessment) is *never* in the student's interests, whether we use multiple-choice or performance-based tests. Because a test, by its design, is an artifice whose audience is an outsider, whose purpose is ranking, and whose methods are reductionist and insensitive.

Our habits run too deep for mere technical scrutiny. The questionable practices used in testing are not rational, no matter how ubiquitous; they cannot be understood on technical or policy grounds alone. Our "modern" testing systems are built upon an ancient human urge to perpetuate a "marking and classification" system, in Michel Foucault's words. (Stephen Jay Gould's history of intelligence testing in *The Mismeasure of Man* makes clear how easily ethnocentric assumptions infected the testing but were hidden by the methods.[10]) Our tests, as the chapter-opening quote from Foucault suggests, still reflect premodern views about the student's (unequal) relationship to the examiner (and hence premodern views about the student's rights). The "rituals" and "roles" of the examination are rooted in a medieval world of inquisitions and class distinctions. The examiner's "methods," then as now, prevent the student from questioning the tester about the questions, the methods, or the results—especially because of "secure" testing, a legacy of the secretive methods employed by medieval guilds. The use of such chicanery as "distracters" on tests and win-lose grading systems are among many practices that mark the testing relationship as morally imbalanced.

When our sole aim is to measure, the child is invariably treated as an object by *any* test, a theme to which I will repeatedly return. The educative role of genuine assessment is always at risk if by *test* we mean a process in which we insist upon *our* questions, *our* timing, and *our* imposed constraints on resources and prior access to the questions and in which we see *our* scoring and reporting needs as paramount. When we isolate the learner's "knowledge" from the learner's character in a test, we no longer feel an obligation to get to know the assessee well (or even to pursue the meaning of an answer). It is no longer obligatory to worry whether we have provided students with the opportunity to have their achievements thoroughly examined and documented; it is no longer obligatory to construct opportunities for them to show what they can do (or, at the very least, to sign off on the results).

There is an *inescapable* moral dimension, in other words, to the assessment relationship—a dimension that we ignore. In school testing as we have always known it, that relationship is inherently tilted in favor of the tester. The tenor of the relationship has little to do with what *kind* of test we use and everything to do with the manner in which testing and other assessment methods treat the student, as we shall see in the chapters that follow. A philosophy of assessment in which student interests are viewed as primary would have us ask, What approaches to assessment are most respectful?

Respectful may seem like an odd word to use in talking about quizzes, tests, exams, grades, and the like, but it is the most apt word with which to initiate the rethinking of our deep-seated habits about testing. The assessor either respects or disrespects the student by the manner in which the relationship is conducted. It is respectful, for example, to be open with people about your intent and methods; a steady dose of secure tests must then be disrespectful and off-putting. It is respectful to allow people to explain themselves when we think that they have erred or when we do not understand their answer. Tests that provide no opportunity for students to supply a rationale for answers reveal that what they think and why they think it is unimportant. It is respectful to give people timely, accurate, and helpful feedback on their "effect," yet most tests provide the student with nothing more than a score—and often weeks later. It is respectful to give people ample opportunity to practice, refine, and master a task that we wish them to do; yet secure, one-shot tests prevent the efficacy that comes from cycles of model/practice/feedback/refine.

The assessment relationship can thus range from being one of complete mutual respect—through ongoing responsiveness, flexibility, patience, and a capacity for surprise in our questioning and follow-up—to one in which the student is only "tested" (and is thus treated as an object), through the imposition of tasks and procedures that provide the student (and teacher, in the case of externally designed tests) with no opportunity to enter the conversation.

The Epistemology of Testing

There are also troublesome epistemological questions that have never been properly addressed by most test designers, be they psychometricians or teachers. What really counts as evidence of "knowledge"? What is it that we want students to be able to do as a result of schooling? The de facto answer, if we examine tests, is that the student must recognize or plug in correct facts or principles to atomistic questions simplified of their natural messiness by the test maker. But is this a defensible view of what constitutes a knowledgeable student or a successful schooling? Clearly not, as we see quickly if we substitute the phrases "know-how" or "wisdom" for "knowledge."

What matters in education is understanding and the habits of mind that a student becomes disposed to use. Conventional testing cannot tell us, then, what we need to know, as I argue in Chapter Two—namely, whether the student is inclined to be thoughtful and able to be effective. Wolf, Bixby, Glen, and Gardner make the same point in quoting from William James: "Be sympathetic with the type of mind that cuts a poor figure in examination. It may be, in the long examination which life sets us, that it comes out in the end in better shape than the glib and ready reproducer, its passions being deeper, its purposes more worthy, its combining power less commonplace, and its total mental output consequently more important."[11] As Wolf and her colleagues argue, we are meant to understand that a thorough assessment requires describing long-term and multifaceted accomplishments. How else will we determine whether essential *habits* exist? (This is a validity question rarely addressed by measurement specialists.)

The problem is clearer still if we ask what counts as evidence that the student *understands* what was taught. A one-shot, secure test in which the student is required neither to produce a work-product nor to engage in discussion is unlikely to tell us whether the student has understanding or not. Correct answers can hide misunderstanding; incorrect answers, without an opportunity to explain oneself, can easily hide deeper insight. In traditional testing, the "number of items correct, not the overall quality of performance, determines the score. . . . It is as if the number of completed

sentences in an editorial mattered more than the overall power of
the argument or the integrity of its perspective."[12] In Chapter Seven,
I consider these issues from the perspective of measurement (what
is validity?) and epistemology (what is the most vital meaning of
"knowing" and "understanding"?).

The uniformity of test questions and the view that mastery
means displaying common knowledge in prescribed forms also represent the persistence of premodern views. Prior to the scientific and
democratic revolutions of the seventeenth and eighteenth centuries,
it was assumed that knowledge was uniform, stable, and "theoretical," attained through didactic teaching, private reflection, and
reading and writing (as opposed to through argument, action,
discovery, or experimentation). Control over "truth" was the student's paramount obligation; intellectual autonomy and meaning-
making—and with them, a *diversity* of understandings—would
have been viewed as heresy. Thus to "test" the student was, and is,
a practice of determining whether the student has mastered what is
orthodox. The absence of opportunities to display one's understanding in one's own way derives from the "slender technique" of
the medieval examination.

A sign that assessment reform is fighting ancient myths
about learning and modern impatience with complex assessment
can be seen in our deeper ignorance of the venerable Taxonomy.
Benjamin Bloom, who developed the Taxonomy, and his colleagues were quite clear that a synthesizing understanding was displayed through diverse and even unpredictable student action: "The
student should . . . be made to feel that the product of his efforts
need not conform to the views of the instructor, or some other
authority . . . [and] have considerable freedom of activity . . . [in-
cluding] freedom to determine the materials or other elements that
go into the final product."[13]

Synthesis is thus *inherently resistant* to testing by multiple-
choice or other methods that assume uniform, correct answers, because it requires the student to fashion a "production of a unique
communication" that "bears the stamp of the person."[14] Not only
is diversity of response to be expected; the correct answer may not
even be specifiable: "Synthesis is a type of divergent thinking: it is
unlikely that the right solution can be fixed in advance." Higher-

order assessment will therefore almost always be judgment-based: "Each student may provide a unique response to the questions or problems posed. It is the task of the evaluator to determine the merits of the responses." (We must develop apt scoring criteria and standards that reward diverse excellence, in other words.) Nor will standardized testing conditions likely be appropriate: "Problems should be as close as possible to the situation in which a scholar/ artist/engineer etc. attacks a problem. The time allowed, conditions of work etc. should be *as far from the typical controlled exam situation as possible. . . .* It is obvious that the student must have considerable freedom in defining the task for himself/herself, or in re-defining the problem or task."[15]

How have we allowed this commonsense point of view to be repeatedly lost? One answer is suggested by Foucault's observation that there is "a whole type of power" in testing. That we glibly talk about "instruments" and "items" is only one indication that the *format* of one type of test has greatly influenced our thinking about what counts as knowledge and as evidence of mastery. Large test companies have made millions of dollars making and selling tests to school systems, claiming that the multiple-choice items test for higher-order thinking and achievement. Whether we consider Bloom's or anyone else's views of higher-order thinking, this is a dubious claim at best: there is plenty of evidence to show that these test-company claims simply do not hold up under disinterested scrutiny.[16] (Why do we allow testers to be judge, jury, and executioner in their own case—a situation without precedent in American consumer affairs?)

The ironic and unfortunate result is that teachers have come to resist formal evaluation of all kinds, given the intellectual sterility and rigidity of most generic, indirect, and external testing systems. Because of that resistance, local assessment practices are increasingly unable to withstand technical scrutiny: teacher tests are rarely valid and reliable, and "assessment" is reduced to averaging scores on tests and homework. We would see this all more clearly if we grasped the implications of the idea that assessment should *improve* performance, not just *audit* it. As long as assessing is just seen as testing, and "testing" amounts only to putting numbers on papers and letters on transcripts, the full harm of our practices to the learner goes unseen. But harm there is. Learning *cannot* take place without criterion-referenced assessment, no matter how good the teaching. Successful learning depends upon adjustment in response to feedback; no task worth mastering can be done right on the first try. Effective adjustment depends upon accurate self-assessment; good self-assessment depends upon the assessor supplying excellent feedback—useful as judged by the performer—and prior insight into the standards and criteria of assessment. (See Chapter Six, which addresses feedback, and Chapter Three, which explores the debilitating impact of a world of testing that precludes the *possibility* of feedback—namely, the use of secrecy before, during, and after the test.)

Apt feedback depends upon the sharp senses of a judge who knows how to assess current performance in light of standards and criteria—that is, the hoped-for results—while remaining mindful of the character of the performer and the context of the assessment. Generic assessment is a contradiction in terms, in other words. Good assessment always involves tact, in the older sense of that word, and tact is always threatened by testing (a notion developed in Chapter Four). Effective feedback—namely, feedback that helps the learner improve—is *impossible* without such tact.

The message of William Barrett's book on philosophy of a few years back, *The Illusion of Technique,* is thus an apt one for summarizing testing in schools: we have made generic what must be relational and situational; we have made what is inherently murky artificially precise.[17] By making a practice that ought to be a focal point for learning into an after-the-fact checkup not worth dwelling upon, we have unwittingly caused the most vital "organ" of pedagogy and genuine intellectual assessment to begin to atrophy in our teachers: human judgment. How? By reducing assessment to testing. This book is about why schools must fight to make assessment of student work primary and testing subservient to a sound assessment strategy.

Assessment Versus Testing

The distinction between an *assessment* and a *test,* made often in the previous pages, is not merely political or semantic (in that derogatory sense of hairsplitting). An assessment is a comprehensive, multifaceted analysis of performance; it must be judgment-based and personal. As Lee Cronbach, Stanford University professor and the dean of American psychometricians, put it over thirty years ago, assessment "involves the use of a variety of techniques, has a primary reliance on observations (of performance), and involves an integration of (diverse) information in a summary judgment." As distinct from "psychometric measurement" (or "testing"), assessment is "a form of clinical analysis and prediction of performance."[18] An educational test, by contrast, is an "instrument," a measuring device. We construct an event to yield a measurement. As Frederiksen puts it, "A test may be thought of as any standardized procedure for eliciting the kind of behavior we want to observe and measure."[19]

But the *meaning* of the measurement requires assessment. Assessment done properly should *begin* conversations about performance, not end them. Even the father of intelligence testing understood that one test was not a sufficient indicator of a person's capacities. Alfred Binet was anxious to see his tests used as part of a thoughtful assessment process. He warned his readers, for example, that, "notwithstanding appearances, [the intelligence tests are] not an automatic method comparable to a weighing machine in a railroad station. . . . The results of our examinations have no value if deprived of all comment; they need to be interpreted."[20] And he warned his readers in the last version of the IQ tests that "a particular test isolated from the rest is of little value; . . . that which gives a demonstrative force is a group of tests. This may seem to be a truth so trivial as to be scarcely worth the trouble of expressing it. On the contrary, it is a profound truth. . . . One test signifies nothing, let us emphatically repeat, but five or six tests signify something. And that is so true that one might almost say, 'It matters very little what the tests are so long as they are numerous.' "[21] This is a warning rarely heeded by teachers. Many students have paid dearly for their teachers' haste and impatience with testing and grading—haste bred by school schedules that demand 128 final grades by the Monday after the Friday exam. (Measurement specialists forget that lots of similar items, using only one format, do not count as "many tests.")

It thus makes sense to distinguish between performance *tests* and performance *assessments* in just the ways suggested by Cronbach, despite the fact that many advocates of performance testing refer to their tests as performance assessments. A performance test is meant to yield a score, albeit one that some believe to be more valid than the score yielded by an indirect test. A performance *assessment,* on the other hand, is meant to yield a more comprehensive judgment about the meaning of this score and performance in general, viewed in various ways. The assessor may or may not use "tests"—of a direct or an indirect kind—as part of any assessment.

We need to keep in mind, therefore, that the central question is not whether we should use one kind of test or another but what role testing should play in assessment. Criticism of testing should be understood as concern for the harm that occurs when (judgment-based) assessment is reduced to (mechanical) testing and conclusions based on test data alone.

The etymology of the word *assess* alerts us to this clinical— that is, client-centered—act. *Assess* is a form of the Latin verb *assidere,* to "sit with." In an assessment, one "sits with" the learner. It is something we do *with* and *for* the student, not something we do *to* the student. The person who "sits with you" is someone who "assigns value"—the "assessor" (hence the earliest and still current meaning of the word, which relates to tax assessors). But interestingly enough, there is an intriguing alternative meaning to that word, as we discover in *The Oxford English Dictionary:* this person who "sits beside" is one who "shares another's rank or dignity" and who is "skilled to advise on technical points."

Technical soundness in student testing is not enough, in other words. In an assessment, we are meant to be the student's moral equal. (At the very least, as Peter Elbow, long-time researcher and thinker on writing and teaching, argued in discussing competency-based teaching, the teacher should move from being the student's "adversary" to "ally."[22]) Such a "sitting with" suggests that the assessor has an obligation to go the extra mile in determining what the student knows and can do. The assessor must be more tactful, respectful, and responsive than the giver of tests—more like "a mother and a manager," in British researcher John Raven's phrase, "than an imperious judge."[23] One might go so far as to say that the assessor (as opposed to the tester) must ensure that a student's strengths have been found and highlighted (irrespective of what weaknesses one also documents). This is precisely what the Department of Labor's SCANS (Secretary's Commission on Achieving Necessary Skills) report on education and the workplace called for in saying that students ought to leave high school with a "résumé," not a transcript.[24]

A *test,* however, suggests something very different. It is an evaluation procedure in which responsiveness to individual test takers and contexts and the role of human judgment are deliberately minimized, if not eliminated. This is intended as an observation, not a criticism. There are well-known virtues to standardizing procedure and minimizing bias, drift, and other forms of error in judgment. Most tests accomplish this mechanization of scoring by taking complex performances and dividing them into discrete, independent tasks that minimize the ambiguity of the result. (We can take off points and count up scores easily, in other words.) As a result, most tests tend to be "indirect" (and thereby inauthentic) ways of evaluating performance, because tests must simplify each task in order to make the items and answers unambiguous and independent of one another. As we shall see, we have paid a price for this inauthenticity, irrespective of the indisputable precision gained by using indirect measures.

An inherent tendency toward simplification is not the only danger in testing. For a variety of policy-related and historical reasons, testing in this country has become generic as well, in the sense of being linked neither to a particular curriculum nor to realistically complex problems and their natural settings. We live in a schizophrenic world of shared national expectations for schools but diverse local cultures and curricula. We have defined *accountability* as comparability on common measures, despite the fact that accountability is not dependent upon tests and is better done at the local level through responsiveness to clients (see Chapter Eight). Because of our diversity, our ability to do accurate comparisons across classrooms, schools, and districts is dependent on questions that are not highly contextual or articulated with local curricula.

But a generic test of understanding is a contradiction in terms. We want to know about *this* child, in *this* setting, in relation to *this* curriculum. It is for this reason that Howard Gardner argues that "what distinguishes assessment from testing is the former's favoring of techniques which elicit information in the course of ordinary performance, and its general uneasiness with the use of formal instruments administered in a neutral decontextualized setting."[25]

As a developmental psychologist, Gardner no doubt was influenced in making this distinction by the work of Jean Piaget in the use of clinical interviews and observations. It was Piaget who first cautioned about the limits of testing in assessment, troubled by the artificiality of forced responses to narrowly defined questions and tasks. The test is modeled on the scientific experiment, he reminds us. Given that, the process must be both controlled and replicable, hence "standardized."[26] One variable—the particular skill or fact—is isolated by the test question even though this isolation makes the test unrealistically neat and clean ("well structured," in measurement jargon).

The clinical assessment, by contrast, can never be rigidly standardized, because the interviewer must be free to diverge from a protocol or strategy of questioning in order to follow up on or better elicit the student's most revealing acts and comments. The specific questions and physical tasks that are used by the assessor are meant to serve as mere prompts to revealing and spontaneous action; we vary the questioning, as necessary, if we feel that the answers are somehow not genuine or revealing. The aim is to use both anticipatable and *unanticipatable* responses to assess the student's actions and comments. (Piaget repeatedly warned about the likelihood of inauthentic responses by the child, whether due to unwittingly suggestive questioning by the adult, boredom on the child's part, or a desire by the child to tell the questioner what the child thinks the questioner wants to hear. Thus varying the questions may be essential to procure authentic responses.[27])

The assessor tries to ferret out all of what the student knows and can do by various means. The tester, on the other hand, demands of the student specific responses to fixed questions of the tester's choosing. The student does not have the freedom (the right, really) to say on tests, "Wait! Let me reframe the question or clarify my answer!" The format of the test may be modeled on modern scientific processes, but the philosophical assumptions that permit the student to be treated as an object of the tester-experimenter are premodern.

At the very least, assessment requires that we come to know the student in action. Assessment requires a "multidimensional attempt to observe and to judge the individual learner in action" using "careful judgment," as the faculty of Alverno College in Milwaukee describe the philosophy and practice of two decades of their renowned outcomes-based liberal arts program.[28] In their materials, they stress repeatedly that the purpose of assessment is to assist and inform the learner. That is why so much of their formal assessment involves a formal self-assessment process as the cornerstone of later achievement and autonomy (a process that I discuss further in Chapter Two).

The Alverno understanding also gives us an insight into why assessment and performance have been historically linked. Self-assessment makes sense only in a world of testing where the criterion performance is known and serves as a clear and focusing goal. (What sense would there be in self-assessment in reference to indirect, one-shot, simplistic tests?) While a test in which the student responds to prefashioned answers tells us what the student "knows," it does not tell us whether the student is on the road to using knowledge wisely or effectively. As the faculty at Alverno put it, "Narrow, one-dimensional probes into a student's mines of stored information do not begin to get at how she learns or what she can do."[29] At Alverno, each student's progress and graduation are dependent upon mastering an increasingly complex set of performance tasks that simulate a variety of professional-world challenges. What assessment entails is insight into academic personality—intellectual character.

We now move from a women's college to wartime recruitment of spies. The idea of using many different tests to conduct an assessment of a person's character and the use of authentic simulations lay at the heart of Office of Strategic Services (OSS) recruitment procedures during World War II. The team of psychologists and psychiatrists charged with identifying the best candidates for work behind enemy lines developed what they called a "multiform, organismic (i.e., holistic) system of assessment: 'multiform' because it consists of a *rather large number of procedures based on different principles,* and 'organismic' (or 'holistic') because it utilized the data obtained through these procedures for attempting to arrive at a picture of the personality as a whole."[30]

Whether or not the term *assessment* first gained wide usage through the OSS "assessment of men" (as Russell Edgerton, president of the American Association for Higher Education, has claimed[31]), we do know that the research team had an explicit and compelling interest in distinguishing between what they called "elementalistic" testing and "holistic" assessing. "Elementalistic" testing is testing as we know it: complex performances are turned into a small set of abstracted "operations," each of which can be objectively scored. The OSS perceived such testing as "scientific" but "abstract and unrealistic."

The realism that the OSS felt to be essential was introduced by a clever series of simulations—what OSS assessors called "situational tests"—designed to replicate not only the challenges but also the conditions the recruits were likely to face. (This was necessary because they routinely found a lack of correlation between certain paper-and-pencil tests and actual performance, particularly where social interaction was central to the task.) The tasks are familiar to many of us now through such programs as Outward Bound and Project Adventure: tackling a ropes course, negotiating a maze, staying in fictitious character throughout an interrogation, bringing a group task to completion (despite planted confederates of the staff, who do their best to screw up the mission and question the recruit's authority), memorizing a map for later use, and so on.

The material gained from clinical interviews and the staff's overall judgment could and did override any mechanical decision made as a result of each test and total scores: "It was one of the noteworthy features of the OSS assessment system that it recognized explicitly the necessity of relating all observations to each other, not in a mechanical way, but by an interpretive process." It was this viewpoint that made the team rely heavily on "additional procedures" beyond traditional tests. They found the use of "autobiography, interviews, situational tests, psychodramas, and projection tests" indispensable in developing a clear picture of the whole person and his or her likely performance.[32]

Testing: Standards and Laws

There is nothing radical or "soft" about an emphasis on the whole person and the need to use judgment in assessing the meaning of scores. The American Psychological Association/National Council on Measurement in Education/American Educational Research Association Standards for Educational and Psychological Testing (hereafter referred to as the APA Standards) are unequivocal on this matter: Standard 8.12 says that "in elementary and secondary education, a decision that will have a major impact on a test taker should not automatically be made on the basis of a single test score. Other relevant information for the decision should also be taken into account by the professionals making the decision."[33] There are also ten standards subsumed under Standard 16 ("Protecting the Rights of Test Takers") that have to do with such matters as informed consent and the right to privacy about scores.

But where under Standard 16 is a discussion on students' right to minimal test security? What about the right of access to test papers after they have been scored? Where are the standards that provide students with the right and realistic opportunity to challenge a score or the aptness of the questions? (Incredibly, the final four substandards under Standard 16 discuss the rights of due process when a test score is thought to be fraudulent! Thus one's "rights" only come into play when one is accused of criminal behavior, not as a consumer or citizen entitled to knowledge concerning decisions affecting one's fundamental interests.) During the 1970s, when consumer rights came to the fore, the APA Ethical Principles in the Conduct of Research with Human Participants did call for specific protection on some of these points; Walt Haney and George Madaus, Boston College measurement experts, quote: "Persons examined have the right to know results, the interpretations made, and, where appropriate, the original data on which the final judgments were made." But in the 1981 and 1985 versions of the Ethical Principles, the section was deleted. (And a decade-old suit by the test companies to keep tests secure after administration still languishes in the courts, in a challenge to New York's law on open testing.) Haney and Madaus also note, in describing the changes in the APA Standards, that "strong vested interests within the APA demanded changes that favored their constituents at the expense of the test taker. . . . The profession has yet to come to grips with how the Standards can work fairly and equitably for developer, user, and test taker without an enforcement mechanism . . . other than the courts."[34]

Indeed, it has been in the courtroom that some of the more sacred testing practices have been questioned. Unbeknownst to most teachers, there are a variety of legal precedents in which the claims of testing companies and test-using institutions about the validity of scores have been successfully challenged. *Debra P*. v. *Turlington* (644F.2d.397[1981], for example, a case involving a failing grade on a state minimum-competency test, yielded a ruling that a test had to *match what the students were in fact taught* for a score to be valid. (For brief reviews of the legal history of testing, see Cronbach, 1990, and the Introduction in Berk, 1986.)[35]

One reason that educators might not be aware of this legal history is that many cases have centered on employment decisions in the adult workplace. Despite the workplace focus, however, the legal precedents might have an effect on the testing debate in schools if teachers, students, and parents were more aware of their rights, because many of those precedents bear on the current interest in performance testing.

Most of the recent court cases grew out of Title VII of the 1964 Equal Employment Opportunity Act and the establishment of the Equal Employment Opportunity Commission (EEOC); they have to do with charges that testing procedures inappropriately discriminate. But what may surprise some readers is that many cases involve successful challenges to the inappropriate content of multiple-choice standardized tests. In those cases, the plaintiff's argument often rested on the claim that the test's content had little to do with the proposed job or performance on it; the companies and/or test makers were cited for the failure to validate their tests through a careful job analysis—that is, to validate the proposed test tasks against the actual abilities, knowledge, and attitudes required by a job. (In one case, not even a job description was viewed as adequate unto itself; nor were supervisors' ratings deemed adequate.) In fact, both the EEOC Guidelines and the APA Standards referred to earlier specify that a thorough job analysis is required in employment- or licensure-focused testing.

Thus in *Fire-fighters Institute for Racial Equality* v. *The City of St. Louis* (616F.2d350[1980]), minority firefighters twice successfully sued on the basis that the skills tested were too dissimilar to those used by fire captains on the job. In another case that went to the U.S. Supreme Court (*Albemarle Paper Co.* v. *Moody*; 422US405[1975]) the court struck down the use of an employer's test because no job analysis had been conducted to show that the skills cited as essential by the company in its own validation study were in fact needed for the jobs listed.

I am not a lawyer. My aim is not to dissect cases but to raise an important question suggested by a cursory look at the legal history: Why have these standards for and concerns with job analysis rarely been applied to educational testing? They are not completely absent, fortunately. In fact, there is a lengthy and important history in testing and curriculum at the *adult* level concerning the need to start with task or role analysis.[36] There are also sweeping changes underway in licensure to make the process more performance-based at the national level.[37] And the role analysis on which such design is based is at the heart of any competency-based education, as many writers have pointed out.[38]

A demand for authenticity is therefore more than just a demand for face validity, despite what some caustic traditionalists have claimed. It is a demand for tests built upon intellectual job analyses. Since the validity of educational tests is now almost universally achieved merely through correlation with other test scores or grades in college, this kind of careful "job analysis" (that is, correlation with the ultimate criterion performances) is rarely done. And the "job" of performing well in professional or civic life has little or nothing to do with the kinds of tasks and content-related questions found on most commercial and teacher-constructed tests. Indeed, this was a central element of the argument made by David McClelland, a Harvard University psychologist, in his renowned critique of testing twenty years ago (discussed in Chapter Seven).[39]

Nor should those who seek to replace multiple-choice testing with performance testing rest easy on the legal front. The courts have consistently found for the plaintiffs in situations where there were no formal guidelines or procedures to ensure interrater reliability in judgment-based forms of testing, for example. (On that ground alone, most of our schools would be found guilty of violating student rights.)

Sound assessments do not differ from tests simply because the former are more complex than the latter. The questions of rights and responsibilities are crucial: in a proper assessment, we put the student's rights first; in an imposed test, with no oversight, we put the tester's interests (not rights, mind you) first. The "assessment" of reading by a portfolio and interview thus easily turns into an overly emphasized and perhaps unreliable test if our primary purpose is to report a single, efficiently gained score to compare with the scores of others. The "test" of Outward Bound or putting on a play is closer to what we mean by true assessment—educative on many levels about both the student and the criterion situation. These challenges are very different in tone and consequence from those "performance assessments" that still seek a single score—just a "better" one.

The Standards of Assessment

None of this should be heard—as I know it often is—as the sanctioning of assessment understood as coddling or merely praising, a flinching from telling the student where the student truly stands. I do not support the efforts of those reformers who see the employing of rigorous criteria and standards as somehow anti-assessment and anti-student.[40] As I have repeatedly argued (in consulting, in workshops, in the CLASS video series on how to undertake assessment reform, and in print), for local work to be both useful and credible, faculties must "benchmark" their grading and work to develop more criterion-referenced procedures and better interrater reliability in their grading.[41] This is especially important in light of the well-known lack of score reliability to be found in the judgments of naive and untrained assessors of complex performance. Vermont's portfolio system, for example, has already run into this problem.

Nor are the arguments for standard-referenced assessment related primarily to school accountability concerns. As I shall argue in Chapters Five and Eight, the *learner's* performance can be improved only when it is measured against "progress," not "growth." And measuring progress means measuring "backward" from the "destination"—that is, the standards and criteria exemplified in models of excellent work. Mere *change* in the student's performance provides no insight into whether that change is likely to lead to excellent adult performance. To both help the learner and inform the parent and the community, the work of assessment must be done in reference to clear and apt criteria and standards.

There is thus no simple, either-or choice about what to test, how to test, and how to assess using tests. Instead, there are unending dilemmas. The challenge is to develop a picture of the whole person using a variety of evidence, including tests, and to do so in the most feasible and helpful (to the student) way. One of the many dilemmas is that testing so easily becomes the entire assessment system instead of being a facet of it; testing is, after all, quicker, cheaper, neater, and cleaner. (This and other dilemmas are mapped out more thoroughly in Chapter Two.) We can see a kind of Gresham's law in education to be eternally resisted: "Efficient tests tend to drive out less efficient tests, leaving many important abilities untested—and untaught."[42] It may well be in the learner's interest to be tested, and the student may well learn something from being tested, but a preponderance of mere testing puts the learner's intellectual interests at risk. What is at stake, then, is whether we will insist on an assessment process in which testing practices respect the student's long-term interests.

This book should be understood, then, as a call to develop policies and principles for the testing of tests in a way that better protects students. There are more than technical and strategic questions at stake in testing. The fundamental quandary is how we can best employ testing as one facet of an overall assessment strategy that serves all "customers for information" but sees the student "customer" as primary. We need to consider the intellectual and, yes, moral consequences of testing—especially the harm inflicted by the pervasive secrecy that dominates testing, the unfairness of scoring systems with built-in disincentives, the ethics of using test "distracters," and the tactlessness involved in using answer keys that admit no ex post facto correction on the basis of an apt but unanticipated answer.

Yet there is undoubtedly a risk in drawing upon the language and logic of morality (and epistemology) in discussing student assessment and testing, because to do so may appear either naive or unhelpful to those who must address the pressing problems of testing and school reform. Nonetheless, it is essential that we take the risk. *Any use of power and its limits involves moral questions and moral consequences, and testers have extraordinary and often unilateral power.* Thus nothing could be more practical than to develop procedures whereby the logically prior questions about the purposes and effects of assessment and testing are thoroughly considered and codified into intelligent policies and practices.

Every test, every grade affects the learner. Every dull test—no matter how technically sound—affects the learner's future initiative and engagement. No, even saying it this way does not do justice to the consequences of our testing practices: every test *teaches* the student. It teaches the student what kinds of questions educators value, it teaches the student what kind of answers we value (correct merely? justified? chosen from our list? constructed by the student?), it teaches the student about intellectual relationship, and it teaches the student how much we respect student thinking.

Toward an Assessment Bill of Rights

We might, then, think of sound assessment and the appropriate use of tests along the lines of the modern judiciary or our own Bill of Rights. Due process is essential in good assessment, just as it is in legal proceedings. What counts as evidence must be acceptable not only to disinterested judges but also to such interested parties as the student and the student's teachers. The student/teacher should have not only the right of appeal but the right to question the questioner (to "cross-examine") and to present other kinds of evidence—in short, to make one's case. (That these rights sound fantastic and impossible, though they are routinely granted in the U.S. higher-education system and the K-12 systems of other countries, shows how far we have come in valuing efficiency over effectiveness, "measurement" over education.)

Cronbach makes explicit what is usually implicit in this regard: "The tester enters into a contract with the person tested. In former days the understanding was left vague. The tester is now expected to be frank and explicit. . . ." Cronbach offers some general guidelines about problematic practices ("Scores that will have an important effect on the person's future should be reported in understandable form," "A procedure for challenging a test report should be available and the test taker should be informed of the procedure," and so on) but warns that "such principles are not easily put into practice."[43]

But demanding that the tester be more "frank and explicit" is not enough. The power is still so unequally distributed and the methods used by the test maker are so arcane that the student (and the teacher, when the tests are external) has no real opportunity to understand the proceedings. As in the legal model, there ought to be not only an appeals process for testing and assessment decisions (as there often is in special education decisions, for example) but also "cross-examination" of test makers as to the compromises and limitations of the test design and the meaningfulness of the scores.

Local educators need greater guidance and more helpful decision-making structures as they attempt to balance the inherently competing interests of test giver and test taker. It is *never* in the student's interests for test questions and answer sheets to remain secure not only before but after administration, yet test companies and teachers have thus far successfully lobbied to retain the right to protect their product and save themselves time and money.

Principles for the conduct of assessment that put the student's rights on a moral par with the technical needs of psychometricians and the policy needs of school-board and community members are long overdue. I know of only a handful of school districts that have testing and assessment policies. And policy makers, educators, classroom teachers, and district administrators need significant help in "testing" the tests—help that takes the typical complaints beyond the merely personal to the principled.

More formal and powerful help could perhaps come from a genuinely disinterested national organization set up to review tests and test-maker claims, modeled along the lines of Underwriters' Laboratory or the Federal Trade Commission—an idea offered by Haney and Madaus and others as a more appropriate venue than the de facto one of courts of law: "[We call for] the establishment of an independent auditing agency that would, without vested interest, evaluate tests and testing programs that profoundly affect the lives of examinees."[44] Legislation may well be part of the solution. In a recent article on what should be done at the federal level to prevent testing-related abuses, Michel Feuer, Kathleen Fulton, and Patricia Morrison of the Congressional Office of Technology Assessment made a similar pitch: Congress might "focus on various proposals to certify, regulate, oversee, or audit tests," including the establishment of an oversight agency.[45]

Feuer, Fulton, and Morrison also argue Congress should "require or encourage school districts to develop and publish a testing policy."[46] Each school district ought to, at the very least, state the permissible uses of such morally problematic practices as test security, scoring work on a curve, the use of nonarticulated and generic tests, the failure to require consistent grading among teachers for the same work, and so on—practices discussed throughout this book. These policies would do more than state the values of the institution; they would provide a local procedure for ensuring that assessment practices of both students and educators were publicly scrutinized, discussed, justified, and improved. Regional service agencies and federally funded educational labs and centers might also be asked to serve as a clearinghouse for policy statements and for guidelines in their formulation.

Here is a sample set of guiding principles from the New Zealand Department of Education:[47]

Principles of Assessment for Better Learning

1. The interests of the students shall be paramount. Assessment shall be planned and implemented in ways which maximize benefits for students, while minimizing any negative effects on them.
2. The primary purpose of assessment shall be to provide information which can be used to identify strengths and to guide improvement. In other words, it should suggest actions which may be taken to improve the educational development of

students and the quality of educational pro-
grammes.

3. Assessment information should not be used for
judgmental or political purposes if such use
would be likely to cause harm to students or to the
effectiveness of teachers or schools.

4. Every effort should be made to ensure that assessment and evaluation procedures are fair to all.

5. Community involvement is essential to the credibility and impact of assessment and evaluation
processes. All parties with a direct interest should
have an opportunity to contribute fully. Self-
assessment is the appropriate starting point.

6. Careful consideration should be given to the motivational effects of assessment and evaluation
practices.

7. In the assessment of intellectual outcomes, substantial attention should be devoted to more sophisticated skills such as understanding of
principles, applying skill and knowledge to new
tasks, and investigating, analyzing, and discussing complex issues and problems.

8. Emphasis should be given to identifying and reporting educational progress and growth, rather
than to comparisons of individuals or schools.

9. The choices made in reporting assessment information largely determine the benefit or harm resulting from the information. For this reason, the
selection, presentation, and distribution of information must be controlled by the principles out-
lined previously.

My own view is that, while these principles represent an
important step toward protecting the student, they are too diffuse
as stated. I would prefer that school systems develop an Assessment
Bill of Rights to protect the inherently vulnerable student from the
harms that testing easily leads to. It would be supported by explicit

audit or oversight policies to ensure that the rights were protected. Here is my rough draft of such a set of rights:

Assessment Bill of Rights

All students are entitled to the following:

1. Worthwhile (engaging, educative, and "authentic") intellectual problems that are validated against worthy "real-world" intellectual problems, roles, and situations
2. Clear, apt, published, and consistently applied teacher criteria in grading work and published models of excellent work that exemplifies standards
3. Minimal secrecy in testing and grading
4. Ample opportunities to produce work that they can be proud of (thus, ample opportunity in the curriculum and instruction to monitor, self-assess, and self-correct their work)
5. Assessment, not just tests: multiple and varied opportunities to display and document their achievement, and options in tests that allow them to play to their strengths
6. The freedom, climate, and oversight policies necessary to question grades and test practices without fear of retribution
7. Forms of testing that allow timely opportunities for students to explain or justify answers marked as wrong but that they believe to be apt or correct
8. Genuine feedback: usable information on their strengths and weaknesses and an accurate assessment of their long-term progress toward a set of exit-level standards framed in terms of essential tasks
9. Scoring/grading policies that provide incentives and opportunities for improving performance and seeing progress against exit-level and real-world standards

I am sorry to report that the idea of an Assessment Bill of Rights has been attacked by more than a few teachers when I have offered it in workshops. Some have actually angrily called for a *prior* list of student responsibilities (though I do not recall such a list in our Constitution). Perhaps nothing better illustrates why these rights are deserving of formal protection, given the uneven balance of moral power in both the testing and teaching relationships as traditionally defined. The implicit hypocrisy in the position of these teachers is easily made explicit when one asks them whether they would be willing to endure a professional performance appraisal conducted under the same conditions as student testing.

Assessment, to be educative and fair, needs to be more a matter of principle and less a matter of good intentions, mere habit, or personality. In the chapters that follow, I explore some of the principles that underlie real and ideal testing and assessment—and the dilemmas that make it a profound mistake to replace sound assessment principles with unthinking procedures or answer keys requiring no judgment.

Notes

1. M. Foucault, *Discipline and Punish* (New York: Vintage Books, 1979), pp. 184-185. Translation Copyright © 1977 by Alan Sheridan.
2. D. P. Resnick and L. B. Resnick, "Standards, Curriculum, and Performance: A Historical and Comparative Perspective," *Educational Researcher* 14 (1985): 5-21.
3. N. Frederiksen, "The Real Test Bias," *American Psychologist* 39 (1984): 193-202, p. 199.
4. See, for example, R. Stiggins, "Assessment Literacy," *Phi Delta Kappan* 72 (1991): 534-539.
5. D. Wolf, J. Bixby, J. Glen III, and H. Gardner, "To Use Their Minds Well: Investigating New Forms of Student Assessment," in G. Grant, ed., *Review of Research in Education* (Washington, D.C.: American Educational Research Association, 1991), p. 31.
6. See H. Berlak and others, *Toward a New Science of Educational Testing and Assessment* (New York: State University of New York Press, 1992), p. 182ff.
7. See, for example, P. Terenzini, "The Case for Unobtrusive Measures," in Educational Testing Service, ed., *Assessing the Outcomes of Higher Education,* Proceedings of the 1986 ETS

Invitational Conference (Princeton, N.J.: Educational Testing Service, 1987).

8. J. Dewey, "Current Tendencies in Education," in J. A. Boydston, ed., *The Middle Works of John Dewey: 1899–1924* (Carbondale: Southern Illinois University Press, [1917] 1985), p. 119.

9. Wolf, Bixby, Glen, and Gardner, "To Use Their Minds Well," pp. 43–44.

10. S. J. Gould, *The Mismeasure of Man* (New York: W. W. Norton, 1981).

11. As quoted by Wolf, Bixby, Glen, and Gardner, "To Use Their Minds Well," p. 51.

12. Ibid., p. 47.

13. B. S. Bloom, ed., *Taxonomy of Educational Objectives*, Vol. 1: *Cognitive Domain* (White Plains, N.Y.: Longman, 1956), p. 173.

14. Ibid., p. 175. Compare B. S. Bloom, G. Madaus, and J. T. Hastings, *Evaluation to Improve Learning* (New York: McGraw-Hill, 1981), pp. 52–56.

15. Bloom, Madaus, and Hastings, *Evaluation to Improve Learning*, pp. 265, 268 (emphasis added).

16. See G. Madaus and others, *From Gatekeeper to Gateway: Transforming Testing in America* (Chestnut Hill, Mass.: National Commission on Testing and Public Policy, Boston College, 1990), and Frederiksen, "The Real Test Bias," for example.

17. W. Barrett, *The Illusion of Technique: A Search for Meaning in a Technological Civilization* (New York: Anchor Books, 1978).

18. L. J. Cronbach, *Essentials of Psychological Testing*, 2nd ed. (New York: HarperCollins, 1960), p. 582.

19. Frederiksen, "The Real Test Bias," p. 199.

20. A. Binet, and T. Simon, "The Development of Intelligence in the Child," in *The Development of Intelligence in Children* (Salem, N.H.: Ayer, [1908] 1983), p. 239.

21. A. Binet and T. Simon, "New Investigation upon the Measure of the Intellectual Level Among School Children," in *The*

Development of Intelligence in Children (Salem, N.H.: Ayer, [1911] 1983), p. 329.

22.   P. Elbow, "Trying to Teach While Thinking About the End," in G. Grant and Associates, *On Competence: A Critical Analysis of Competence-Based Reforms in Higher Education* (San Francisco: Jossey-Bass, 1979). See also P. Elbow, "One-to-One Faculty Development," in J. F. Noonan (ed.), *Learning About Teaching*. New Directions for Teaching and Learning, no. 4. San Francisco: Jossey-Bass, 1980.

23.   J. Raven, "A Model of Competence, Motivation, and Behavior, and a Paradigm for Assessment," in Berlak and others, *Toward a New Science of Educational Testing and Assessment*, p. 100.

24.   Department of Labor, *What Work Requires of Schools: A SCANS Report for America 2000* (Washington, D.C.: U.S. Government Printing Office, 1991).

25.   H. Gardner, "Assessment in Context: The Alternative to Standardized Testing," in B. Gifford, ed., *Report to the Commission on Testing and Public Policy,* (Boston: Kluwer Academic Press, 1989), p. 90.

26.   Critics of the multiple-choice test often do not grasp the fact that in *all* testing we "standardize" the conditions of test administration. We hold those conditions constant and we isolate knowledge to obtain a fixed answer to our specific question as the means of isolating a specific aspect of achievement with precision.

27.   Whether developmental schemes such as Piaget's and Kohlberg's should be viewed as implicit systems of the "evaluation" of intellectual and moral behavior is an interesting and nettlesome question. In other words, should we say that empirical descriptions of growth constitute intellectual/moral progress, so that a "higher" score is "better" performance? Kohlberg thought so; Piaget did not (though Kolhberg thought he did). Gilligan, of course, thinks both schemes were empirically and conceptually flawed by the absence of adequate data and analysis of girls' moral and intellectual experience. See C. Gilligan, *In a Different Voice: Psychological Theory and Women's Development* (Cambridge, Mass.: Har-

vard University Press, 1982), and C. Gilligan and G. Wiggins, "The Origins of Morality in Early Childhood Relationships," in J. Kagan and S. Lamb, eds., *The Emergence of Morality in Young Children* (Chicago: University of Chicago Press, 1987).

28. Alverno College Faculty, *Assessment at Alverno College,* rev. ed. (Milwaukee, Wis.: Alverno College, 1985), p. 1. (Other material is also available from the college.) For a comprehensive analysis of the assessment system at Alverno (and such competency-based programs in higher education more generally), see G. Grant and Associates, *On Competence: A Critical Analysis of Competence-Based Reforms in Higher Education* (San Francisco: Jossey-Bass, 1979).

29. Ibid., p. 1.

30. Office of Strategic Services, *Assessment of Men: Selection of Personnel for the Office of Strategic Services* (Troy, Mo.: Holt, Rinehart & Winston, 1948), p. 28 (emphasis added).

31. R. Edgerton, "An Assessment of Assessment," in Educational Testing Service, eds., *Assessing the Outcomes of Higher Education,* Proceedings of the 1986 ETS Invitational Conference (Princeton, N. J.: Educational Testing Service, 1986), pp. 93–110.

32. Office of Strategic Services, *Assessment of Men,* p. 53.

33. American Psychological Association, "Standards for Educational and Psychological Testing" (Washington, D.C.: American Psychological Association, 1985), p. 54.

34. W. Haney and G. Madaus, "The Evolution of Ethical and Technical Standards for Testing," in R. K. Hambleton and J. N. Zaal (eds.), *Advances in Educational and Psychological Testing: Theory and Applications* (Norwell, Mass.: Kluwer, 1991).

35. L. J. Cronbach, *Essentials of Psychological Testing,* 5th ed. (New York: HarperCollins, 1990), and R. A. Berk, ed., *Performance Assessment Methods and Applications* (Baltimore, Md.: Johns Hopkins University Press, 1992).

36. See D. Riesman's insightful history, "Encountering Difficulties in Trying to Raise Academic Standards," in Grant and Associates, *On Competence.*

37. See, for example, the various papers from a recent conference

on performance assessment in the professions: Educational Testing Service, ed., *What We Can Learn from Performance Assessment for the Professions*, Proceedings of the 1992 ETS Invitational Conference. (Princeton, N.J.: Educational Testing Service, 1993).

38. See, for example, Elbow, "One-to-One Faculty Development"; Elbow, "Trying to Teach While Thinking About the End"; and R. Nickse and others, *Competency-Based Education* (New York: Teachers College Press, 1981).

39. D. McClelland, "Testing for Competence Rather than for 'Intelligence,'" *American Psychologist* 28 (1973): 1–14.

40. See, for example, F. Smith, *Insult to Intelligence: The Bureaucratic Invasion of Our Classrooms* (Portsmouth, N.H.: Heinemann Educational Books, 1986).

41. See G. Wiggins, "Standards, Not Standardization: Evoking Quality Student Work," *Educational Leadership* 48 (1991): 18–25; compare G. J. Cizek, "Confusion Effusion: A Rejoinder to Wiggins," *Phi Delta Kappan* 73 (1991): 150–153.

42. Frederiksen, "The Real Test Bias," p. 201.

43. Cronbach, *Essentials of Psychological Testing*, pp. 74–75.

44. Haney and Madaus, *The Evolution of Ethical and Technical Standards for Testing*, p. 34.

45. M. Feuer, K. Fulton, and P. Morrison, "Better Tests and Testing Practices: Options for Policy Makers," *Phi Delta Kappan* 74 (1993): 530–533, p. 532.

46. Ibid.

47. Department of Education, *Assessment for Better Learning: A Public Discussion Document* (Wellington, New Zealand: Department of Education, 1989).

2 | Assessment Worthy of the Liberal Arts

Assessment of *what?*[1] Assessors cannot exercise judgment or use any tools unless they are clear about the criteria and standards to be used in the judging. In other words, we must determine the aim of education before we can determine what we should assess and what kind of evidence we should seek.

Despite what many testing programs implicitly assume, the aim of education is thoughtful action, not "knowledge." Our syllabi are means to a larger end: developing the "disciplines" that are at the heart of each discipline. A capacity for autonomous learning and a thirst for unending education are more important than accurate recall or simplistic application of the particular knowledge taught. The implications for assessment are fundamental: we need to be assessing primarily for mature habits of mind and a thoughtful and effective use of knowledge.

Consider, therefore, the first known assessor of intellectual achievement. I am thinking, of course, of Socrates—the Socrates of the dialogues of Plato, in which we regularly see those who either appear to be or profess to be competent put to the "test" of question, answer, and (especially) sustained and engaged conversation. Socrates the assessor: he is certainly an odd one by conventional standards. He does not seem to have nice answer keys or scoring rubrics by his side. And his dialogues never lead to "knowledge" or the kind of closure favored by traditional teachers and assessors. Rather, what is at stake is determining whether those with whom Socrates speaks have the right habits of mind—the "disciplines" of the liberal arts.

These aims and methods can be seen through the Platonic dialogue called "Meno."[2] Meno, a brash young fellow, comes up to Socrates and abruptly asks a question. The first lines of the dialogue are: "Can you tell me, Socrates, whether virtue can be taught, or is acquired by practice, not teaching? Or if neither by practice nor by learning, whether it comes to mankind by nature or in some other way?" Meno apparently needs to know—now. Socrates responds in a very annoying and typically Socratic way. He says that he cannot answer the question because he does not know what virtue is. Meno is clearly astonished to learn that a bona fide, certified sage does not know what *everybody* knows—namely, what it means to be good. But after Meno makes the foolish mistake of venturing to tell Socrates what virtue is, Socrates proceeds to undress him two or three times.

Finally, in exasperation at having his own accounts of virtue turned inside out and found wanting, Meno says something that goes to the heart of the distinction between conventional testing and an assessment worthy of the liberal arts. Meno says, "Well now, my dear Socrates, you are just what I have always heard before I met you. Always puzzled yourself and puzzling everyone else. And you seem to me to be a regular wizard. You bewitch me. You drown me in puzzles. Really and truly, my soul is numb. My mouth is numb. And what to answer you I do not know." For our concerns, it is the next line that is most important: "Yet I have a thousand times made long speeches about virtue before many a large audience. And good speeches too, as I thought. But I have not a word to say at all as to what it is."

Meno's ironic comment highlights the difference between merely dutiful learning in school and real intellectual excellence. Meno is reduced to speechlessness, he thinks, because of the sophistry of Socrates' questions and analyses; the thoughtful reader knows, however, that Meno does not really know what he is talking about. He is unable to move beyond clichés, he fails to see the contradictions in his diverse arguments, and he cannot justify his opinions when asked. Yet the dialogue presents Meno as a conventionally successful student. How do we know? The real-life Meno was, in fact, a successful young military man. And throughout the dialogue, Meno is constantly dropping references—the ancient equivalent of student footnotes—to all the famous people who say this and that about virtue (and whom he, of course, agrees with). It may be true, as Meno claims, that he can be a successful speaker—passionate, convincing.

One of Plato's intentions here, then, is to challenge the views of the Sophists: competent presentation is not adequate evidence of intellectual mastery; rhetorical skill, using borrowed ideas, is not understanding. Mere learnedness or eloquence is not what a liberal education is about. As Plato has Socrates say elsewhere, education is not "putting sight into blind eyes" but liberating the mind from mere opinion and hackneyed thinking.

Meno is really like so many students—a memorizer, able to make effective speeches with references to famous people, sayings, and works. We are meant to know that his name is used throughout the work as a pun. It is very close in Greek to the word for memory: μɛνον (Meno), μνɛμον (power). Is that not what too much of our assessment is already about? Do we not too often fail to assess whether the student can do anything more than cite borrowed quotes, arguments, facts, and figures?

We also know from history that the real Meno was a nasty fellow: clever, effective, ruthless. It was no coincidence, then, that Plato titled a dialogue about morality and education as he did. He clearly meant for us to recall Meno's actual character while hearing his mind at work. Meno's impetuosity in the conversation and his desire to merely buttress his unexamined opinions with what wise men say make a dangerous combination. Plato wants us to see, through Socrates, that conventional education can be quite dangerous. As we get better and better at our lessons and our craft, we may become less and less likely to question what we know.

We are meant to see that there is an inescapable moral dimension to all learning (even abstract academic learning) and to our assessment of its success. An education is not merely a training; skill can be used for good or for ill, thoughtfully or thoughtlessly. A thoughtful assessment system does not seek correct answers only, therefore. It seeks evidence of worthy habits of mind; it seeks to expose and root out thoughtlessness—moral as well as intellectual thoughtlessness. Sometimes, therefore, it is not factual error but the student's *response* to error that reveals either understanding or lack of it.[3] Focusing squarely on such habits of mind as openness to ideas, persistence, and willingness to admit ignorance makes different demands upon the student than focusing on the test criteria of the current system—and different demands upon the assessor as well. At the very least, judgment must be seen to be an essential element of assessment: mere right answers to uniform questions are incapable of revealing its presence or absence.

"Thoughtless mastery" (as I have elsewhere termed it) really does exist; it is not a contradiction in terms, though typical testing cannot easily discern thoughtful from thoughtless mastery.[4] For what must be assessed is not whether the student is learned or ignorant but whether he or she is thoughtful or thoughtless about what has been learned. Our assessments tend unwittingly to *reinforce* thoughtless mastery as an aim by failing to distinguish between "thoughtful use" and "correct answer" and by routinely valuing de facto the latter. A now-famous test question from the National Assessment of Educational Progress (NAEP) in mathematics, discussed by Alan Shoenfeld of Berkeley, makes this clear: "'An army bus holds 36 soldiers. If 1128 soldiers are being sent by bus to their training site, how many buses are needed?' Of the students who worked the problem 29% wrote that the number needed is '31 remainder 12' while only 23% gave the correct answer."[5]

Unthinking habits run deep: a steady dose of decontextualized problems with right numerical answers leads students to not question the idea of a "remainder 12" bus. We dare not too quickly blame the student-victim. This is not mere carelessness on the student's part. It is learned thoughtlessness, induced by an assessment system composed of tests containing decontextualized items whose answers have no real consequence or real-world meaning and that are not meant to be lingered over.

Eight Dilemmas of Student Assessment

This tension between unthinking learning and thoughtful (re)consideration is the first of eight dilemmas at the heart of the assessment of intellectual progress. Much learning paradoxically *requires*

unthinking learning of pat formulas, drills, and declarative statements. But understanding is something different than technical
prowess; understanding emerges when we are required to reflect
upon achievement, to verify or critique—thus to rethink and re-
learn—what we know, through many "tests" of experience, action,
and discussion (knowledge-in-use). Understanding involves questioning, as Socrates so often did, the assumptions upon which prior
learning is based.

Consider physical mastery. One of my passions is baseball,
and in George Will's wonderful book *Men At Work,* on the craft of
playing and managing major-league baseball, there is an odd but
insightful phrase, "muscle memory," that well describes thoughtless prowess. Good hitters talk about not thinking too much at bat.
What has to take over the hitter is "muscle memory"—a wonderful
phrase for the kind of unthinking skill that we admire. On the other
hand, if hitters whose batting average is falling want to genuinely
understand hitting and alter a set of habits that no longer serve
them, they must study hitting, analyze it, and reconstitute it in the
form of new habits—"second nature," in that apt phrase—using a
feedback loop of constant assessment and adjustment to ensure that
the new habits work. Similarly, I do not want my brain surgeon to
be thinking about what health really is while I am under the knife.
But to truly understand and honor the Hippocratic Oath, every
doctor must repeatedly undertake deep meditation on the nature of
care. And to avoid unthinkingly seeing my case as merely a subset
of a predictable condition, the doctor needs to be responsive—pos-
sessing what Freud called "free-floating attention."

We can put this first dilemma in the language of relationship. Artistry requires habit-induced skill but also tact and good
judgment, the nontechnical inclination to be alert to the perhaps
unique elements of the present situation. No assessment system
worthy of the liberal arts assesses mere knowledge or skill; it assesses
intellectual character, good judgment—the *wise* use of know-how
in context. We are therefore derelict if we construe assessment as
only the act of finding out whether students learned what we
taught. On the contrary, one could argue that assessment ought to
determine whether students have effectively reconsidered their recently learned abstract knowledge in light of their experience. (This

is why the case method and problem-based-learning methods in law, business, and medicine are now so common and apt.)

Schooling aims to transmit what is known; we should thus assess for knowledge of what was taught. But schooling also aims at intellectual autonomy and the generation of future knowledge and personal meaning; we must assess, then, for what may be generative of future knowledge (which *may* have little to do directly with testing what was taught). Therein lies our second dilemma in assessment: we must worry about what students know, but we must also worry about whether what they know now has any meaning. To put this in old, familiar language: the higher-order act of synthesis in the Taxonomy is a creative act of connection making; synthesis is *not* necessarily achieved or better assessed after knowledge is exhaustively taught and assessed (that is, by marching through the Taxonomy in chronological fashion, something against which Bloom in fact vainly argued.)

We certainly *say* we would like to see more "real" thinkers, and we bemoan doltish behavior in our students, but I think we do protest too much. Our testing and grading habits, which give us away, show that we do not negotiate the dilemma well. Look how often, for example, students give us back precisely what we said or they read. It is too easy to come to school and college and leave both one's own and the teacher's prejudices unexamined. If in so doing students "succeed" (get A's), they are left with the impression that assessment is merely another form of jumping through hoops or of licensure in a technical trade. And yet school and college offer us the socially sanctioned opportunity, indeed the *obligation,* to disturb and challenge students intellectually, using knowledge as a means, not as an end, to engender more effective and self-reflective thought and action. That view is at odds with the habit of using uniform tests of the content of the syllabus.

Do not make the mistake of hearing this last point as an ode to evaluation-free schooling. On the contrary, I think effective education is impossible without constant, rigorous assessment that results in good feedback. But we should require more than rigorous testing, as I said in Chapter One. We should require respectful and responsive forms of assessment, in accordance with our deeper objectives.

We have the obligation to "test" and "examine" each student's supposed achievements. But we must do so in a way that is ennobling, fair, and responsive to the student's intellectual needs. This is our third dilemma, introduced in the previous chapter: a test is designed to standardize and simplify our assessment, but to rely on tests is to ensure that students' "knowledge," not their intellectual progress as thinkers and producers, gets assessed. A more enlightened concern for students' need to "show off" what they know (to use Theodore Sizer's fine phrase) would make us more sensitive to their need for regular opportunities to *shape the terms of evidence of mastery*—a contract between the student and the assessor to deliver evidence of progress that is mutually acceptable. This is a dilemma because it wreaks havoc with efficient testing of many students at once and with the possibility of comparable assessment results—values that we also hold dear.

The fourth dilemma involves the tension between our need to probe and our obligation to be respectful. To "examine" what the student knows requires me to be mistrustful, in a sense. I put the student's knowledge to the test; I suspend my naive faith in the student's apparent mastery. What does the student *really* know? My aim is to ferret out not only what the student knows but what the student seems or claims to know but in fact does not—as Socrates did with Meno and all the other discussants. Compounding the ill effects of our inherent mistrust, we often employ many disrespectful practices: we employ secrecy about what is tested and graded, for example, we use tricky questions and answers ("distracters"), and we rarely give the student adequate opportunity to justify an odd or *seemingly* incorrect answer. (These practices are discussed more fully in Chapter Four.)

We must replace these practices with the tact of Socrates: tact to respect the student's ideas enough to enter them fully—even more fully than the thinker sometimes—and thus the tact to accept apt but unanticipatable or unique responses. Like Socrates, we must be prepared to give up control of the conversation and the order of our questions. That is what a dialogue is, after all: a mutually respectful and responsive (hence nonscriptable) shared inquiry. So often we are disrespectful in the sense of having one question, one sort of answer, and one protocol in mind. We rarely treat the student as a respected colleague.

Whatever the lure of standardization, therefore, it is opposed to the flexible settings that evoke personalized understanding. Establishing high standards that are adapted to each child and circumstance of assessment is very difficult: How many of us can be a Socrates, a Piaget, a Freud? But at what cost to *our* understanding—hence to validity—do we settle for held-in-common answers—those that are the most easy to obtain?

That the tension between rigor and respect, standardization and humanely held standards is real can be seen in the various uneasy compromises played out in traditional schools and alternative schools. "Good" schools have teachers who "grade hard" (and on a steep curve) and test a lot. But with what rationale and at what cost? In one "good" district in which I worked, science teachers gave to their seventh- and eighth-graders a final exam that contributed 15 percent of the final grade. The questions—over 100—were picayune, and the test was unreliable: the average test grade was a full letter grade lower than the year's grade for students of all abilities. What does the student take as a lesson from such a system about academic rigor, academic values, and fairness?

On the other hand, I often hear the wish of faculties to do away with formal evaluation, tests, or grades—sometimes even in these "good" schools—in the supposed interest of students. Some alternative-school faculties seem to go further, viewing all formal assessment and grades as antithetical to their mission—as if competence could somehow be developed without formal feedback. These well-meaning folks often end up confusing effort with achievement, individual growth with genuine progress.[6] If I had to choose between, on the one hand, mickey mouse "gotcha!" tests with norm-referenced scoring and grading and, on the other hand, an absence of uniform tests and grades, I *might* go with the alternative schools; but it is a bad choice, and it shows that we have not understood and negotiated the dilemma.

So we must think more carefully about how to balance the nurturing of diverse intellectual urges with the need for maintaining and inculcating standards—a quest for humane yet effective rigor, standards without mere standardization. In the proper drive for more authentic forms of assessment, we have to ensure, for example, that the cry does not lead to mere "projects" with no clear or valid standards. We must do something more than simply find a more hands-on way of engaging students; these new performance tasks must provide clear insights and discriminations about who has and has not mastered essential tasks and outcomes.

A fifth dilemma is that, despite our desire to test what was learned in a dispassionate fashion, no test is ever neutral—about epistemology. Tests *teach*. Their form and their content teach the student what kinds of challenges adults (seem to) value. If we keep testing for what is easy and uncontroversial, as we now do, we will mislead the student as to what work is of most value. This is the shortcoming of almost all state testing programs. Generations of students and teachers alike have fixated on the kinds of questions asked on the tests—to the detriment of more complex and performance-based objectives that the state cannot possibly test en masse. A person from India described a more harrowing result: when teachers try to do interesting things in their secondary classes in India, he has heard students protest, in loud voices, "Not on the test! Not on the test!" In other words, students then easily come to believe that knowledge is a repository of sanctioned information instead of a "discipline"—a flexible and context-sensitive way of thinking and acting.

Furthermore, tests *should* teach the student, not only about how school tests parallel the "tests" of professional knowledge and understanding but about the questions and challenges that define a given field. Otherwise, an unrelenting dose of efficient, "proxy" forms of assessment teach the student misleading lessons about what an intellectual test is, and they reduce the likelihood of marginal students being interested in intellectual work.

Testing that teaches what we *ought* to value is technically difficult, time-consuming, and dependent upon the kinds of sophisticated task analysis that teachers have little time for. Therein lies the dilemma: few teachers and school systems can imagine what a comprehensive "examining" system might look like—a system that gives each student many options for assessment and that "tests" the most complex aspects of performance and production. Such approaches are more routine in other countries. The Italians, for example, require all students to take oral exams, even in mathematics. Victoria, in Australia, makes locally generated student work part of the state assessment. The International Baccalaureate includes an "extended essay" as a graduation requirement; the work is judged by disinterested readers. Some U.S. schools, particularly the more progressive or alternative, have similar requirements—most notably, Central Park East Secondary School in New York and Walden III in Racine, Wisconsin, both of which require elaborate portfolios and orals for graduation. All of these entities have had to make sacrifices and readjustments to run their assessment systems. Ultimately, of course, what we assess is what we *really* value.

A sixth dilemma inherent in assessing student achievement is balancing testing for the mastery of the ideas and products of other people against testing for the mastery of one's emerging ideas and products. Why is this a dilemma? Why not stress both? Elementary and graduate teachers often do, as I noted in Chapter One. But because an education that centers on doing one's *own* work well is inherently idiosyncratic, the instruction and the assessment cannot, in principle, be standardized in the conventional sense. An unfortunate teacher habit also enters here: too many people believe incorrectly that students must gain control of common knowledge *before* they can be creative with or critical of knowledge. To paraphrase Thomas Kuhn's view, one must have complete control over the existing "paradigm" if dramatic new paradigms or original thoughts are to occur.[7]

Whatever Kuhn's merits as a historian and philosopher of science, I think he is dead wrong about education. I think it is vital to ensure that students immerse themselves, from the word *go*, in pursuing their own work and questioning established "truths" as they learn. Otherwise, they may have a *long* wait, and their critical judgment and imagination may atrophy. Many bright and able minds drop out mentally or physically because they cannot wait so long for intellectually stimulating challenges of that sort. And the ones that *do* stick around may be more dutiful than thoughtful.

Inevitably, if we first demand knowledge of the orthodox facts and opinions, we run a moral as well as an intellectual risk: the risk of letting students believe that Authority and authoritative answers matter more than inquiry. We may well end up convincing students that "knowledge" is something other than the result of personal inquiries built upon questions such as theirs. And many students *do* believe that: there is "knowledge" over here and there are "questions and ideas" over there, and never the twain shall meet.

The problem can be reframed as a classic one and put forth as our seventh dilemma: the distinction between utilitarian and nonutilitarian (or liberal) knowledge. We are in fact not training historians, scientists, or mathematicians. Too many teachers act as if they were providing technical training to apprentices. There is an important sense in which the liberal arts *are* useless, summed up in that comment supposedly made by Euclid 2,000 years ago when someone complained that geometry was not good for very much. He said, well, give him three drachmas if he has to get him some usefulness out of the study. Schooling is not the same as trade school.

But there is a more important truth in students' desire for an education with more apparent usefulness. We often fail to hear this lament for what it is: a request for more *meaning* in their work (as opposed to relevance). There are many instructional and assessment challenges that are not relevant to students' immediate practical concerns and interests. They nonetheless offer enticing, insightful, and ennobling challenges. For example, I have watched a class of geometry students happily spend two hours on the question, Is the Pythagorean theorem true if one uses shapes other than squares on the legs of the triangle? Adults often disappoint in the other direction, by pandering to students—that is, pursuing ideas that are *too* relevant because they are transitory and ultimately without either meaning or significance.[8] Test and syllabus designers are perpetually insensitive to students' need for genuine problems to chew on, not packages of predigested "knowledge" or artificially simple and unengaging drills.

The dilemma about the liberal arts can be restated in a way that makes clear why a liberal education is problematic. We all need to feel competent, and we want to believe that our education is providing us with something of value. From school competence comes confidence and, we think, greater clarity and direction about one's future; from such confidence comes greater risk taking and thus even greater competence. The trouble with a really *good* education, however, is that it often fails to satisfy this need for self-satisfaction and vocational direction in the short term (if at all). We have to recognize that an education that aims at deep understanding may cause anxiety or impatience in students; the urge to shun or resist schooling may be well founded. Our dropouts may actually be the tip of the iceberg, more extreme cases of the psychic dropouts who inhabit all our schools and colleges. (Socrates notes that the man liberated from his chains in the Cave *resists* the steep, rough ascent to intellectual freedom.)

The unending questions at the heart of a good education are always disturbing. Meno, you will recall, warns Socrates not to travel to foreign lands, where people would very likely not take kindly to his strange questions. (The allusion to the fate of the real Socrates is clear.) Most students do not deal well with the ambiguity and uncertainty that are the hallmark of a genuine education: I recall a Harvard medical student, shown as part of a group of students experiencing problem-based learning on an episode of "Nova" on PBS, who said defensively, "I didn't come all this way to spend this kind of money to teach *myself*." It is thus naive and misguided to argue that intellectual standards are self-evidently desirable. Our *best* learners at lower levels (where learning is more rote) may balk at the upper levels. Setting high intellectual standards without providing incentives to persist, opportunities to fail and improve, and the tact, wisdom, and guiding model of a mentor is a cruel and hypocritical stance.

The eighth and final dilemma follows from this tension between setting standards and providing incentives to meet them. We aim to maximize everyone's achievement, but we cannot imagine how to do so without lowering or compromising our standards. We demand excellence from all, but we do not expect it. We establish mission statements under the assumption that all children can learn what we have to teach, but we test and grade under the assumption that some will do well and most will not.

The prejudices that underlie these expectations go very deep—far deeper than any contemporary biases, as Michel Foucault reminds us in describing the constant, elaborate, and deliberate ranking of pupils within French schools in the seventeenth and eighteenth centuries.[9] We may set out initially to uphold high standards, but many of our assessment practices unwittingly exaggerate differences and become self-fulfilling prophecies about our inability to do so. The standard curve could have been used as often as it is only under the assumption that uniform excellence due to deliberate education is impossible. All one need do to see the error of such thinking is to note the across-the-board quality performance that occurs through military, athletic, musical, or dramatic training in the best programs or to remember that in the original mastery learning research, the key finding was that "equal time spent on task" is a more important variable than aptitude for yielding a wide range of performance results; varying the learning time allowed leads to a significant decrease in range of results and often to across-the-board mastery of material.

On the other hand, the evidence that uniformly high standards *can* be upheld and met by everyone is usually dependent upon external assessments of some kind, as the examples suggest: we are delighted when everyone gets a 5 on an Advanced Placement exam. Yet educators *within* "good" schools are convinced that standardization in assessment will lower standards, and the minimum-competency movement seems to bear out their fears. On the other hand, idiosyncratic (and often eccentric or perverse) testing and grading easily result in schools and colleges where external standardization is resisted. This undermines a common concern for quality and student respect for standards. Is it not possible for a faculty to set high standards for all students and also make it possible for all students to meet those standards without charges of fraud or perversion of standards? (Is that not what the best colleges and private schools do?) Is there, in fact, such a thing as *one* standard? Could one not argue that there are as many standards as there are aspirations and programs?

Some Postulates for a More Thoughtful Assessment System

Our task, then, is more difficult than we perhaps first imagined. The quest is not for "better" tests, as if a mere technical deficiency or ignorance lay at the heart of our current problems in assessing for ultimate educational aims. We have to bring to consciousness and thoughtfully examine our deep-seated habit of seeking superficially correct answers to uniform questions. Technical improvements in performance testing will never obviate the need for careful judgment in the use of such testing, because the dilemmas just discussed are unavoidable. Are testers not therefore obligated to more carefully consider the dangers and limits of their techniques? How might we more effectively grasp and negotiate these dilemmas? Let me offer nine postulates, with some examples for each, as a way of considering these dilemmas and questions more carefully.

Postulate 1: Assessment of thoughtful mastery should ask students to justify their understanding and craft, not merely to recite orthodox views or mindlessly employ techniques in a vacuum.
We suffer from an impoverished conception of what it means to *know* something. Understanding is not displayed by "correct" answers to questions and problems out of context; on the contrary, misunderstanding is easily hidden behind thoughtless recall. Mastery of the liberal arts is not a mastery of orthodoxy but an ability to effectively *justify* one's answers and arguments—to a real audience or client, and in specific contexts where generic answers are not adequate.

Our schools, but especially our universities, are schizophrenic in this regard. Their traditions often reveal their roots in the rigid religious training of premodern times. But they now exist to foster research. There was and is an irresolvable tension between promoting orthodoxy and promoting inquiry. Whatever our modern ideology about inquiry, we still lean pretty heavily on the orthodoxy side in our assessment: up until the graduate experience, students have to first demonstrate their control over other people's knowledge in all subject matters. And K-12 schooling is filled with assessments that require the student to master an orthodox format (for example, the five-paragraph essay or three-step math proof), irrespective of the quality of the student's thinking. But this academic orthodoxy has little to do with the ultimate aim of developing effective inquirers, researchers, and scholars as exemplified in the ultimate educational "test"—the dissertation and oral in defense of a thesis.

A dissertation, high school history term paper, or third-grade book report does not provide adequate evidence of mastery; it is the *defense* or *discussion* of that product that reveals whether or not understanding is present. We must remember that all assessment should point toward the last stages of education and our assessments in the final stage (original research and defense against critics), so as to give the student both frequent warning of the need to *justify* opinions that are developed as a result of teaching and frequent opportunities to do so.

An effective examination is most certainly not "gotcha!" testing. The assessor is meant to probe, reframe questions, and even cue or prompt an answer, if necessary, to be sure of the student's actual ability and to enable even a poor performer to learn from assessment. In many orals, for example, the first answer (or lack of one) is not deemed a sufficient insight into the student's knowledge.[10] Not only is a first answer not decisive in the evaluation; there is a clear commitment to determine what it is the student really understands underneath apparently wrong or odd answers. The student is properly *rewarded* for self-corrections and self-conscious clarification of earlier responses.

Speaking logistically, a wholesale move toward more oral examinations would be difficult (though they are a routine part of subject exams in other countries). But there are other, less time-intensive measures that are feasible—measures that would allow us to honor the obligation to examine students' responses to follow-up questions and probes of their ideas, not merely to note and evaluate their first answers. The obligation implies, for instance, that in assigning a paper and evaluating it, the student should have to respond to our criticism (or the criticism of some other audience, perhaps of peers), to which we then respond *as part of the formal assessment process*—not as a voluntary exercise after the test or paper is completed.

To teach students that we are serious about intellectual standards, we must always assess their ability to see the limits of what is learned; they need to have the chance to punch holes in our own or the textbook's presentation. They have a right to demand justification of our point of view. That is what a liberal education is about. It also sends the right moral message: we are both, student and teacher, subservient to rational principles of evidence and argument.

Postulate 2: The student is an apprentice liberal artist and should be treated accordingly, through access to models and feedback in learning and assessment.

Any novice or apprentice needs models of excellence, the opportunity to imitate those models, and the chance to work on authentic scholarship projects.[11] Students should be required to recognize, learn from, and then produce quality work in unending cycles of model-practice-feedback-refinement. They should not get out of our clutches until they have produced some genuinely high-quality work of their own.

As I mentioned earlier, the International Baccalaureate (I.B.) has such a requirement—an "extended essay" involving student research in any I.B. subject. Students explore such diverse topics as the physics of a golf ball or the images in Jamaican poetry. (The I.B. even publishes a high-quality book containing some of the best essays from around the world.) What is instructive and gratifying about the I.B. assignment is the insistence that the student have a personal stake in the research. The guidelines explicitly discourage the kinds of sweeping, overambitious (and hence superficial and uninteresting) papers that our students too often produce. For example, under the guidelines for economics and for literature, the following advice is offered: "An unacceptable essay is one in which there is no personal research, which is dependent entirely on summarizing secondary sources. . . . Encourage: 'Price Theory and hairdressing in my town.' Discourage: 'OPEC 1980–1990.' " "Candidates should avoid topics which are general or vague. These usually lead to a superficial survey, often borrowed directly from textbooks, which has little or no educational value. Examples of topics to avoid: the origins of Romanticism, the use of nature in poetry, Greek mythology in English literature, etc."[12]

An apprentice must see and understand progress in a given craft—in this case, knowledge production. Paradoxically, that means, in part, learning to see one's past standards as now unacceptable. One of my favorite assignments when I taught at Brown was to ask students in their final paper for a rewrite of their first paper, based on all that they had since learned or thought. A number of the seniors told me that it was the most important event in their four years. They were astonished to see how their thinking had changed and to discover how sloppy their "complete" work seemed to them in retrospect.

Further, they were learning that thinking does not stand still—and that it *should* not. In demanding intellectual excellence of novices, we begin to focus our assessment on what Aristotle called the "intellectual virtues." Does the student display a sense of craftsmanship, perseverance, tolerance of ambiguity? Can the student display empathy when everyone else is critical, or be critical when everyone else is empathetic? Can the student, *without prodding,* rethink and revise a paper or point of view? An education is ultimately about those intellectual virtues. When all of the knowledge has faded away, when all of the cramming has been forgotten, if those intellectual dispositions do not remain, we have failed.

While some people get very squeamish about assessing such things as perseverance, style, craftsmanship, and love of precision, I do not. If we value something, we should assess it. The best way to assess such habits is indirectly: to devise tasks that require them, tasks that can be done well only if the requisite habits are present and well tapped by the student.[13] As I noted above, this indirect assessment was used by the OSS in testing spy candidates. All assessment would be much improved, in fact, if we thought of it as a kind of intellectual Outward Bound. It should never be possible to do an end run around those desirable habits. Students who can get A's by missing class, cramming, or articulateness and native ability only are telling us something about the failures of our assessment system.

Sometimes improved assessment involves as subtle a shift as sending the message day in and day out that quality matters—not just because teachers say so but because the situation demands it. Consider one simple strategy purportedly used by Uri Treisman at Berkeley in his successful work with minority mathematics students. He demands that every piece of work that students hand in be initialed by another student; students get both the grade for their own paper and the grade for the paper on which they signed off. This grading policy makes it clear that one is responsible for one's work, as both a producer and an editor; there are consequences for failing to adequately self-assess one's work or critique the work of others properly. One can go further by designing tests in which *situational* consequences occur through one's success or failure: if the problem in physics involves a model bridge needing to withstand a certain load; if the persuasive essay genuinely has to persuade a professional editor; if the student studying German has to order specific merchandise and request information from a German firm, then grades become apt symbols for real qualities and consequences. (This kind of "authentic simulation" and "quality control" is possible only when we also provide students with useful feedback as part of the assessment process, as we shall see in Chapter Six. *All* assessment should be thought of as "formative," to put it glibly.)

Postulate 3: An authentic assessment system has to be based on known, clear, public, nonarbitrary standards and criteria.

The student cannot be an effective apprentice liberal artist without models. There is no way to empower the student to master complex tasks if the tasks, criteria, and standards are mysterious (or are revealed, but not in advance). It is no wonder, then, that the ubiquitous one-shot, secure test and the often-secret scoring criteria undermine our educational aims.

When we look at the performance world (as opposed to the academic world), we see how much easier it is for performers to be successful, because the "tests" are known from day one. The sheet music, the script, the rules of debate, the rules and strategies of the game are or become known: genuine mastery involves internalizing public criteria and standards. Unfortunately, in education, especially in higher education, the primary vestige of our medieval past is the use of secret tests. (The novices always had to *divine* things.) I was disappointed to learn, when I was a teaching assistant at Harvard, that undergraduates are still not officially allowed to see their blue books after the final exam. But it could be worse: I was told that at Oxford and at Cambridge, they burn blue books!

This unfortunate and deadly tradition is a legacy of tests used as mere gatekeepers or as punishment/reward systems, not as empowering and educative experiences designed for displaying all that a student knows. Most people would likely say, if asked, that it is the *student's* responsibility to figure out what will be tested, not the teacher's responsibility to make it unambiguous. But why would we not require the school or university to meet students halfway and give them a chance to play from their strengths?

Possible solutions include strategies as simple as giving students the option of alternative forms of the same assignment or handing out in advance a long list of possible questions from which a few will be chosen for the exam (a practice common in colleges and graduate schools). Other solutions include the supplying in advance of scoring rubrics, model papers, or videotaped model performances—anything that would give students an insight into the standards in force. Here is an example of a scoring rubric from a past Advance Placement (AP) exam in U.S. history:

> *Question:* "The economic policies of the federal government from 1921 to 1929 were responsible for the nation's depression of the 1930's." Assess the validity of this generalization.

> *Scores*

> 13–15 An accurate, well-written response that directly assesses the validity of the generalization. Demonstrates a clear understanding of governmental economic policies; for example, tariffs, pro-business legislation, and foreign debt. Uses at least three specific examples or covers many topics with an intelligent conclusion.

> 10–12 A good answer that attempts with some detail to assess the validity of the statement, if only implicitly. Should cover at least two areas of economic policy, but may contain a few minor errors of fact.

> 07–09 A reasonably coherent discussion, but with little analysis of economic issues. Answer is not fully developed; may discuss only one issue beyond the level of assertion; for example, laissez-faire policies. Or may give a coherent discussion of concepts without citing specific acts or policies.

04–06   Little if any assessment of the statement. An
overgeneralized answer, without supporting
evidence. . . . The stock market crash must be
seen as not merely an event but a consequence
of prior policies. . . .[14]

It is expected that the AP teacher will have gone over past
essay questions and scoring systems with the student (indeed, books
are available from the AP program in which past questions, scoring
rubrics, and sample essays are provided, with commentary). Note,
however, that the language of the rubric is *inherently* vague, representing as it does the generalizations of strengths and deficiencies
found in the many different papers judged by readers to be of equivalent value. The student, to understand and effectively use the
rubric, needs to see samples of the papers that correspond to the
scores.

What is less noble in the AP experience, of course, is the fact
that the student has neither advance knowledge of the question that
will be asked nor access to resources in answering the question.
What, then, are we really assessing here, insofar as the student cannot be expected to be an expert on every conceivable question that
the AP examiners might propose? I pursue this problem thoroughly
in Chapter Seven, where I argue that "authenticity" often depends
more on the constraints of the test and its administration than on
the task itself.

*Postulate 4: An authentic education makes self-assessment
central.*

The means for dispelling secrecy are the same means for
ensuring a higher across-the-board quality of work from even our
most worrisome students: teaching students how to self-assess and
self-adjust, based on the performance standards and criteria to be
used. Alverno College, mentioned earlier, has successfully made
self-assessment central to its program. In one of my favorite examples, assessment of the communications competency, a student must
early on give a videotaped talk. One's first hunch might be that it
is the talk that is going to be assessed. No: after the student gives
the talk and it is videotaped, the student is assessed on the accuracy

of her self-assessment of that videotaped talk![15] If we want people
to gain control of important habits of standards and habits of mind,
then they have to know, *perhaps first of all,* how to accurately view
those things and to apply criteria to their own work; they cannot
always be dependent upon another person for assessment. (Here
again we see the importance of not treating Bloom's Taxonomy as
a chronology for teaching: "evaluation" is taught from the beginning at Alverno and in other competency-based programs.) Habit
development depends upon constant self-assessment, but you need
to know what you are *supposed* to be doing before you can do it.

One practical implication of this postulate is that we should
require students to submit a self-assessment with all major pieces
of work. (Alverno requires each student paper to have clipped to it
a self-assessment and one of the subscores given by the teacher is for
the accuracy of the self-assessment.) The Advanced Placement art
portfolio is a different example of such a system: students submit
both a letter and a set of works to the reviewers. The letter explains
their intent; the works reveal the actual effect. The judges determine
whether, in their professional judgment, the students' intentions
were fully realized in the work in question. (This also shows how
it is possible to score work rigorously where the work submitted by
a group of students is not superficially comparable.)

*Postulate 5: We should treat each student as a would-be
intellectual performer, not as a would-be learned spectator.*

Most courses (and almost all traditional tests) treat the student as a would-be learned spectator rather than as an apprentice
intellectual performer. The student must metaphorically "sit in the
bleachers" or do drill on the sidelines while others (professors,
teachers, and writers of textbooks) "perform." But a liberal education aims at the student's ability to employ knowledge effectively
and gracefully, in the context of authentic problems and interactions.

Too many schools define *mastery* as accurately remembering
and applying what others say in a plug-in sort of way. This anti-
intellectual posture easily induces passivity and cynicism in students. To unendingly postpone the students' doing of their own
work is to turn powerful ideas and challenges into drudgery. In an

education aimed at would-be performers, on the other hand, students experience the "tests" that face the expert in the field right from the start—having to find and clarify problems, conduct research, justify their opinion in some public setting—while using (other people's) knowledge in the service of their own opinion.

One of the finest classes that I have ever seen taught at any level, which illustrates this point, was at a high school in Portland, Maine. A veteran teacher offered a Russian history course for which the entire syllabus consisted of a series of chronological biographies. It was then each student's job to put the course together, by becoming each person, in turn, and in two senses: through a ten-minute talk and then through an interactive simulation in character. After four or five students had presented their talks (and been assessed by other students on those talks), they had a Steve Allen "Meeting of the Minds" press conference chaired by the teacher; the "journalists" were the other students. Each member of the panel scored the others on their performance.

A striking thing about the in-character reports I heard in that classroom was their engaging quality. I have sat through my share of dreary student reports. These were as delightful, personalized, and informative as any I have ever heard. In response to my query about why, the teacher said that it was very simple: students knew that there were only two criteria by which they were going to be judged—whether the talk was accurate and (more important) whether it was interesting. How difficult can it be to ask for what we really want? Yet how many rubrics have you seen that put a premium on the interest level of student writing or on the persuasiveness of student presentations? Our assessments are mechanical and disengaged. No wonder student performances often are too.

Postulate 6: An education should develop a student's intellectual style and voice.

As suggested by the previous point, what a liberal artist will be, if he or she has "made it," is somebody who has a style. Somebody whose intellectual "voice" is natural, compelling, and clearly individual. Read the turgid prose that we receive *and accept,* and you can see that we are failing to develop style, voice, and an engaging point of view. (Read our own professional writing in academic journals.) Students are convinced that we want merely the party line and that insights cast in compelling prose are an option, not a requirement.

There are a number of ways to get at this style component of assessment. Some writing assessments now score papers for "voice," not just mechanics and organization.[16] Consider, for example, Exhibit 2.1.—the rubric from a Canadian assessment—noting especially the caution to judges at the bottom.

Another approach might ask students, after they have written a lengthy research paper (with all the requisite footnotes and bibliographical information), to turn the same research into a one-page paper to be delivered, in an engaging and insightful way, to an audience of laypersons such as Rotarians.

Do not misunderstand me. This is not just an aesthetic issue, this issue of style or voice. It is an issue of one's inner voice. It is the serious problem of how to strengthen one's faint intellectual intuition in a sea of loud professorial or textbook opinions, how to nurture the seed of a new idea that is easily crushed if not allowed to grow. This is related to the idea of conscience, and it is no coincidence that Socrates talked about his little voice as his most trustworthy guide.

It is easy, as a student, to lose that little voice. But that voice is not just a "personal" voice, irrelevant to "academic" accomplishment. It is the voice of common sense and of inchoate hunches. It is the voice that can turn around and question the importance of what one has just spent two months working on. In other words, it is the little voice that says, Ah, come on, is this really *that* important? It is the little voice that says, You know, there is probably another way to look at this. It is the little voice that says, I have a feeling that there is something not quite right about what the teacher is saying—what Neil P. Postman and Charles W. Weingartner, in great sixties' fashion, called a "crap detector." It is the little voice that most of us do not hear in our students (or ourselves) unless it is asked for. An assessment should ask for it.

There are ways of assessing such seemingly intangible capacities. I saw an English teacher do essentially what I am describing through a peer editing process. He told his students that they should turn back any paper that was boring or slapdash and mark the exact spot where they began to lose interest. The paper was not "finished"

**Exhibit 2.1. Alberta, Canada,
High School Leaving Exam: Writing Assessment.**

Section I: Personal Response to Literature—Scoring Guide

Thought and Detail

When marking **Thought and Detail**, the marker should consider how
effectively
  • the assignment is addressed
  • the detail supports and/or clarifies the response

5   *Excellent:* An insightful understanding of the reading selection(s) is
    effectively demonstrated. The student's opinion, whether directly stated
    or implied, is perceptive and is appropriately supported by specific
    details. Support is well defined and appropriate.
4   *Proficient:* A well-considered understanding of the reading selection(s)
    is appropriately demonstrated. The student's opinion, whether directly
    stated or implied, is thoughtful and is supported by details. Support is
    well defined and appropriate.
3   *Satisfactory:* A defensible understanding of the reading selection(s) is
    clearly demonstrated. The student's opinion, whether directly stated or
    implied, is conventional but is plausibly supported. Support is general
    but functional.
2   *Limited:* An understanding of the reading selection(s) may be evident
    but is vaguely demonstrated or is not always defensible or sustained.
    The student's opinion may be superficial, and support is scant and/or
    vague, and/or redundant.
1   *Poor:* An implausible conjecture concerning the reading selection(s) is
    suggested. The student's opinion, if present, is irrelevant or incompre-
    hensible. Support is inappropriate, inadequate, or absent.
INS *Insufficient:* The marker can discern no evidence of an attempt to fulfil
    the assignment, or the writing is so deficient in length that it is not
    possible to assess thought and detail.

*It is important to recognize that student responses to the Personal Response
Assignment will vary from writing that treats personal views and ideas
analytically and rather formally to writing that explores ideas experimen-
tally and informally. Consequently, evaluation of the personal response on
the diploma examination will be in the context of Louise Rosenblatt's
suggestion:*
The evaluation of the answer would be in terms of the amount of evidence
that the [student] has actually read something and thought about it, not a
question of whether necessarily he has thought about it in the way an adult
would, or given an adult's "correct" answer. (Rosenblatt, Louise. "The
Reader's Contribution in the Literary Experience." An interview with Li-
onel Wilson in *The English Quarterly 1* (Spring, 1981): 3–12.)

Source: Alberta Education (1993). *1993–94 School Year, English 33
Information Bulletin, Diploma Examinations Program.* Edmonton, Alberta. Reprinted with the permission of Alberta Education.

in the peer review process, as a revised draft, until the peer readers were able to read to the end of the paper without placing that mark. That sort of assessment sends a message to students about writing and its purpose—a message that technical compliance with formal criteria is a means to an end, not our aim as writers.[17]

There is another point to this issue of voice and style. The thing that is so ghastly about academic prose is that one really does sense that it is not meant for any real or particular audience. (Of course, sometimes it isn't, in the sense that rhetorical or aesthetic qualities apparently count for nil, as judged by editors.) It seems to me that if we are serious about empowering students, we must get them to worry about audience in a deeper way. We must demand that their work be *effective*. We must demand that it actually reach the audience and accomplish its intended purpose. There is nothing more foolish, in my view, than saying, "Write a persuasive essay" without making students persuade anybody of anything. So let us set up situations in which the student has to persuade readers, or at least get judged by an audience on more than just accuracy. Even Socrates knew, within the clash of Reason and Rhetoric, that teaching had to be not merely truthful but effective.

Postulate 7: Understanding is best assessed by pursuing students' questions, not merely by noting their answers.

Too often in assessment, we worry about whether students have learned what we taught. This is sensible, of course. But let me take an unorthodox position: such a view of assessment, taken to extremes, is incompatible with the "test" of the liberal arts. One important purpose of those "arts that would make us free" is to enable us to criticize sanctioned ideas, not merely retell what was taught.

A less confrontational way to make the point is to remind ourselves that it is the astute questioner, not the technically correct answerer, who symbolizes the liberal artist. We would do well to recall a point made by the philosopher Hans-Georg Gadamer (with his explicit homage to our friend Socrates), who argued that it is the dominant opinion, not ignorance, that threatens thinking.[18] Ensuring that the student has the capacity to keep questions alive in the face of peer pressure, conventional wisdom, and the habit of our own convictions is what the liberal arts must always be about.

Admittedly, *some* knowledge is required before we can ask good questions and pursue the answers we receive. But if we are honest about this, we will admit that the kind of exhaustive expertise we typically expect of students up front is overkill. After all, children are wonderful and persistent questioners. Indeed, academic types are invariably prone to making the mistake that philosopher Gilbert Ryle called the Cartesian fallacy: assuming that a complete "knowing that" must *always* precede and serve as a condition for "knowing how."[19] No person who creates knowledge or uses knowledge to put bread on the table would ever be guilty of this fallacy. All apprentices and would-be performers learn on the job. Given that, as teachers, we therefore tend to overteach or "front load" knowledge, a good pedagogical rule of thumb is this: teach the minimum necessary to get the students asking questions that will lead to your more subtle goals.

We would do well, then, to think of our task as introducing the student to cycles of question-answer-question and not just question-answer—with the aim of a course being, in part, to make the student, not the teacher or text, the ultimate initiator of the cycle. To continually postpone the students' ability to ask important questions in the name of "mastery" is to jeopardize their intellect. Good judgment and aggressive thinking will atrophy if they are incessantly postponed while professors profess. In any event, the most important "performance" in the liberal arts is to initiate and sustain good question-asking.

Some very practical points about testing can be made out of this esoteric argument. We rarely assess students on their ability to ask good questions. Indeed, we rarely teach them a repertoire of question-asking strategies for investigating essential ideas and issues. If what we assess is what we de facto value (irrespective of what we say), then it should become obvious to students through the demands of the course and our assessment strategies that question-asking is central. Too often, however, our assessments send the message that mastery of the "given" is the exclusive aim and that question-asking is not a masterable skill but a spontaneous urge.

The problem goes deeper. Our scope-and-sequence curriculum-writing (and the tests that follow from it) suggests a very inert and atomistic view of knowing. How, then, will students' naive understanding of the same subjects across the years of education become developed, tested, and integrated? How will we know whether students are becoming not merely "knowledgeable" but also more sophisticated in their understanding of the same important ideas unless we persist in asking the same important questions over time? Jerome Bruner suggested in his seminal book *The Process of Education* that any subject could be taught in a credible and effective way, at any cognitive level.[20] I would go further: the younger student will never make it to the upper levels of academe without being repeatedly confronted with the most important questions and perspectives on those questions, beginning at the earliest levels of education.[21]

Postulate 8: A vital aim of education is to have students understand the limits and boundaries of ideas, theories, and systems.

To paint the starkest picture of the difference between a "liberal" and a "non-liberal" view of the disciplines, we in the liberal camp might see our task as teaching and assessing the ability to gauge the strengths and weaknesses of every major notion we teach—be it a theorem in math, a hypothesis in science, or a literary theory in English. We need to know if students can see the strengths and weaknesses of theories and paradigms. This would include not only the limits of a theory within a unit or subject but across disciplines, as when we apply the rules of physical science to the human sciences.

A few years back, as part of my work with the Coalition of Essential Schools, I made reference to so-called essential questions as a way of formalizing this idea, and a number of schools (most notably, Central Park East Secondary School) developed an entire framework around the idea.[22] There is no novelty in the concept, however. Bruner talked about "guiding conjectures," and Joseph Schwab, many years ago, wrote about and taught from a similar concept at the University of Chicago.[23] He termed the ability to move back and forth across these questions and limits the art of the "eclectic" and I encourage a return to his essays for numerous suggestions on how to help students explore the merits of sanctioned truths and the boundaries of subject-area insight.

I fear that we no longer know how to teach science (or any

established body of knowledge) as a liberal art. To present the sciences as merely logical and technical is to make it increasingly unlikely that nonscientists will profit from studying science enough to support intelligent science policy as adults (and to make science students insufficiently critical). As it stands now, too little of learning science or other subjects involves doing science and too much to do with mastering orthodox algorithms—learning metaphysics instead of physics, as it were; mastering sanctioned (hence inert) truths instead of learning and being assessed on the truth of the matter: the truths are provisional, yielded by intellectual methods and questions that *transcend* the current results.

I know this weakness in our science students firsthand from my high school teaching days. My best students did not understand, for example, that error is inherent in science and not merely the fault of immature students or poor equipment. (Many believed that when the "big boys and girls" do their measuring, the results are exact.) Nor did many of them realize that words such as *gravity* and *atom* do not correspond to visible "things".

Students can be helped to see the limits of ideas by talking about the history of a subject. We still do a poor job of teaching and assessing students' grasp of the history of important ideas, and yet I know of no method by which inappropriately sacred truths can be more effectively demystified and thoughtfully reconsidered. What questions were Newton and then Einstein trying to answer? What did the first drafts of a history textbook look like, and why were they revised? To ask these questions is to open up a new and exciting world for students. To be smug about our knowledge and to distance ourselves from "crude" and outdated theory is to ensure that we repeat the mistakes of our smug and parochial elders.

Consider the history of geometry, the very idea of which strikes many people as an oxymoron. Many college students are utterly unaware of the problems that forced Euclid to develop an awkward parallel postulate (which was instantly decried by his colleagues). So much for "self-evident truths," that glib phrase found in superficial textbook accounts of Greek mathematics!

The practical consequence of our failure to reveal to students the history of important ideas and assess their understanding of that history is twofold. For one, students easily end up assuming that axioms, laws, postulates, theories, and systems are immutable—

even though common sense and history say otherwise. This fundamental confusion seems not to disturb enough people: when I was
a consultant to the Connecticut performance assessment project in
math and science, I proposed the following challenge as a worthy
task for assessing understanding of geometry:

> Two mathematicians had a debate. The first said that
> the postulates of geometry are like the rules of games:
> a system of rules and a mental model for thinking
> about space, but not "real." The second disagreed,
> saying that geometry is more like the features of the
> world and the textbook therefore more like a roadmap,
> a guidebook to what space "really" is like. Professor
> A's views seem to imply that geometry was *invented*
> *by mathematicians,* while Professor B seems to suggest
> that geometry was *discovered* (in the same way that
> America and the roundness of the earth were discov-
> ered). Who do you think was more correct and why?
> You work for a national student-focused magazine.
> Your editor wants you to come up with a lively article
> on the debate, giving examples most supportive of
> each side, interviews with audience members on their
> different reactions, and reasons why a reader of the
> magazine should care about the debate.

Only Steve Leinwand, the head of secondary mathematics
education for Connecticut (and a delightfully unorthodox thinker
in his own right), grasped both the importance of my prompt and
the alarming implication of its rejection by all the teachers.[24] Can
a student truly be said to *understand* geometry who is unaware of
the limits of the system or the reasons behind the extraordinary
move away from thinking of geometry as "real" to thinking of it
as axiomatic? Even our best math students are unaware that non-
Euclidean geometries can be proven to be as logically sound as
Euclid's; fewer still are helped to understand the sea change in our
thinking about what knowledge is that resulted when geometry
could no longer be viewed as a system of truths.

The second result of our failure to teach and test for the
history of ideas is that it does lasting harm to intellectual courage

in all but our feistiest students. Students never grasp that "knowledge" is the product of someone's "thinking"—thinking that was as lively, unfinished, and (sometimes) muddled as their own. One major reason for the intellectual poverty in this country is that most students become convinced either that they are incapable of being intellectual or that they are uninterested in being intellectual, thinking that it involves only the arcane expertise of a narrowly framed and inert subject.

Some practical assessment implications? First, we should require that students keep notebooks of reflections on coursework, their increasing knowledge, and important changes of mind about that knowledge. Second, we should assess this work as part of the grade. I did so for many years and found the notebooks to be the most important and revealing aspect of the students' work. I also learned a lot about how their thinking evolved in a way that improved the courses I taught. Third, the most technical of trainings should ask students to do critical research into the origins of the ideas being learned, so that students can gain greater perspective on their work. To fail to do this, whether out of habit or rationalization that there is no time for such reflection, is to risk producing a thoughtless batch of students.

Postulate 9: We should assess students' intellectual honesty and other habits of mind.

To worry about whether understanding is "thoughtful" or "thoughtless" is ultimately to concern ourselves with whether students are honest or dishonest about what they know and how they have come to know it.

I am not referring to the obviously heinous crime of cheating—something we know to be all too common. Rather, I am talking about the moral obligation of the student to emulate Socrates' trademark: his cheerful admission of ignorance. Alas, our students rarely do admit their ignorance. Thus one of our primary tasks should be to elicit (and not penalize) the admission. But the student's willingness to risk the admission depends upon *our* willingness. It is only after both teacher and student have admitted ignorance, as the Meno dialogue reminds us, that mutual inquiry and dialogue become possible; only then are we placed on equal moral footing as thinkers. Unfortunately, our inclination to "profess" is always in danger of closing the doors through which our students can enter the liberal conversation without excessive self-deprecation: so many of our students preface a wonderful idea by saying, "I know this sounds stupid, but. . . ."

Let our assessments therefore routinely encourage students to distinguish between what they do and do not know with conviction. Let us design scoring systems for papers that heavily penalize mere slickness and feigned control over a complex subject and greatly reward honest admissions of ignorance or confusion. And let us ask students to write a paper in which they critique the previous one they wrote.

Intellectual honesty is just one aspect of self-knowledge. Another important aspect is the absence of self-deception. This too can be furthered through assessment. One of my favorite notions along these lines was something the atomic physicist Leo Slizard is reputed to have said about how to assess doctoral candidates. He argued that students should be assessed on how precisely and well they know their strengths and limitations and felt that it was a mistake to err greatly in *either* direction. I am not arguing for teachers to become counselors or depth psychologists; I *am* arguing for their responsibility in improving the students' ability to self-assess in the deepest sense. We must ensure that students have neither excessive nor deficient pride in their work, either of which closes off further intellectual challenges and rewards.

The inherent danger of all scholarship is not so much error as blind spots in our knowledge—blind spots hidden by the increasingly narrowed focus of our work and the isolation that can then breed worse: arrogance. Excessive pride leads us not only to ignore or paper over our doubts but more subtly to be deceived about the uniqueness and worth of our ideas. We forget that it was a conversation with others in the coffee shop or an article in a recent journal that sparked the idea. A few collaborative assessment tasks, with some required reflection on every student's part about the roles of each contributor, would provide useful perspective for everyone. Similarly, students in the ARTS PROPEL program in Pittsburgh were required to thoroughly document the "biography" of a work—from the germ of the idea written on the back of an envelope, to peer criticisms, to the final draft—so as to see how ideas unfold and are influenced by others.

Given the importance of collaboration, we should also assess class discussions more thoroughly than we do. We again fail to assess what we value when we make it possible for students to learn everything that we deem necessary just by listening to us and doing the reading. Over the years, I have developed materials for assessment (and self-assessment) of class discussions, one example of which is found in Exhibit 2.2. (Each student fills out an evaluation after each major discussion, and the teacher fills out a simplified version on a weekly basis for each student.)

Which brings us back to Socrates, the discussant as teacher. What casual readers of Plato—(and even some overly analytic philosophers) always fail to grasp is that the dialogues invariably are about the role that character plays in intellectual development; they are never about mere "theories" of virtue, knowledge, or piety. The twists and turns of dialogue, the sparring with Sophists or young know-it-alls ultimately are meant to show that character flaws, not cognitive defects, impede the quest for a lifelong education. It is our *attitude* toward knowledge that ultimately determines whether we become wise (as opposed to merely learned.)

As Socrates repeatedly reminds us, we must love wisdom enough to question our knowledge—even our pet ideas, if need be. By extension, the more we gain confidence in our ideas, the more we must become vigilant about finding knowledge in unexpected places: we must imagine that those who seem incapable of wisdom might teach us something (as our students often do).

It is therefore not a canon—of ideas or books—that defines the liberal arts, but a set of very hard-won virtues. Like all sophisticated dispositions, these liberal habits are typically revealed only when they are challenged. It is only when peer pressure is greatest— be it in the classroom with students or at conferences with our peers—that we learn who has the power to keep questions alive. (Remember Gadamer's reminder that it is not ignorance but dominant opinion that is the enemy of thoughtfulness.) The liberal arts, properly speaking, do not *make* you free; they *keep* you free. Wisdom—as Socrates knew—reveals itself when persistent inquiry is threatened: externally by custom and such remarks as, "Oh, *everyone* knows . . . ," and internally by the tendency to rationalize our own habits, beliefs, and fears.

How much do students really love to learn, to persist, to

Exhibit 2.2. Discussion Rating Scales.

How did you feel about today's discussion?

Class's treatment of issues
superficial   1   2   3   4   5   thorough and deep

Helpfulness of discussion to your understanding
low   1   2   3   4   5   high

Your own level of engagement
low   1   2   3   4   5   high

The class's overall level of engagement
low   1   2   3   4   5   high

Quality of your own participation
poor   1   2   3   4   5   excellent

Quantity of your spoken remarks relative to your normal performance
low   1   2   3   4   5   high

Degree of your own understanding of material
limited   1   2   3   4   5   full

Facilitator's Success
too much input   1   2   3   4   5   too little input

too much control   1   2   3   4   5   too little control

great respect for   1   2   3   4   5   too little respect for
others   others

Comments:

---

passionately attack a problem or task? How willing are they, like
many of the great Native American potters of New Mexico, to watch
some of their prized ideas explode and to start anew? How willing
are they to go beyond being merely dutiful or long-winded? Let us

assess such things, just as good coaches do when they bench the talented player who "dogs" it or when they thrust the novice into the lineup because the novice's pluck impresses them more than the lack of experience.

We must make habits of mind—the intellectual virtues—central to our assessment. It is to our detriment and the detriment of the liberal arts that we feel squeamish about saying and doing so. The Scottish are not so squeamish: one report card I saw assessed students in terms of achievement, perseverance, and *flair!*[25] For that matter, most references requested of teachers by college admissions offices involve an assessment of those virtues. Consider, for example, the "universal" form used by a large group of private colleges (see Exhibit 2.3).

Let us thus routinely "test" students in the same way that a mountain "tests" the climber—through challenges designed to evoke the proper virtues, if they are present. And if they are not present, the quality of the resultant work should seem so inadequate to the *student* that little need be said in the way of evaluative feedback.

Let our assessments be built upon that age-old distinction between wisdom and knowledge, then. Too subjective? Unfair? Not to those who have the master's eyes, ears, and sense of smell—who have *tact,* in the old and unfortunately lost sense of that word. For these intellectual traits are as tangible as any fact to the true mentor, and they are more important to the student's welfare in the long run. It is not the student's errors that matter, but the student's responses to error; it is not mastery of a simplistic task that impresses, but the student's risk taking with the inherently complex; it is not thoroughness in a novice's work that reveals understanding, but full awareness of the dilemmas, compromises, and uncertainties lurking under the arguments he or she is willing to tentatively stand on.

If our typical testing encourages smug or thoughtless mastery—and it does—we undermine the liberal arts. If our assessment systems induce timidity, cockiness, or crass calculations about grades and the relevance of each assignment, we undermine the liberal arts. If our assessments value correctness more than insight and honesty, we undermine the liberal arts. If our assessments value ease of scoring over the important task of revealing to students the

Exhibit 2.3. One Form for Assessing the Intellectual Virtues.

Please feel free to write whatever you think is important about the applicant, including a description of academic and personal characteristics. We are particularly interested in the candidate's intellectual purpose, motivation, relative maturity, integrity, independence, originality, leadership potential, capacity for growth, special talents, and enthusiasm. We welcome information that will help us to differentiate this student from others.

Ratings

	No basis	Below average	Average	Good	Very good	One of the top few encountered in my career
Creative, original thought						
Motivation						
Independence, initiative						
Intellectual ability						
Academic achievement						
Written expression of ideas						
Effective class discussion						
Disciplined work habits						
Potential for growth						
Summary Evaluation						

Academic skills and potential

errors or tasks that matter most, we undermine the liberal arts. Let us ensure, above all else, that our tests do just what Socrates' tests were meant to do: help us distinguish genuine from sham authority, the sophists from the wise. Then we will have assessments that are worthy of our aims.

Notes

1. This chapter is a substantial revision of a speech given to the American Association of Higher Education convention in Washington, D C., in June of 1991.

2. *Plato: Laches, Protagoras, Meno, Euthydemus,* W.R.M. Lamb, trans. (Cambridge, Mass.: Harvard University Press, 1962).

3. This is made quite clear in other Platonic dialogues. Theaetetus, for example, falls into some of the same self-inflicted logical errors made by Meno, but he is more aware of and honest about his mistakes, prompting Socrates to commend him on his forthrightness and adaptation to the conversation. See *Plato,* W.R.M. Lamb, trans.

4. G. Wiggins, "A True Test: Toward More Authentic and Equitable Assessment," *Phi Delta Kappan* 70 (1989a): 703–713.

5. A. H. Shoenfeld, "Problem Solving in Context(s)," in R. Charles and E. Silver, eds., *The Teaching and Assessing of Mathematical Problem Solving* (Reston, Va.: National Council of Teachers of Mathematics/Erlbaum, 1988), p. 84.

6. Many critics of alternative assessment are also convinced that the critics of conventional testing are against all testing. See J. Cizek, "Confusion Effusion: A Rejoinder to Wiggins," *Phi Delta Kappan* 73 (1991): 150–153. I confess that the conservative has a valid point here: many critics of standardized tests reveal themselves to be against all formal evaluation in reference to standards. That is a mistake, and it is one reason that alternative school people end up shooting themselves in the foot: they sometimes produce free spirits who are not very capable.

7. T. S. Kuhn, *The Structure of Scientific Revolutions,* 2nd ed. (Chicago: University of Chicago Press, 1970), pp. 165–166.

8. *Meaning* and *significance* are *not* synonyms, as C. K. Ogden and I. A. Richards's classic treatise on the meaning of meaning reminds us. (See C. K. Ogden and I. A. Richards, *The Meaning of Meaning*, 5th ed. [Orlando, Fla.: Harcourt Brace Jovanovich, 1938].) Meanings, they argued, are "objective," because they are derivable from the text or facts at hand. Significance, however, is more personal—projective and contextual. Whether or not this view is sound for literary criticism (consider the arguments between deconstructionists and hermeneuticists, for instance), it has a commonsense appeal. Thus the Pythagorean theorem may not have much significance to the average fifteen-year-old, but a great deal of important meaning and connection can be found in reference to it.

9. M. Foucault, *Discipline and Punish*. (New York: Vintage Books, 1977), pp. 181–184.

10. See Chapters Four and Five for more on the relationship between assessment, incentives, and tact.

11. See A. Collins, J. S. Brown, and S. E. Newman, "Cognitive Apprenticeship: Teaching the Crafts of Reading, Writing, and Mathematics," in L. B. Resnick, ed., *Knowing, Learning, and Instruction: Essays in Honor of Robert Glaser* (Hillsdale, N.J.: Erlbaum, 1989), on cognitive apprenticeship, and H. Gardner, *The Unschooled Mind: How Children Think and How Schools Should Teach* (New York: Basic Books, 1991).

12. From International Baccalaureate Examination Office, Extended Essay Guidelines (Cardiff, Wales: International Baccalaureate Examination Office, 1991).

13. See G. Wiggins, "Creating Tests Worth Taking," *Educational Leadership* 49 (1992): 26–33, and Center on Learning, Assessment, and School Structure, *Standards, Not Standardization*, Vol. 3: *Rethinking Student Assessment* (Geneseo, N.Y.: Center on Learning, Assessment, and School Structure, 1993), for more on the design of performance tasks.

14. From the 1983 Advanced Placement exam in U.S. history.

15. A vivid picture of such self-assessment in action can be found in G. Grant and W. Kohli, "Assessing Student Performance," in G. Grant and Associates, *On Competence: A Critical Analysis of Competence-Based Reforms in Higher Education* (San

Francisco: Jossey-Bass, 1979). This comprehensive study of college competency-based programs is essential reading for K-12 educators, especially those involved in outcomes-based education programs.

16. See P. Elbow, *Writing with Power: Techniques for Mastering the Writing Process* (New York: Oxford University Press, 1981).

17. No one has written more compellingly and informatively on this subject than Elbow in *Writing with Power*. See Chapter Six where I discuss his ideas further.

18. H.-G. Gadamer, *Truth and Method* (New York: Crossroad, 1982).

19. See G. Ryle, *The Concept of Mind* (London: Hutchinson House, 1949).

20. J. Bruner, *The Process of Education* (Cambridge, Mass.: Harvard University Press, 1960/1977).

21. This line of argument has profound consequences for scoring rubrics. There is a need to ensure that the scoring rubric is written "backwards" from the deepest and most penetrating understanding, therefore. The case for "developmental" and "progress" (longitudinal) assessments is discussed in Chapter Five. Such a system is now in place in Great Britain.

22. See G. Wiggins, "Creating Tests Worth Taking."

23. See J. Schwab, *Science, Curriculum, and Liberal Education* (Chicago: University of Chicago Press, 1978).

24. For readers interested in understanding the historical importance of this debate, see M. Kline, *Mathematics in Western Culture* (New York: Oxford University Press, 1953), and M. Kline, *Mathematics: The Loss of Certainty* (New York: Oxford University Press, 1980).

25. D. Archbald and F. Newmann, *Beyond Standardized Testing: Authentic Academic Achievement in the Secondary School* (Reston, Va.: NASSP Publications, 1988).

3 | The Morality of Test Security

It is so common that we barely give it a second thought: the tests that we and others design to evaluate the success of student learning invariably depend upon secrecy.[1] Secrecy as to the questions that will be asked. Secrecy as to how the questions will be chosen. Secrecy as to how the results will be scored. Sometimes secrecy as to when we will be tested. Secrecy as to what the scores mean (if we are not given back our tests and an answer key). Secrecy as to how the results will be used. What a paradoxical affair! Our aim is to educate, to prepare, to enlighten, yet our habits of testing are built upon procedures that continually keep students in the dark—procedures with roots in premodern traditions of legal proceedings and religious inquisitions.

As with all deep-seated habits, we have lost sight of the questionable aspects of the practice beneath our rationalizations: "Surely we want the student to be able to grapple with the unexpected. . . . How could we *possibly* give the student access to the questions in advance? . . . There is no way to obtain validity without test security. . . . Hasn't testing *always* been done this way? . . . Isn't our secure testing system more 'fair,' since it ensures that everyone is judged in the same way?" The unthinking character of these responses would be plain if not for the ubiquity and seductive ease of the use of secrecy. We need only look at technical guides on how to enforce test security to become alert to the moral and intellectual dangers inherent in the practice. For example, in an old

textbook on testing, we are advised to "deny the examinee information concerning the rightness or wrongness of his response" as a
way of keeping the test secure for other potential test takers—
though the harm to the learner is inescapable and overt in such a
procedure.[2]

Why would we take for granted that students do not have a
right to full knowledge and justification of the form and content of
each test and the standards by which their work will be judged? The
student's (and often the teacher's) future is at stake, yet neither has
an opportunity to question the aptness or adequacy of the test, the
keying of the answers, or the scoring of the answers. Why would we
assume that any test designer—be it a company or a classroom
teacher—has a prior right to keep such information from test takers
(and often test users)? Why would we assume, contrary to all accepted guidelines of experimental research, that test companies (and
teachers) need not publish their tests and results after the fact for
scrutiny by independent experts as well as the test taker? Maybe the
better advice to test makers is that offered twenty years ago by performance assessment researchers Robert Fitzpatrick and Edward
Morrison: "The best solution to the problem of test security is to
keep no secrets."[3]

Whatever the technical reasons for test security, it clearly does
unintended harm to students. Steady doses of such secrecy may well
beget a lasting form of student furtiveness in response. Students
learn to fear admitting ignorance or being creative. Questionable or
imaginative responses, rather than being valued by students as the
building blocks of thoughtful understanding, are viewed nervously
as potential mistakes. The aim becomes not personal knowledge but
figuring out "what they want"—better safe than sorry, though the
loss of intellectual autonomy and honesty may be deeply regretted
later in life. If by *character* we mean intellectual courage and moral
integrity, then character may well be threatened by tests that are
perpetually secret. The legacy of cramming, cheating, and "teaching to the test" may be imitative responses on the part of students
and teachers to a sanctioned deceptiveness.

Adults have lost their empathy here. We no longer feel the
useless anxiety the student feels in a world of tests that are valid only
because of the prior (and often subsequent) secrecy of the instru-

ment. Though we at some level "know" that risk taking and high-level performance do not emerge in a climate of secrecy, we fail to see how our test rituals sanctify such a stance. Yet if we think of public policy or personal histories, the danger becomes clear: "Secrecy can debilitate judgment whenever it shuts out criticism and feedback, leading people to become mired down in stereotyped, un-examined and often erroneous beliefs and ways of thinking."[4]

In this chapter, we will examine the different kinds of secrecy found in testing situations everywhere. The case will be made that, while each form of secrecy can be appropriate in specific contexts, there is a need for much greater clarity as to the limits of each. We have a duty to ask, Should the assessor be assumed to have the right to employ such secrecy, irrespective of its impact on students, teachers, and schools? *Or is the* tester *obligated to justify the practice or its extent?*

The euphemism "secure test" hides the fact that an always morally questionable practice lies at the heart of testing as we know it. By using the word *security,* we imply that we have a property that needs to be kept safely in our possession, as a fundamental right. But is the test maker's property inherently more important than the test taker's right to openness and due process in assessment? After all, the "secure" test reflects a form of unilaterally exercised power that cannot be examined or easily contested by the test taker. The use of secrecy is more than a matter of technical tactics. Casting the matter in moral and legal language alerts us to the problems *inherent* in the practice. Due process is threatened when *any* "judge" does his or her work in secret. Imagine, for example, the harm to our political system and to citizen insight into and faith in our legal principles if Supreme Court judges did not have to publish opinions to support their decisions. (Consider how much better tests might be if every test had to be justified in writing in the same way that court decisions are made.[5])

There may well be times, in the classroom as well as at the state and national levels, when test security can be justified. What can no longer be justified, however, is the unspoken view that psychometricians and teachers have the right to make such secrecy a cornerstone of test methodology.

The Emperor Revisited

The practice of test security is so much a part of the educational landscape that a few stories and vignettes may be required to cast the problem in a fresh, revealing light. Because secure testing is omnipresent, we may no longer see how our judgment has become impoverished or our conduct stereotyped. We might do well, therefore, to consider our unthinking use of secret tests as a modern version of "The Emperor's New Clothes."

You no doubt recall the story. Rascals posing as tailors "wove" a suit of the finest "cloth" for the king, earning riches by fashioning an illusion—an illusion not only about the garment itself but about their skill in serving the king. The king's nakedness, there to be seen by all, remained unseen. A sham that should have been obvious worked precisely because of the tailors' warning: only boorish, crude folks would fail to recognize the quality of the incredibly fine yarn. And so the townspeople rationalized their perceptions of nakedness and their secret doubt; they, like the king's retinue (who feared for their honor), praised the king as he paraded in his "finery." The king too, "knowing" that *he* was not a commoner, was sucked into the self-deception.

It was an innocent child, unaware of the "secret" and of the need to maintain secrecy, who exposed the hoax. "But he has nothing on!" exclaimed the child. But that is not the end of the story— and it is the ending that shows how harmful to judgment secrecy and the uncertainty about what we "should know" can be. The townspeople did not immediately come to their senses; the elders initially dismissed the remark of the young "innocent." Eventually, though, the child's words were repeated enough that their truth cut through the self-deception and doubt. But the Emperor, thinking that the now-skeptical townspeople must be right, "thought to himself, 'I must not stop or it will spoil the procession.' So he marched on even more proudly than before, and the courtiers continued to carry a train that was not there at all."[6]

The tale is instructive about current testing policy on many levels. We *still* do not want to spoil the procession. Testing increases, though few useful results emerge from the investment. We are *still* dismissing the remarks of the "innocents." We do not see through the eyes of students as they prepare for and take the tests that we buy and realize how debilitating those tests are to intellectual engagement, courage, and imagination. Nor do we see through the eyes of employers, teachers, and administrators and realize how rarely they study test results to *understand* applicants' and students' abilities or the meaning of their errors. We are so self-deceived that we often comment, when discussing test reform, "But *we* made it through the system, didn't we? . . ."—as if these high-stakes secure tests were nothing more than the harmless indignities of a freshman initiation of years gone by.

Commercial test makers literally profit from the illusion that, like the clothes made from the tailor's yarn, all "fine" tests must be built with a specialist's mysterious skill. Testing, rather than being a common practice of assessing student performance on the tasks we value, becomes an arcane science that is entrusted—and apparently only entrustable—to statisticians.[7] Critics of such tests fear looking like the crude folks that the tailors warn people their critics will be; wary practitioners are routinely made to feel ignorant of the true "finery" in test validity and reliability.

The harm of any long-standing secret is its power to cause self-deception—as the story shows so clearly. The utter simplicity of the test items is like the king's nakedness: *so* obvious as to make one feel certain that some complex and unknown set of standards must render the seemingly nonexistent test "garment" substantive. Like the townspeople in the story, everyone—from teachers to superintendents—ends up talking as if the real capacities we value were being directly observed in detail (instead of by means of one or two proxy questions with simplistic answers, as is always the case). The supposed necessity of secure test questions eventually becomes "obvious" to everyone—as if all the important tests and criteria in life (for getting employed and getting a raise, writing a successful dissertation for a doctorate, obtaining a driver's license, winning the big game, or submitting a winning engineering or graphics-design bid) also involved secret tasks, criteria, and standards. The mystery of test-maker authority ensures that private doubts remain inchoate; highfalutin (but hazily understood) technical language comes to dominate our conversation.[8]

The inevitable happens: teachers imitate the form of secure

standardized tests, forgetting (or never realizing) that the technology is limited in its capacity to assess what we value. Even teachers who talk of the foolishness or harm of secure simplistic tests end up employing their own versions of them—the true sign of the tests' mythic rather than rational power. The arcane (but misunderstood) procedures of the "tailors" take root and are poorly mimicked by the uninitiated: any inspection of local tests reveals that almost all of them are of questionable validity and reliability.[9] Grades that teachers then give become increasingly less justifiable (even as they become more precise) as so-called objective tests proliferate. And the school transcript remains as unreliable as it ever was. The call for sounder standardized tests then naturally increases from the outside critics, and the vicious circle continues.[10] Bring in the tailors! Let the king march more proudly! But pity the poor student. For, contrary to the story, the child's voice—common sense—remains unheard or unheeded still.

The One-Sidedness of Secrecy

Secrecy is not inherently wrong, as Harvard University professor of philosophy Sissela Bok stresses in her fine treatise on the subject. But because there are moral consequences at stake in any use of secrecy, some overarching principles are necessary both to inform and safeguard our judgment and to inform technical policy and practice.

In professional, personal, and social matters, mutual respect must underlie any justified use of secrecy. Because a student starts with limited rights in any formal educational relationship, and those rights are further restricted by the traditional testing context, test makers and users are obligated to be more respectful of the student's position than they tend to be. This obligation is easier to see if we think of secrecy in relation to adult citizens or consumers, as Bok suggests: "No just society would . . . allocate controls so unequally. This is not to say that some people might not be granted limited powers for certain purposes . . . but they would have to advance reasons sufficient to overcome the initial presumption favoring equality."[11] The right of the persons affected to control what is kept secret becomes more compelling at the level of social institutions: "When power is joined to secrecy, the danger of spread and abuse . . . increases. In all such cases the presumption shifts [away from the assumption of a right to secrecy]. When those who exercise power . . . claim control over secrecy and openness, it is up to them to show why giving them such control is necessary and what kinds of safeguards they propose. . . . Even where persuasive reasons for collective practices of secrecy can be stated, accountability is indispensable."[12]

Bok does not address the issue of secrecy in testing in her book—a surprise, when one thinks about the inequities of power at stake in testing. She does, however, discuss the danger and moral harm of secretly intrusive psychological research, particularly research based on deceit by the researcher. And she approvingly quotes Margaret Mead's criticism of such research—criticism that was in part based on the fact that such methods "damage science by cutting short methods that would responsibly enhance, rather than destroy, human trust."[13]

No person or group should thus be assumed to have unilateral power to control what is kept secret. But this principle has always been difficult to honor when dealing with children (or others who seem "inferior" to us in terms of rights). We do, however, now take the right to be protected from secrecy for granted when dealing with judicial inquiries and the rights of the accused, and children can now sue their parents or be protected from abusive parents by the state. Due process certainly requires that secrecy be minimized in these arenas. But it was not always so. The insistence on mutual respect and openness in formal inquiries is recent, as Foucault notes. His history of legal investigation and examination in seventeenth-century France is a reminder of how difficult moral equality is to uphold in practice:

> In France, as in most European countries, with the notable exception of England, the entire criminal procedure, right up to the sentence, remained secret: that is to say, opaque, not only to the public but the accused himself. . . . [K]nowledge was the absolute privilege of the prosecution. The preliminary investigation was carried out as "diligently and secretly as

may be," as the edict of 1498 put it. According to the
ordinance of 1670, which confirmed . . . and reinforced the severity of the preceding period, it was impossible for the accused to have access to the documents of the case . . . impossible to know the nature
of the evidence . . . impossible to make use of the documents in the proof.[14]

The combination of secrecy and unilateral respect could justify even deceit in the judge's conduct—a result that we would now
find morally repugnant: "The magistrate, for his part, had the right
to accept anonymous denunciations, to conceal from the accused
the nature of the action, to question him with a view to catching
him out, to use insinuations. . . . The secret and written form of the
procedure reflects the principle that . . . establishment of truth was
the absolute right and the exclusive power of the sovereign and his
judges."[15]

It is not pushing the argument too much to ask the reader
to reread these two passages and think of the student as the accused
and the test maker as the judge. ("Knowledge as the privilege of the
assessor," "impossible to know the nature of the evidence," "to
question him with a view to catching him out" [as with the use of
distracters in tests], and so on.) At the heart of Foucault's analysis
is the view that such one-sided practices have been common to all
the areas in which we seek to "discipline" humankind (law,
military, education, and psychiatry). Foucault explicitly links the
judicial and educational "examination," which "combines the
technique of an observing hierarchy and those of a normalizing
judgment." While he argues that "investigation" has become mod-
ernized through the methods of science, the "examination is still
caught up in disciplinary technology."[16] Sue E. Berryman at
Teachers College, Columbia University, notes, for example, that
tests are "obscure, opaque, inaccessible"; "these tests and their results carry no intuitive meaning to anyone besides educators. . . .
They thus fail to measure objectives that parties with interests in the
outcomes of our educational system can understand, 'see,' and
debate."[17]

The legacy of secrecy in student testing is of course long-standing, with its roots in the world of autocratic religious power and the hierarchical, guild mentality of the Middle Ages—a world filled with many adult "secret societies."[18] The secret test as we know it came from this world, where professors saw themselves as members of a guild, where status transcended rights and was granted by "degrees" to only a few, where the assessor had the historically unquestionable right to demand (orthodox) answers of the test taker without justifying either the questions asked or the evaluation of the answers. Whatever modern justifications are made for test security on validity grounds, there is little doubt that the roots of the practice derive from this earlier assumed right to keep vital information from the examinee.

The modern world's unwillingness to tolerate such one-sided secrecy becomes clear when we examine the policies that have arisen around the use of secure tests in the hiring and promotion of *adults*. Irrespective of the wishes or habitual practices of testing specialists, the courts have been quite clear that the assessee has a right to more information (and more stringent, user-friendly tests of validity) than testers have historically wanted to provide (as we saw in Chapter One).[19]

It seems to me no coincidence that we continually and un-thinkingly retain the use of blanket secrecy in dealing with minors. To put it charitably, we know better than they what is in their interest. To put it somewhat cynically, children will never likely be protected from excessive secrecy (or any other practice that depends upon moral inequality), because they will always be without adequate political clout to ensure that their moral equality is codified into law. Thus Walt Haney, Boston College researcher and co-head of the National Center for Testing, who has been an expert witness in the long-standing lawsuit over whether test companies are obligated to release individual completed and scored tests (as opposed to just scores), told me that in his opinion the original test disclosure law would not have been passed if the major class of litigants had been schoolchildren, not medical students.[20]

The Formal Positions of the Professions on Test Ethics

We look in vain for adequate guidance from the affected professions on the ethics of secrecy in student assessment. As we saw in Chapter

One, the APA Standards for educational and psychological testing were designed to provide criteria not only for the evaluation of tests but for "testing practices, and the effects of test use."[21] These APA Standards note that the "interests of the various parties in the testing process are usually, but not always, congruent." The only example given of noncongruent interests has to do with testing for admission to highly selective jobs, schools, or programs. But why wouldn't many teachers and older students cite secure tests as not congruent with their interests or specific programs? Secrecy is certainly not in the interest of a would-be performer who is going to be judged.

In neither the technical nor the ethical standards do we find discussion of the test taker's rights with respect to adequate advance knowledge and preparation. (In fact, many of the standards under both test administration and test-taker rights have to do with the maintenance of test security!) And there is no discussion of what role, if any, student test takers and teacher test users should have concerning a test's validity for their particular context. The bulk of the standards deal with the test taker's rights of confidentiality and the harm of unobtrusive testing—that is, testing conducted without the test taker's knowledge: the issue of informed consent, more generally construed.[22] The only standard relevant to test security is Standard 16.2, which states that "test users should provide test takers . . . with an appropriate explanation of test results and recommendations made on the basis of test results in a form they can understand."

This "form they can understand" need not include, however, direct access to the answered and scored test. An intriguing historical change of mind that relates to access to one's scored test has in fact occurred in the APA Standards for ethics in research. In a recent paper, Haney and Madaus ruefully point out that a key clause of the 1977 ethics guidelines was *deleted* in the most recent (1981) edition.[23] Beyond the test taker's "right to know results" and "interpretations made" on the basis of results, the new version no longer contains the following clause from the earlier document: the test taker was deemed to have the right, "where appropriate, [to] the original data on which final judgments were made." It was this "right" that led to the test disclosure law in New York—a law bitterly fought by test companies then and still a matter of litigation today (in a lawsuit fought on the grounds that the test company's copyright is more salient than the test taker's right to the completed test and answer key).

While ex post facto test disclosure has been debated in this way for years, only recently have arguments been made for greater openness *prior* to the test. Following up on an idea presented by Jerrold Zacharias years ago, Judah Schwartz of Harvard has been among the most vocal and eloquent in arguing that the complete item bank from which any test might be constructed also be made public.[24] Given that any test is a sample; and given that the item bank can be made large enough to encompass the domain of possible questions and thus prevent narrow cramming and invalid inferences about results, there is little reason to maintain perpetual security, and there are many good reasons for making that bank of questions open for public inspection. We could easily develop "large publicly available data bases of reviewed and signed problems in a wide variety of school subject areas. . . . School systems and state boards of education and other responsible authorities would use these data bases as the sources of the questions and problems in the accountability [systems]."[25]

Schwartz proposes that the state or district make clear which sections of the data base would be tapped and what the criteria would be for the selection of particular questions. The data base would be available in all "libraries and bookstores," with the clear advantage of such a "sunshine" procedure: "If the pool of problems from which examinations are composed is publicly available in advance, then any group in society that feels ill-served by the substance or language or context of a question can raise a prima facie objection in advance of the use of the question and not have to rely on the vagaries of statistical analyses to claim bias or prejudice after the fact."[26]

The Student's Perspective: Some Revealing Vignettes

We need to be reminded that there exist ways of examining that do not rely on total test secrecy. Indeed, in any system designed to produce high-quality performance by all participants, such secrecy is antithetical to the success of the enterprise, as the military, the performing arts, and athletics reveal. And in the adult world of performance appraisal, we see that not only are such "tests" possible but that there exist laws and regulations that protect adult test takers from the kind of excessive secrecy we routinely foist upon students and teachers.

Consider first the following fanciful scenarios, all written from the test taker's point of view. They illustrate both how students experience the effects of unrelenting test security and how counterproductive secrecy is to would-be performers and performance systems.

Vignette 1

Imagine the student as the manager of a warehouse, where organization of incoming material and the ability to pull together future orders are paramount. But reflect on what the manager's job might be like if he or she did not know what kinds of materials would be arriving each day, the quantity of those materials, or the kinds of orders that would later have to be filled. This is the student's position in school.

Each day, new material arrives, sometimes too quickly for the student manager to organize it on the shelves. After a week of sorting through and ordering the contents, new and unexpected material arrives, compelling the student to completely rethink the system used in storing—with no assurance that the revised system will compensate for future, unknown deliveries.

After months of storing and organizing catch-as-catch-can, the student managers are warned by the central office that they must be prepared to correctly fill dozens of (unknown) orders on the spot, without access to the notes and resources that serve as their data base. The managers will be "tested" on their ability to predict the order and fill it from memory—not the more authentic and vital ability to plan for, refine, and routinely process a wide range of known and varying orders.

One can see from this vignette why cheating can easily become a way of life for those who cannot develop a trivia-oriented memory or psych-out-the-test-maker tricks on their own. The arbitrariness of the test and the inappropriate reliance on memory encourage the test taker to consider all possible means for mastering the challenge—especially since "rehearsal" has been ruled out by the design of the test. This focus is especially tragic since, as it is now, students are rarely taught to learn how to learn—that is, how to "manage" knowledge so as to effectively store and retrieve it for thoughtful, flexible use—nor are they assessed in such a way as to test their ability to manage available resources.

Vignette 2

To better appreciate how excessive secrecy in testing corrupts relationships, consider what our response as adults would be to a job evaluation process in which the employer could do what test makers routinely do: without our knowledge or consent, pick a few tasks from the hundreds we have learned and performed over the years, demand an on-the-spot performance, and assess that performance only. It is telling that, with adults, the practice would be regarded as unjust and likely illegal. Why does it not seem so when we deal with children?

 A principal in the Buffalo, New York, area took me aside at a workshop to share with me a story that illustrates the potential for hypocrisy here. He recently negotiated a forward-looking and humane performance appraisal system with his teachers—an open system involving peer consultation and teacher self-assessment through a portfolio process. It occurred to the principal that the process was generalizable: such a system might well be extended to the performance appraisal of students. The teachers (especially the high school teachers) would hear none of it.

Vignette 3

Consider how the combination of security and proxy (indirect) secret items ultimately corrupts performance. Consider a performance system, such as a professional sport league. What would happen if baseball were played as usual all season long, but then the pennant races were decided by one-shot, secure tests designed by statisticians and resulting in one aggregate score? Thus on the last day of the season, specially constructed secure tests would be given to each player, composed of static drills and game situations. The pennant races would be decided each year by a new test and its results. Who believes that this secrecy, so necessary to the test's validity, would not end up corrupting both the game and the players' motivation? (Note that the students' current situation is actually worse, because students are usually not allowed to "play the game" of knowledge but must endure syllabi composed of drills and contrived and discrete game situations ordered in "scope and sequence" fashion. Not ever learning the "game" of knowledge through actual use, students are even less likely to predict the kind of real-world challenges they will ultimately face.)

More than the first two vignettes, this third one reveals how unwittingly and inappropriately powerful the possessors of secret testing knowledge and criteria can be—even if their aim in life is to be helpful statisticians. The test designer here supposedly seeks only to design a valid sampling-test of all the important elements of performance as specified by others. The secrecy is "justified," because without it the test would be corrupted: coaches would "teach to the test"—in the bad sense of shortchanging the players' overall education so as to artificially raise the score and distort its meaning. Yet we easily see how such a system would corrupt coaching and the game itself anyway. Not only the players but also the coaches would be robbed of the capacity to concentrate on the time-consuming task of developing excellent play beyond drill in discrete skills—just as in the classroom, teachers never end up asking students to use knowledge in complex, integrated ways, given the demands of preparing for the multiple-choice test.[27]

Vignette 4

Imagine that student musicians have to wait until the day of the concert to know the music that they will be playing together. And suppose, in keeping with typical testing, that the test of musical skill is made using isolated musical "items" (bits of pieces, not a whole work). Assume too that students play their instruments through microphones connected to other rooms—microphones that allow judges to listen but prevent students from hearing themselves play. And assume also that the scoring is norm-referenced: weeks later, the students receive a single score telling them where they stand relative to all the clarinet or trumpet players in the state and a computer printout summarizing the stylistic and technical areas they should work on. (From this information, teachers and students are meant to improve!)

This vignette reminds us that a one-shot, secure test cannot, *in principle,* reveal whether the student has and uses a repertoire for mastering complex performances. In what sense does the musician learn about where he or she stands from such a test? What would "normed scores" reveal about the quality of musicianship in the region? How can the musician *master* a secure performance played once? What have we gained by such artificial precision if neither students nor judges can equate the assessment results to the criterion performance and its standards?

While it is true that I have chosen the vignettes to illustrate what I trust are commonsense objections to test security, my aim is really to jog our thinking about this thoughtless habit of ours. Where, other than in schools, do officials *willingly* turn over accountability to outsiders who use secret "audit" procedures that are insensitive to local goals and practices? How can schools be held accountable by such tests if teachers and students do not know, have a say in, or trust the standards by which they will be judged? Where but in schools are teachers assumed to have the right to construct any old test they please, using items that require security before and after the test? Why should we *tolerate* such secrecy at the local level, given ample opportunities to design a set of tasks for reliability and the ability to demand multiday work on substantial projects that do not require security.

The Various Kinds of Test Secrecy

Given our unthinking reliance on secrecy in testing and the obvious harm that such secrecy inflicts on performance rehearsal and later improvement, it is worth our while to think through the issue of its necessity. Let us begin by considering the most basic question, then: In what sense *is* a "test" secret, and in what sense *must* a test be secret (in order that it not be compromised)? And whether or not a test is compromised by being no longer secure, when is such secrecy unfair to the test taker or test user? Where do the test taker's rights become predominant, in other words, in a conflict of interest over security in testing? We will consider a variety of practices in which the testing that takes place in schools is predicated on a degree of secrecy about what will be assessed, what methods of assessment will be used, the value of those methods, what the results mean, and the value of those results.

Everyone has experienced the most obvious answer to the question of what is a secret in conventional testing. Each of us has entered many classrooms not knowing the specific questions that were going to be asked. Such secrecy is so common that it has a profound hold on our consciousness. "Secret up until the day it occurs"—that is what a test *is,* for most of us. The mythic power of this practice was made very clear in a story told to me by Sharon P., a student teacher who tried some novel approaches to instruction and assessment in her student-teaching practicum. She designed a culminating unit in her English course in which the students, in small groups, devised a selection of would-be questions for the final exam, according to certain criteria supplied by Sharon. The reaction of two teachers in the faculty room at her school summed up the irrational hold that the practice of test security has upon us: "But then the students will cheat!" they protested in unison. Nor were they convinced of the wisdom of such a policy even after a lengthy discussion.

If we examine more closely such situations and the issues raised, we see that there are diverse aspects of test secrecy that occur before, during, and after a test. I can think of eleven kinds of secrecy built into conventional testing. The first three occur *before* the test is taken:

- The *specific* questions that will be on the test are usually secret, known only to the test maker.
- A larger set of questions from which the later secure test will sample is often secret, although students sometimes have access to these (or to the data base described above).
- The timing of an upcoming test is sometimes secret, a common feature of the high school or college "quiz"—usually described

euphemistically by the teacher on the day in question as "unannounced."

The following kinds of secrecy may exist *during* the test:

- The test itself can be secret, in that the student is actually unaware that a test is taking place. (In the technical literature, this is called "unobtrusive" testing.)
- The scoring criteria and standards can be secret (when the questions are not multiple-choice or equally weighted in value), in that the student is unaware of the scoring criteria, descriptors for the range of answers, and the "anchor performances" being used to set standards.
- Whether or not one is on the right track in understanding a question or forming an approach to it is secret. The student cannot converse with the test maker or test administrator, in other words, to check on the meaning of a question or the aptness of an approach to answering it.
- The resources for constructing and double-checking possible answers are kept secret (to stretch the term a bit), in the sense that the real-world resources that would be appropriately available are explicitly kept from the student during the test. This type of security extends to the use of other people as resources, including not only students but any adults present.

The following kinds of secrecy refer to what is not revealed *after* the test:

- The meaning of the results may be kept secret, as when the tester does not release the actual test paper. Students are thus unable to confirm or critique their score or the test itself. As I mentioned in the previous chapter, undergraduates frequently do not receive back their blue books after an exam.
- Even if the students get their papers back, the results remain somewhat secret if students are not allowed to see the answer key or sets of exemplary test papers against which to compare their answers.
- The significance of the national or state multiple-choice test is

kept secret by virtue of its indirect nature. It almost never has obvious relevance to local curriculum or "face validity" to the student and teacher. And when technical validation for the test tasks and standards does exist, it is rarely meaningful to the student and the teacher.

• The value of the test for future learning and aspirations remains secret in testing that is one-shot, not scaled using longitudinal scoring criteria and standards, and composed of indirect items.

There are arguments for the use of each one of these secrecy practices in certain instances. What we seek, however, are some principles for judging the boundary lines in each case. In what contexts is each type of secrecy appropriate and in what contexts is it not? How might we better judge when any particular use of secrecy in assessment goes over the line and becomes unjustified?

To address these questions, two prior sets of questions must be kept in mind. The first set is technical and will be addressed further in Chapter Seven, in a reconsideration of validity. The questions in that set boil down to this: What are we *really* testing by relying on so much secrecy? In other words, leaving aside correlations with similar types of tests, can we really be said to be testing for scientific or historical understanding, for example, if the student has no prior knowledge of the question, no opportunity to use resources, and no opportunity to ask questions? A second set of questions is moral, and it is these questions that are the focus of our consideration in this chapter: What educational values are at stake with (and perhaps threatened by) the persistent use of such secrecy by adults with children? To what extent might even a form of secrecy in testing that is defensible on technical grounds *inherently* threaten teacher-student and student-subject relationships—with all that such a threat implies for the potential harm to the student's faith in the school, its agents, and its standards?

Pretest Secrecy

The technical argument for pretest secrecy is fairly straightforward. The validity of all short-answer tests (though not necessarily examinations and most authentic assessments) is typically compromised if the test questions are known in advance. Why should this be so? For two different reasons. First, the student would then be in a position to "know" the correct answer without necessarily knowing why it is so, given the format. Knowing many questions in advance would enable the student to short-circuit the learning process. Students could simply memorize the questions and correct answers, perhaps even gaining the answers from someone else. But this result would render invalid the inference that the student who does well on the test "knows and understands" the subject matter tested![28]

Second, insight into the student's breadth of knowledge may be jeopardized. Since most tests involve a necessarily small sample of the total domain of a subject and what was taught, knowing the questions in advance can make the student wrongly appear to have a very expansive knowledge. (Put differently, in most testing situations, we want and expect to be able to generalize about the breadth of mastery beyond what was tested—just as we generalize to the whole nation from a sample of 1,100 in a Gallup poll.) Instead of making an effort to successfully gain control over the domain of all *possible* important tasks or questions, the student need only concentrate on the small sample of questions now known to be on the test. Note that a test of a few essay questions or performance tasks puts the teacher or test maker more at risk for such an invalid inference than does a multiple-choice test (if the essays are the entire test). Since the student need only prepare for one or two essay questions— versus the typical hundred or more questions on a multiple-choice test—the validity of any inference about student control of all the important topics may be severely compromised by advance knowledge of the questions.

This is a solvable problem, however, if the student is given access to a representative set of possible test questions and if we acknowledge that most tests overrely on low-level, information-focused questions. The model of distributing a set of possible questions in advance is, after all, a common feature of graduate and undergraduate education. The student studies all the questions carefully, in a methodical and comprehensive review of the priority questions of the course, and knows that some of those questions will compose all or most of the final examination. Some questions would admittedly go unasked if this were to be a common practice, but we would do well to consider why we feel the need to ask those kinds of questions.

There are shades of gray as well. If we say that the questions should be secure, do we hold the same view about the *format* of the questions? At present, it is considered sound policy for teachers or testing companies and agencies to describe the types of questions to be asked (definition, true-false, and/or essay, for example) and to provide samples of each type of question for review. (It is just this kind of modest "declassifying" that enables SAT and ACT preparation services to function and thrive. If this sort of revelation is deemed a fair practice, why should we not offer some opportunities for students to practice some of the particular questions—for example, as a take-home part of an exam?) It would seem unfair on the face of it for the student not to know the various types of questions and their approximate importance in the whole test; it seems to violate basic principles of due process and equal access. (And a failure to ensure prior access to the test format might upset the technical validity of the results, if some students are familiar with the format and others are not.) Similarly, it would seem inappropriate for the student to not know the weight of a subscore or the criteria or standards being used when the test involves judgment-based scoring. How would I know how to apportion time or judge the length or depth of my response without such information?

But prior openness can be taken further, as Judah Schwartz's suggestion for a regional, state, or national data base makes clear. We could ask all classes of questions and have open testing, without compromising validity, if we defined *openness* as prior knowledge of the complete domain of all specific questions or tasks that we have in our collective possession. It would no longer be feasible to "cheat" on the validity issue, because it would not be practical to master each question in advance; students would still have to worry about the whole domain of knowledge that the test would tap. In many cases at the high school and college level, all possible test questions are known in advance course by course; what is "secret" is which few ones from the larger list will actually be used.

Indeed, if we thought of the "portfolio" as a set of products and performances meeting certain criteria with respect to range of genre, topic, or type of product, then it would be quite possible to dispense with most security. Consider the performance-based course requirements shown in Exhibit 3.1, all of which could (and should) be known in advance and "taught to," without compromising the breadth of the domain, while making it possible for students to know their performance obligations.

We certainly should feel comfortable asking districts (or regions, using regional service agencies that exist in each state) to develop such a set of portfolio categories and/or a complete data base over the years, subject to some of the principles mentioned at the end of Chapter One (in the Assessment Bill of Rights).

One uncontroversial implication concerning this kind of openness of the domain and secrecy of the sample is that we would no doubt improve the quality of all tests and test questions. If all test makers, including teachers, had to publicly provide a larger pool from which the test would sample, the current preponderance of low-level recall questions having little to do with genuine competence in a field of study would be undercut. Thoughtful and deep understanding is simply not assessable in secure testing, and we will continue to send the message to teachers that simplistic recall or application, based on "coverage," is all that matters—until we change the policy of secrecy.

In short, we should not let the test maker off the hook with only the most superficial form of openness; we should require more. To be sure, it might engender more chaos and greater cost in testing if tests were not secure, but we should at least explore a cost-benefit analysis, given how clearly test openness is in the student's interest.

At the very least, we should require, as a criterion of good testing, that any educational test be as open *as is possible.* This would not take us very far in determining the limits, of course, but it would at least make the matter more explicit and therefore more subject to scrutiny and external review. It would compel test designers to think through the matter of the student's right to proper rehearsals more clearly, for example. And it would likely lead to tests that have varying components, some of which are appropriately known in advance and others which are not. (We see such a model used all the time in performance competitions such as Odyssey of the Mind, formal debates, and music competitions.)

It is of course the case, however, that in fields that involve the vagaries of human interaction, one cannot know precisely what

Exhibit 3.1. Major Tasks for a Global Studies Course.

---

1. Design a tour of the world's most holy sites.
   - Include accurate maps.
   - Prepare a guidebook, with descriptions of local norms, customs, etiquette.
   - Analyze the most cost-effective route and means of transportation.
   - Write an interesting-to-students history of the sites.
   - Compile an annotated bibliography of recommended readings for other students.
2. Write an International Bill of Rights.
   - Refer to past attempts and their strengths and weaknesses: Helsinki Accords, Communist Manifesto, U.S. Bill of Rights, and so on.
   - Convince a diverse group of peers and adults to "sign on."
3. Write a policy analysis and background report on a Latin American country for the secretary of state.
   - What should be our short-term policy goals with that country?
   - What are that country's economic and political prospects?
4. Collect and analyze media reports from *other* countries on U.S policies in the Middle East.
   - Put together a "briefing book" of photocopied press clips for the president, with commentary on the accuracy of each story.
   - Videotape/audiotape a simulated newscast summarizing world reaction to a recent U.S. policy decision.
5. Compile an oral history on a topical but historically interesting issue:
   - Interview recent American immigrants.
   - Talk to veterans of Operation Desert Storm, Vietnam, and World War II about America's role as a police officer for world affairs.
6. Design a museum exhibit, using artifacts and facsimiles.
   - Exhibit links between a European country's geography and its economy.
   - Illustrate the local area's role in the industrial revolution.
   - Display patterns of modern emigration and their causes.
7. Write and deliver, on videotape, two speeches: the first, by the visiting head of an African country on the history of U.S.-Africa relations; the second, in response, by President Clinton's spokesperson.
8. Take part in a formal debate on a controversial issue of global significance—for example, aid to Russian republics or the U.S. role in the fall of communism.
9. Create a model United Nations (with groups of two or three representing each country) and enact a new Security Council resolution on terrorism.
10. Write a textbook chapter titled "The Primary Causes of Revolution: People, Ideas, Events, or Economic Conditions?" in which you weigh the various causes of revolution and reflect on whether the most important revolutions were "revolutionary" or "evolutionary."

---

the "test" will require: there are inherently unanticipatable aspects to real-world tests. The client does the unexpected; the other team seeks to outwit us; difficult weather conditions demand unusual piloting maneuvers, and so on. Some would use this as an excuse for retaining complete pretest security, but the real-world situation is quite different: the adult always has the opportunity to adjust, consult resources, ask questions, bring in others, or even seek a delay. And the diligent student can rehearse the task effectively even if in the "real" test the facts, problems, or contexts are varied. This rehearsal is what coaches of athletes, performing artists, and teachers of medicine and law help students do: know the difference between what is inherently anticipatable and what is not, work on what is, and train for the imaginable unanticipatable events. As General Schwarzkopf, the commander of Operation Desert Storm put it: hope for the best; plan for the worst.

Secrecy During the Test

The rationale for standardizing test conditions and materials is clear enough: fairness and validity require each student to have equal opportunity to answer a question correctly. If test makers do not standardize what resources can and cannot be used and develop a standard protocol for what test administrators can and cannot say during the test, then we run the risk of invalid inferences about performance and unreliable scores.

But that rationale hardly justifies the regular practice of for-bidding almost all human interaction and the use of contextually appropriate resources—particularly if our aim is to make tests educative and authentic and to determine whether students can intelligently use resources.

One form of concurrent secrecy, unobtrusiveness (that is, testing without the student's knowledge), while seemingly desirable, is often harmful. "Informed consent"—the antithesis of unobtrusive testing—is an ethical principle we value; it is included in the APA ethical and technical guidelines as a desirable standard. Yet as I note in Chapter Four, the British have deliberately made such unobtrusiveness a goal of (imposed) testing as a way of ensuring that tests are more authentic and more seamlessly interwoven with daily instruction (and thus less likely to produce needless test anxiety). The goal of unobtrusiveness seems ironically problematic: as psychometricians Jay Millman and Jennifer Greene have pointed out, "An examinee's *maximum* performance might not occur when testing is unobtrusive."[29] But "unobtrusiveness" in the British sense involves avoiding an abrupt departure from the kinds of challenges and problems that face a student in the classroom. Surely that is a worthy aim, given that part of what is wrong with traditional models of testing is that the student has to gear up for methods and formats that have no carryover to authentic learning or real-world tests. On balance, then, it would seem that an attempt to minimize obtrusiveness while still honoring the basic principle of informed consent is the proper guiding principle.

With respect to the secrecy of resources during the test, the technical constraints requiring the standardizing of test conditions invariably seem to inappropriately outweigh the pedagogical ones. Keeping the essential tools of research and reference unavailable compromises the construct validity of a test, in my judgment. If the nature of the simplified items used in tests prevents the use of books or student notes—resources that would invariably be available during those times when the student is "tested" in the world of intellectual performance—then what are we testing? And what lessons about adult standards and authority are learned if resources are arbitrarily withheld—*arbitrarily* in the sense that the student knows full well that during all genuine work situations, resources are available. Here we see most clearly that the use of tests, combined with secrecy, causes a moral imbalance that needs to be closely monitored.

Shades of gray exist with respect to possible access to resources. One physics teacher I know allows each student to bring to the final exam an index card filled out as he or she sees fit. Not only can this device sharpen and focus prior study; it may provide the teacher with an additional assessment: Do the students know which facts, figures, and formulas are of most worth as resources? (An unintended outcome, of course, is that students learn to write in superhumanly small script!) Some state exams go halfway by "standardizing" the resources. New York's earth science exam, for example, provides a booklet of tables and charts for students to use during the exam.

Whatever the technical merits in forbidding the use of resources, another pedagogically harmful aspect of the prohibition is the implicit lesson that what other people know that might be of help must remain secret as students wrestle with difficult challenges. Our testing, wittingly or not, daily makes clear the dysfunctional lesson that intellectual assessment must be conducted in silence and in isolation from others. To ensure the validity of the inference that a person's score is truly that individual's, such a practice may well be defensible in many instances. But another kind of validity may thereby be sacrificed. What are we actually finding out about our students if the most basic feature of adult work life— namely, that we can use all resources, including other people, as necessary to get the job done—is never assessed? We should not only not discourage the use of people resources; we should actively encourage it. We can, for example, build the effective seeking of advice into a test: many district writing assessments and performance science tests are now multiday, and they build into the process the possibility of collaboration after an initial rough draft in isolation.

There is potentially a deeper moral harm to the student when the only option for collaboration is an accomplice or cheater. Years ago Piaget went so far as to suggest that exam-oriented schooling, where educators "have found themselves obliged to shut the child up in work that is strictly individual," reinforces all the child's most self-centered instincts and "seems contrary to the most obvious requirements of intellectual and moral development."[30]

What, then, of the student's presumed right to ask questions of the assessor? Here is a problem of profound moral significance: How can we better honor the right of the questioned to question the questioner? But that right threatens traditional standardization and technical concerns for comparability. We know that tests that permit assessor/student interaction are easily corrupted unless there are strict protocols and guidelines by which adult judgment about intervention is informed. But we can turn the question around: How can the scores on inherently complex and ill-structured test questions be adequately reliable if, despite the invariable ambiguity of test questions, the student cannot clarify the questions or double-check a proposed solution (as would be allowed in any realistic setting)?

All these situations call for test makers to develop more sophisticated questions and dynamic/interactive tasks, with a protocol for test administration that lays out in some detail the permissible and impermissible interactions. This has already been done in IQ testing and in a good deal of qualitative research (such as moral development interviews). And we should demand of test companies as well as teachers the inclusion of certain questions and tasks that permit the use of resources that are specified in advance (such as textbook, dictionary, calculator, and student notes)—questions that could be given out after a preliminary secure section, perhaps. (Students could procure the resources they brought [and/or resources provided by the tester] from another room during a break, after handing in their first efforts, in anticipation of the more open part of the test. Then there would be no compromise to the secure first part of the test.)

After-Test Secrecy

As for ex post facto security, there can be little justification for it, especially at the local level. While it is true that certain proprietary interests might be threatened by such a policy, I would argue that those concerns must be of secondary importance in almost all cases, because it is surely detrimental to the student's (and teacher's) education for the test papers to remain a secret. Arguments that such a policy imposes an undo hardship on test companies do not seem very compelling, when New York State, the International Baccalaureate, and the Advanced Placement programs make their tests and student papers public each year.

Being unable to inspect the test after the fact means that the value of the test—its formal validation—remains an inappropriate secret, especially when students and teachers never see nontechnical (and nonintimidating) evidence and argument for the validity of the test in the first place.[31] In the long run, this can become an issue of educational equity and access: the student test taker is prevented from gaining not only the incentives but the insights that come from tests that are authentic and thus educative—tests in which tasks and scoring standards instruct the student about real-world tasks and standards.

Ex post facto test security may well contribute to the routine design of tests as isolated, one-event experiences—a design that is never in the student's interest. Under such conditions, the real meaning of each test score, and the significance of that score for the student, can therefore be said to be inappropriately "secret." The student receives what are, in effect, noncomparable scores over time (as opposed to navigating a system of recurring assessments, scored in terms of continuous progress in reference to known, stable standards; see Chapter Four). This practice is thus linked to the greatest moral harm in secure tests (especially those of the indirect or "proxy" kind): the inherent failure of such tests to provide powerful, immediate, and useful feedback to all students as to the nature of their errors, the validated importance of such errors, and diagnostic help in how the errors might be eradicated.

The usual criticisms of the multiple-choice test thus miss the most potentially damaging consequences of the format. It may well be that the items adequately and appropriately discriminate. But mustn't unending secrecy about those items induce a debilitating quest for mere correctness and cramming instead of evoking and soliciting the best of what the student can do? Unending test security easily breeds student insecurity (and teacher insecurity, when the multiple-choice test is externally designed). Students can never feel confident, going into a secret multiple-choice test, that this odd sample of test items will reflect their prior work, achievements, or intellectual strengths.

Piaget's Insight: The Development of Respect for Standards

Deprived of both prior and after-the-fact insight into test tasks and scores, students end up lacking more than a rationale for what they must undergo. They are deprived of the opportunity to fully understand, master, and respect the standards for judging intellectual excellence. Testing is thus seen as an arbitrary act, a game, something to be "psyched out," in the words of older students. The persistence of such a system sends a decidedly irrational and disrespectful message to students: we claim that our test questions are valid and our keyed answers are correct, though we need never justify or explain them to you (or even show you the answers later). Let us call this what it is: deeply disrespectful—and ultimately dysfunctional.

It was Piaget who astutely argued that mutual respect between adults and children has consequences for more than just the student's social development. He argued that *intellectual* standards (and a lived commitment to them) evolve out of a particular *moral* experience: a genuine, open, and ongoing dialogue among mutually respectful equals. Mere exposure to good assessing and "correct" answers does not produce in us a respect for the intellectual standards that underlie good answers. Autonomy develops only "when the mind regards as necessary an ideal that is independent of all external pressure . . . and appears only with reciprocity, when mutual respect is strong enough." Only in habitual discussion among relational equals arises the inward recognition of intellectual standards as "necessary to common search for truth."[32]

Developing the habit of feeling *self-obligated* to intellectual standards, Piaget argued, depends therefore on the experience of the constant need for justification that obliges everyone—in other words, the "rules" that require and enable *all* equal parties to agree with a result. But clearly such an experience is predicated on a mutual sharing of arguments, not on received opinions. To understand the value of the assessor's tasks, answers, and methods, I must be respected enough to have access to their rationale. The assessor must feel obliged to put me on an equal footing with respect to the *why*, not just the *what*, of that which I am asked to do.

With that mutual respect and willingness to justify comes a risk, of course: the assessor is now open to being proven mistaken or being seen as lacking an apt rationale. "One must place oneself at the child's level, and give him a feeling of equality by laying stress on one's own obligations and one's own deficiencies." The unwillingness to take such a risk is all too common, however—a fact constantly decried by Piaget: "It looks as though in many ways the adult did everything in his power . . . to strengthen egocentrism in its double aspect, intellectual and moral."[33]

The student's alienation from adult authorities who avoid

this risk is the inevitable result, and this alienation undermines more than just our trust in adults, according to Piaget; it also undermines our ability to grasp intellectual standards *as worthy in their own right*. An ongoing implicit appeal to Authority (for Authority's sake) by our adult judges, instead of an explicit appeal to shared principles, strengthens our "natural" egocentrism and keeps us from understanding what the expert knows. We come to assume that answers are right or wrong merely because some expert says so, not because there is verifiable evidence or justifiable argument supporting those answers.

We therefore may not ever come to see that the criteria of knowledge—*logic* in the broad sense (that is, rules of evidence and argument)—are verifiably worthy and that they merit being our own internal criteria for distinguishing the true from the false or the proved from the unproved. And this remains a danger no matter what our age or sophistication.[34] The combination of secrecy and power in all adults, but especially in the teacher/assessor, provides the conditions of later student cynicism and disrespect for both intellectual and moral standards. The *credibility* of the test and what the test is meant to represent—namely, adult standards—is at stake, and it is dependent upon the test maker's willingness to justify the test to takers and users and to accept questions and criticisms about the test's value from test takers.

In the absence of a mutually respectful relationship with the assessor, the student cannot appreciate the assessor's reasoning and internalize it. Paradoxically, according to Piaget, *even if I respect the assessors, the authority figures, I am unlikely to effectively uphold their standards*. Intellectual and moral standards, no matter how often "taught" or invoked by Authority, remain "external to the subject's conscience, [and] do not really transform his conduct" if the standards are adhered to by force of character or inequality of relationship only.[35] Is this not what we see and decry in students all the time? Is it not just what we mean when we talk about "thoughtless" student behavior? Listen also to our students' language as they discuss work turned back: "My English teacher doesn't like my writing," for example, conveys the view that the subjective and hazy desires of Authority are being taught, not clear standards. But if the correctness of answers and arguments is justified only because Authority says so, careless and thoughtless work is the inevitable result. So is passivity: students learn by such mysterious and one-way assessment that they cannot reframe questions, reject questions as inappropriate, challenge their premises, or propose a better way to prove their mastery. The moral and political harm is significant. Too many students learn to just "give them what they want" and to accept or acquiesce in bogus but "authoritative" judgments.

Excellence is not (and must never seem to be) about satisfying elders and their inexplicit and apparently contradictory tastes. Excellence must be seen as the meeting of known and justifiable demands—what (objectively) *works*.[36] We then come to understand a lesson that is morally as well as intellectually empowering: the judge too is subservient to intelligent principles.

Testing the Test for Excessive Secrecy

Various overarching criteria for the use of secrecy in testing surface out of this discussion. Students are entitled to the minimal secrecy necessary. To be autonomous (meaning, as the word's roots imply, "self-regulating"), students must confront assessment procedures that are *maximally transparent*—that is, procedures that are rehearsable to the greatest possible extent without compromising the test's validity or the purposes of school learning.[37] Students have a right to practice well the central tasks and standards by which they will be judged. In addition, they must know that what the assessor wants is of objective intellectual worth. Students must always be able to verify the aptness of the test, the score, and the assessor's use of secrecy. Otherwise, they resort to merely guessing or to calculating what the teacher "wants." In practice, this requirement of verification means that testing contexts should always make it possible for the student to self-assess and self-adjust before it is too late. It might even extend to building in a self-assessment of performance as part of the test. (A preponderance of inaccurate self-assessments might well cast doubt on the validity of the test.)

High-stakes and large-scale secret tests (such as the SATs), in which the only apparent judges are electronic, threaten intellectual integrity even further, because they heap harmful suspicion on human judgment. Intellectual freedom is thus threatened by secure testing in the same way that it is threatened by political rule that emphasizes ritual and secrecy above the consent of the governed. Is it cavalier to suggest that the centrally mandated and secret testing of students in this country parallels the centrally planned and secret-dominated political systems now collapsing throughout Eastern Europe? I think not, for in Poland and Czechoslovakia, workers and citizens learned to do what many students and school districts regularly end up doing here: obey the letter of the law only; do no more and no less than the state directives require; see no incentives—indeed, see many disincentives—to set and honor more authentic standards. Nor do the makers and buyers of tests ever have to provide anything more than a public relations answer to critical questions raised by skeptics.

Ultimately, we must recognize that there is a fundamental cultural inequality at work in sustaining this harmful overreliance on test security. Pervasive test security is not necessary. One's place in the educational and professional hierarchy matters more than some theoretical concern with validity and feasibility in test construction. Our tolerance for incomparable results is suddenly much higher when the adults and powerful institutions are being assessed.[38] Much test security is required merely to enable the test to be uniform, simple, cheap, and widely used. But personal and institutional idiosyncrasies, complex quality-control procedures, and local autonomy—properly considered virtues of higher education, the professions, and the marketplace—are all compromised by generic secure tests. Continued reliance on secure proxy tests is thus possible only when schools and students have inadequate power to protest their overuse. Perhaps more to the point, such moral inequality is counterproductive (a theme to be picked up in Chapters Seven and Eight in an analysis of the differences between authentic standards and mere standardization).

A clear alternative approach is already being practiced in various U.S. school districts and in countries other than our own: Return control of assessment to teachers or their representatives; make the assessment more credible, contextual, and fair. Develop districtwide and statewide "task banks" of *exemplary* assessment tasks—tests worth teaching to and emulating in one's design. Develop clear and validated district performance standards through benchmarking and a community-discussion process. Develop oversight and audit functions to ensure the soundness of the system. When a pool of questions and tasks that is large enough to prevent corruptive teaching has been developed, make those questions and tasks public, as if to say to teachers and students alike, "These represent the range of tasks that you must be good at to graduate. Now that you know this, the responsibility becomes yours [just as responsibility is assigned to the athlete, drafting student, artist, and debater]. We will coach you until you know how to self-assess and perform well enough that we become obsolete as 'teachers' and upholders of standards. Then you will have become, quite properly, our colleague." No mystery or secret there—which is just as it should be if our aim is to empower students and teachers instead of merely to check up on them and keep them in check.

Notes

1. This chapter is a substantially revised version of "Secure Tests, Insecure Test Takers," in J. Schwartz and K. A. Viator, eds., *The Prices of Secrecy: The Social, Intellectual and Psychological Costs of Testing in America*, a Report to the Ford Foundation (Cambridge, Mass.: Educational Technology Center, Harvard Graduate School of Education, 1990).

2. R. W. Highland, *A Guide for Use in Performance Testing in Air Force Technical Schools* (Lowry Air Force Base, Colo.: Armament Systems Personnel Research Laboratory, 1955).

3. R. Fitzpatrick and E. J. Morrison, "Performance and Product Evaluation," in F. L. Finch, ed., *Educational Performance Assessment* (Chicago: Riverside/Houghton Mifflin, [1971] 1991), p. 127.

4. S. Bok, *Secrets: On the Ethics of Concealment and Revelation* (New York: Random House, 1983), p. 25.

5. See the "Environmental Impact Statement" developed by the national watchdog group Fair Test for an example of how such a process might work.

6. As translated by N. Lewis, *Hans Andersen's Fairy Tales: A New Translation* (London: Puffin Books, 1981), p. 42.

7. Consider, by contrast, the recent manifesto behind Britain's new

national assessment design (which will rely heavily on classroom-based, teacher-overseen assessment): "A system which was not closely linked to normal classroom assessments and which did not demand the professional skills and commitment of teachers might be less expensive and simpler to implement, but would be indefensible in that it could set in opposition learning, teaching, and assessment." From Department of Education and Science, Assessment Performance Unit, *Mathematical Development,* Secondary Survey Report 1 (London: Her Majesty's Stationery Office, 1980), para. 48, p. 220.

8. The vaunted college admissions test, the SAT, is a lovely example of what happens when secrecy shrouds the testing process. It is *not* an achievement test, but it is used to whip districts and states into a frenzy about school achievement—despite explicit warnings in ETS material not to do so and the obvious fact that such tests depend heavily on socially constrained views of "intelligence" (and thus socioeconomic status). And who recalls that the SAT was developed as an *aptitude* test, for *equity* reasons—namely, to find students with potential in the hinterlands whose achievement might be limited by local schooling?

9. See R. Stiggins, "Assessment Literacy," *Phi Delta Kappan* 72 (1991): 534–539.

10. Educators in other countries derisively refer to our fetish for multiple-choice tests as "the American solution" to educational problems.

11. Bok, *Secrets,* p. 27.

12. Ibid., p. 110.

13. M. Mead, as quoted in Bok, *Secrets,* pp. 244–245.

14. M. Foucault, *Discipline and Punish.* (New York: Vintage Books, 1979), p. 35.

15. Ibid.

16. Ibid., p. 227.

17. S. Berryman, "Sending Clear Signals to Schools and Labor Markets," in J. Schwartz and K. A. Viator, eds., *The Prices of Secrecy: The Social, Intellectual, and Psychological Costs of Testing in America* (Cambridge, Mass.: Educational Technol-

ogy Center, Harvard Graduate School of Education, 1990), p. 43.

18. See Bok, *Secrets*, chap. 4.

19. See a discussion of this legal history in R. A. Berk, ed., *Performance Assessment Methods and Applications* (Baltimore, Md.: Johns Hopkins University Press, 1986).

20. See Chairman of the New York State Senate Higher Education Committee, *Truth in Testing: A Study in Educational Reform*, revised report (Albany, N.Y.: New York State Senate, 1984); A. Strenio, *The Testing Trap* (New York: Rawson, Wade, 1981); and G. Blumenstyk, "Federal Court Ruling that Public Disclosure of Test Violates Copyright Law Seen as a Blow to 'Truth in Testing' Movement," *Chronicle of Higher Education*, Jan. 31, 1990.

21. American Psychological Association, "Standards for Educational and Psychological Testing" (Washington, D.C.: American Psychological Association, 1985), p. 2.

22. This argument against unobtrusive testing is ironic in light of the new British assessment of students; unobtrusiveness is now an explicit aim of formal British testing programs. See Chapter Five, on incentives, for related discussion. See also J. Millman and J. Greene, "The Specification and Development of Tests of Achievement and Ability," in R. Linn, ed., *Educational Measurement*, 3rd ed. (New York: American Council on Education/Macmillan, 1989), for another view on the questionable ethics of test unobtrusiveness.

23. W. Haney and G. Madaus, "The Evolution of Ethical and Technical Standards for Testing," in R. K. Hambleton and J. N. Zaal, eds., *Advances in Educational and Psychological Testing: Theory and Applications* (Norwell, Mass.: Kluwer, 1991).

24. Schwartz and Viator, eds. *The Prices of Secrecy*.

25. Ibid., p. 115.

26. Ibid., p. 116.

27. For an excellent discussion of authentic assessment and how to maximize the beneficial impact of tests on schooling—"systemic" validity—see J. R. Fredriksen and A. Collins, "A Systems

Approach to Educational Testing," *Educational Researcher* *18*, 1989, 27–32.

28. Note that tests are not valid or invalid, in other words; inferences about results on tests are valid or invalid. Our failure to keep this point in mind is both common and unfortunate. See Chapter Seven for a further discussion of validity.

29. J. Millman and J. Greene, "The Specification and Development of Tests of Achievement and Ability," p. 347.

30. J. Piaget, *The Language and Thought of the Child,* trans. M. Gabain (New York: New American Library, [1932] 1965), p. 405.

31. Most educators do not seem to realize that establishing test validity is not merely a technical matter, based on technical rules and criteria. Validity can be established only by showing that the test results can be used to derive broader inferences about the value of the test scores vis-à-vis the wider world. Test makers need to *justify* their claims, ironically enough, by appealing to empirical evidence, not just statistics—something few school officials and policy makers require.

32. J. Piaget, *The Moral Judgment of the Child* (New York: Macmillan, [1932] 1965), p. 196.

33. Piaget, *The Moral Judgment of the Child*, pp. 137, 190. Piaget also suggests that schools reinforce the harmful effects of this constraint by overrelying on unverifiable didacticism, where "words are spoken with authority"; instead, adults should "discuss things on an equal footing and collaborate" with the child and lead the child to respect for both answers and their rational grounds (p. 194).

34. Piaget's sobering words were somehow lost on Kohlberg and others, who became convinced that intellectual development about moral matters was synonymous with irreversible moral progress. See C. Gilligan and G. Wiggins, "The Origins of Morality in Early Childhood Relationships," in J. Kagan and S. Lamb, *The Emergence of Morality in Young Children* (Chicago: University of Chicago Press, 1987).

35. Piaget, *The Moral Judgment of the Child*, p. 62.

36. The reader should not hear this in a utilitarian or mechanical sense. Art teachers often talk this way: Does the student's prod-

uct work in its own way to accomplish the artist's end? And the AP art portfolio assesses for such things as a sense of focus, style, and personal direction.

37. See Fredriksen and Collins, "A Systems Approach to Educational Testing."

38. The exception, admissions tests for graduate schools, is a reminder that the function of most tests is to expedite the work of the gatekeepers at a "higher" point in the system. Contrary to popular belief, competitive college and graduate admissions offices run offices of *rejection,* not admission: a candidate's low test scores enable the readers of many folders to shorten their work considerably by reducing the "maybe" pile (barring counterevidence from transcripts or references.)

4 | Testing and Tact

It was once a commonplace that tact is an essential capacity for teachers—*tact* in the sense described by William James as the "ingenuity to tell us what definite things to say and do when the pupil is before us . . . that tact for the concrete situation."[1] Socrates had this tact: each dialogue in which he participates is unique (as true dialogue must be); each move on his part derives from the unanticipatable response or objection from the other discussant.

It is just this tact that teaches students to respect the teacher in return. The teacher who is interested enough to ferret out what we are thinking, who persists in trying to understand our unexpected and opaque answers, and who sometimes understands our answers better than we do ultimately provides powerful incentive for us to develop the self-discipline required to refine our thinking and our answers. We develop a respect shown for intellectual standards based on the respect for our answers and the rules of evidence modeled by the standard-bearer. As Bruner once put it, "It requires a sensitive teacher to distinguish an intuitive mistake—an interestingly wrong leap—from a stupid or ignorant mistake, and it requires a teacher who can give approval and correction simultaneously."[2]

What, then, of the *assessor's* obligations? Is it not reasonable to ask that a tester be tactful? Well, of *course* testers ought to be tactful, you might say, but how is this even an issue in paper-and-pencil testing? As we have seen in previous chapters, a test is insensitive and unresponsive (by design) to answers deserving follow-up

or to questions that properly demand personalization by the answerer. Thus a tester, without intending to do so, treats the student
as an object while tacitly demanding, "Answer *my* question, *my*
way. You have one try in which to do it; and you get no opportunity
to rethink your answer based on feedback, because you'll get no
feedback." In a relationship, such a demand would be viewed (properly) as tactless, insensitive, overbearing. I would argue that it is
equally inappropriate in a test situation. The student may lose respect for someone who behaves this way (whether in a relationship
or in a classroom); the student may lose respect for and interest in
what is assessed in such a manner. Perhaps the efficacy of such a
method, and not just its ethics, is thrown into question.

This is not a hopelessly romantic idea. Binet and Piaget were
adamant about the assessor's need to adapt the climate and questioning to the child's needs and to unanticipated results. Invalid
inferences result when an assessment fails to honor Binet's caution
that "the attitude to be taken in regard to the child is delicate; first
of all, there must be good will; one must try to remain in touch with
him; excite his attention, his self respect."[3] Second, there is an *unavoidable* ambiguity to mere answers, even if blackened in with
finality by a #2 pencil: we do not know why the student selected a
correct or incorrect answer. A correct answer might be due to irrelevant or lucky thinking; an incorrect answer might hide a thoughtful
and apt response that, if pursued, would change our judgment as
to the student's knowledge. Tact is a moral description of the obligation to validate our test results by exploring the reasons for
answers. Being tactful in the assessment or testing relationship itself, especially when one has a singular goal in mind for one's work,
is far harder than it appears. But it is essential that we become more
tactful in assessment if our aim is to learn what the student really
knows and to induce the student to care to know and reveal more.

Primum non nocere is the Latin phrase for the key element
of the Hippocratic Oath: First, do no harm. But obeying the oath
in all clinical settings is more difficult than it seems, since harm is
usually caused by the unseen gap between our intentions and our
actual effects. Teachers do not set out to be boring; they too often
are. Test makers do not set out to influence learning negatively; they
often do. (Stanford University professor of education Lee Shulman

once told me, in a discussion about this problem and his ongoing research into teaching, that the better teachers can often be distinguished by a seemingly mundane trait: they more accurately describe what goes on in their classroom than do less successful teachers; in other words, they *see* that gap between intention and effect.) The inclination to rationalize what occurs is ever-present when our intent is noble.

Consider a cautionary tale from the history of medicine as a reminder of how difficult this "tact for the concrete situation" can be. We go back to a time when doctors were struggling to treat a horrible new kind of problem, the wounds inflicted from a then-novel technology of war—the gun. Doctors proposed a cure for gunshot wounds based on the plausible view that the bullet poisoned the body. It was necessary, from this perspective, to treat gunshot wounds the way doctors treated any serious infection: the body needed to "undergo a cleansing with boiling oil." As one historian of medicine has put it, "Not only was the theory erroneous, but the treatment was ferociously traumatic. The resultant pain was as intolerable as was the destruction of tissue . . . yet the therapeutic iniquity persisted, enforced by the wrong-headed dogma."[4]

It took a young barber-surgeon, unschooled enough to trust his senses, and the lucky depletion of oil at a critical moment in battle to overcome the "theory." Ambroise Paré, who became the personal surgeon to a general of Francois I, was compelled to develop an unusual method of treatment during the siege of Turin in 1537, when the oil habitually used to cleanse wounds ran out with the unexpectedly high casualties. He had the "inspiration to design a battlefield clinical experiment. . . . [T]his novice surgeon hit upon the idea of making up a bland soothing lotion." As he noted, "I was constrained to apply a digestive of yolkes of eggs, oil of roses, and turpentine. . . . [Rising early in fear of whether my own method would work] beyond my expectation I found those to whom I applied my medicine, to feele little paine, and their wounds without inflammation: the others to whom was used the boiling oil, I found them feverish, with great pain and swelling. And then I resolved with myself never so cruelly to burne poore men."[5]

It may seem like the worst kind of disrespect and exaggeration to imply that test makers and test users are scarring their students in similar ways. But testers, like doctors, are *inevitably* prone to lose their tact when they rely primarily on their technical expertise and theory.[6] How rarely we see the harm of uniform testing and its presumed practices, after all. The theory of testing—like the theory of cleansing gunshot wounds—is strong enough and sanctioned enough to blind us to its effects.

We might see this potential harm more clearly if we thought of the test maker (and test user) and the test taker as in a relationship. The question to ask, then, is whether or not the tester is respectful and tactful in this relationship. If assessment is not something we do *to* students but something we do *with* them, then considering what is good or ill for the student in the assessment relationship is an essential obligation. Is it not, for example, intellectually disrespectful when a test maker feels no obligation to make test tasks thought-provoking enough to be worthy of the students' time and engagement? And what if the tester seems not to care whether students regularly get right answers for the wrong reasons (or vice versa)? What of the routine use of test security, distracters, and other questionable practices that seem both demeaning and liable to undermine students' faith in the assessor? What if we found out that certain often-administered tests and formats were perceived by students or teachers as boring, onerous, or not consistent with the experienced curriculum? What if an indirect and decontextualized form of testing is always less engaging than a direct method of assessment but is nonetheless more common?

And what of the student's relationship to knowledge itself? What disrespect is implied when we offer only generic, decontextualized, set exercises with right and wrong answers, as opposed to problems that demand judgment in the use and adaptation of knowledge? What bad lessons about the intellectual world are provided by tactless procedures that permit no student questions, no reframing of questions, and no opportunity to defend an odd or unorthodox response? If students (and the teacher, in the case of externally constructed tests) see no value in a test (and thus decide not to give the test their all), then what is the test actually measuring? Do test takers and test users have a right to be part of the validation process, just as all parties in a relationship are entitled to a say when the conduct of the relationship affects them (something we acknowledge with even small children)? At the very least, we need to consider how the design of any test adversely or positively affects each student's conception of learning and its value, as well as the student's "aspirations, motivation, and self-concept" (in the words of Benjamin Bloom, George Madaus, and Thomas Hastings).[7]

In this chapter, I propose to address questions of this sort—questions that should make us increasingly uncomfortable with the inherently unresponsive nature of most tests. I am fully prepared for some readers to find such a discussion naive and idealistic. But the reader would do well to reflect upon the consequences of a system of intellectual assessment that perpetually misleads the student about what knowledge is, how it is validated, the role that dialogue plays in real-world appraisals, and what kind of know-how and initiative in problem solving is really wanted in the adult world. At the very least, the reader should consider the disincentives provided by a testing system in which only sanctioned, uniform answers are desired and in which the assessor is never obliged to honor the student's wish to clarify questions and to critique or agree to the worth of the test.

Students' Relationship to
Knowledge as Defined by Testing

If the "doing" of science or history is inherently more engaging than the learning of other people's conclusions, what consequences does this have for assessment? Or, to put it negatively, what should we make of what Howard Gardner has noted—namely, that "one of the most objectionable, though seldom remarked upon, features of formal testing is the intrinsic dullness of the materials. How often does anyone get excited about a test or a particular item?"[8] I note in Chapter Five that John Goodlad found most students to be more inclined to find value and pleasure in the arts, physical education, and vocational courses than in the traditional educational core. He discovered that the school activities that students found most pleasurable were those that "involved them actively or in which they worked with others. These included making films, building or drawing things, making collections, interviewing people, acting things out, and carrying out projects."[9] And as I noted in Chapter One, Bloom described synthesis as the "production of a *unique* communication" that "bears the stamp of the person." Synthesis is the place in the Taxonomy "which most clearly provides for creative behavior on the part of the learner."[10] Work that involves this creative behavior is clearly of greater value to the learner.

There is no better way to consider the impact of the test tasks themselves on student engagement than to compare different tests of the same subject. Consider the mathematics questions presented in Exhibit 4.1. Who cannot see the inherently engaging qualities of the m&m's problem? In addition, it may do a more thorough job of assessing for the outcome in question: understanding of volume.

I have used the m&m's problem shown in Exhibit 4.1 with many middle and high school classes after the appropriate (though fairly traditional) units had been completed by their teachers. What was striking to the teachers observing the students work through the problem each time was the intense interest demonstrated by even the poorest-performing students. In fact, in two cases, the "worst" students were among the last to leave the room, and they were in the top group of performers! And one pair of "poor" students pleaded with their teacher for another piece of posterboard so that they might work with it after school. (The teacher's jaw dropped visibly.)

Contextual detail and even ambiguity heighten engagement, because one's judgment, style, and wit are tapped, not just one's textbook knowledge. Consider, for example, the case method used to teach law, medicine, and business. Anyone who has witnessed the use of the case method in action, as I have in problem-based-learning medical courses (where students are confronted with cases requiring diagnosis and given only a list of symptoms and readings gained in emergency room admissions), is immediately struck by the heightened student engagement generated. The richness of the case, the need for deft judgment and application of knowledge—these are the very things that provide each student with incentive to enter into and grapple with the case.

Why does it make sense to call this engaging of students an issue of tact? Because a simplistic, generic test item out of context is both alienating and unresponsive to the realities of diverse human intelligence. (Is it too farfetched to say that we have had a

Exhibit 4.1. Two Approaches to Testing in Math.

Standardized Test Questions on Volume

1. What is the volume of a cone that has a base area of 78 square centimeters and a height of 12 centimeters?
   a. 30 cm^3
   b. 312 cm^3
   c. 936 cm^3
   d. 2808 cm^3

2. A round and a square cylinder share the same height. Which has the greater volume?

A Multiday Performance Assessment On Volume

Background: Manufacturers naturally want to spend as little as possible, not only on the product, but on packing and shipping it to stores. They want to *minimize* the cost of production of their packaging, and they want to *maximize* the amount of what is packaged inside (to keep handling and postage costs down: the more individual packages you ship, the more it costs).

Setting: Imagine that your group of two or three people is one of many in the packing department responsible for m&m's candies. The manager of the shipping department has found that the cheapest material for shipping comes as a flat piece of rectangular paperboard (the piece of posterboard you will be given). She is asking each work group in the packing department to help solve this problem: *What completely closed container, built out of the given piece of posterboard, will hold the* largest volume *of m&m's for safe shipping?*

1. Prove, in a *convincing* written report to company executives, that both the *shape* and the *dimensions* of your group's container maximize the volume. In making your case, supply all important data and formulas. Your group will also be asked to make a three-minute oral report at the next staff meeting. Both reports will be judged for *accuracy, thoroughness,* and *persuasiveness.*
2. Build a model (or multiple models) out of the posterboard of the container shape and size that you think solves the problem. The models are *not* proof; they will *illustrate* the claims you offer in your report.

---

gender gap in mathematics because the testing, not just the teaching, is so decontextualized and thus arelational?) The reason for using moral language to discuss this issue is that technical demands may not require designers to sweat over these kinds of "aesthetic" and contextual details. After all, they might well gain valid results from more morally questionable methods. My aim is to alert test users to the fact that test designers invariably work at a distance from students, literally and relationally; they are too infrequently asked to consider the moral and intellectual quality of their relationship to the student, as mediated by the test. The tester's intellectual interests are not those of the student, and yet *both* sets of interests should be considered. And not just in terms of the "social" implications of testing: while I applaud the work of Samuel Messick, senior researcher at Educational Testing Service, and others in bringing "consequential validity" as an issue before the measurement community, a "social" perspective may be as tactless and impersonal as a "merely technical" perspective. We need to better consider the differences between students and the unanticipatable but apt answers of students; this is what I mean by *tact*.

In the case of the test tasks themselves, we need to consider the student's relationship to the domain being assessed—to knowledge itself—as operationalized in the test. Dewey was one of the first and most vociferous of modern thinkers to argue that learning must always consider this relationship—the student's relationship to ideas and adult insights. Like any human relationship, the student's relationship to knowledge can be authentic or inauthentic, nurturing or distancing. His criticism of textbook-driven syllabi and tests rested in part on the harm to motivation that he saw resulting from inauthentically presenting knowledge as a fixed and settled compendium instead of as methods of inquiry and their (always tentative) results.[11]

Testing that operationally defines mastery in terms of the student's ability to recognize sanctioned answers makes clear that the student's contributions as a *thinker* are unimportant. Since "the child knows perfectly well that the [tester] and all his fellow pupils have exactly the same facts and ideas . . . he is not giving them anything at all new." It is not too extreme to suggest that the student is then treated as (and made to feel like) a mere object in the test relationship: "As a consequence of the absence of the materials and occupations which generate real problems, the pupil's problems are not his; or rather, they are his only as a pupil, not as a human being. . . . Relationship to subject matter is no longer direct. . . .[T]he occasions and material of thought are not found in the arithmetic or history or geography itself, but in skillfully adapting that material to the [tester's] requirements."[12]

Anyone with common sense or with experience in school can bear witness to the student as object. We naturally want to contribute, to produce, to perform, to make a difference, to use our wits and style; we naturally are made frustrated, passive, or cynical by doing work that does not appear to be in our interests and is barely personalized. And in terms of validity concerns, higher-order thinking typically requires performance challenges that truly engage, as was noted above. (A concern for the student's relationship to knowledge must, therefore, be viewed in part as a demand for a more robust and authentic approach to construct validity, as I argue in Chapter Seven.)

Given that direct testing is more engaging and educative than indirect testing, we need to ask a fundamental question: Is the student *entitled* to the most "direct" forms of measurement possible, irrespective of the technical and logistical hurdles? After all, there are grounds for worry about the link between the nature and import of a test and student motivation. Paul Burke, the author of a recent paper that was part of a major congressional study of national testing, argues that there is a good deal of anecdotal and circumstantial evidence to show that NAEP results are of questionable worth, because students have no perceived interest in the test and its results.[13] Regrettably, Burke suggests that the only solution is to avoid tests that are "penalty-free"—as if only threats motivate eighth- and twelfth-graders to care about their work.

The dilemma is further illustrated in a curious passage in Diane Ravitch and Chester Finn's book describing the first NAEP U.S. history and literature test. In the pilot of the test, NAEP had included the option "I don't know" among the test responses. Although Ravitch and Finn advocated keeping that option in the multiple-choices items, "in accordance with its usual procedure, NAEP did not include 'I don't know' as a potential answer. It is the test maker's judgment that this response is somehow inappropriate, that it confuses the analysis of the test results."[14] But that is not the full story. As one of the ETS researchers who worked on the project told me, the "confusion" is due to the fact that too many kids choose "I don't know" to mean "I don't care" (since the NAEP test has no bearing on their school grades or future aspirations).

We can cite a happier example to show the positive intrinsic incentives possible in formal testing challenges. New York has now for three years had a hands-on test of basic science skills as part of the fourth-grade program evaluation. The test is given to all students and is composed of five activities organized as separate "stations" to which the students rotate for a fixed period of time until all stations have been completed.[15] Douglas Reynolds, director of science for the state, tells a story echoed by many fourth-grade teachers I have worked with in New York: he visited on test day one of the first schools at which the test was given, and as the test ended, three students excitedly crowded around the teacher to ask, "Can we do this again tomorrow?"

Issues of Respect: The Unexamined
Ethics of the Assessment Relationship

Whatever our view about the assessor's obligation to provide authentic forms of assessment and to give a voice to the test takers and test users, there remain other ethical concerns about testing that have been ignored in most overly technical discussions. Whether we consider the secrecy described in Chapter Three or the universal reliance on test formats that do not permit the test taker to ask questions, consult resources, or justify an answer, we ought to consider the link between technical practices of questionable merit and their possible negative impact on student performance, motivation, and trust.

Distracters and Other Forms of Deceit

Consider, for example, our unending reliance on deception in testing. Every test that provides a full range of possible answers from which the student selects involves chicanery—legal trickery—on the part of the test maker. The student must choose between answers that are (and are meant to be) similar in appearance, though only one is correct (or "best"). We rarely consider the morality and the efficacy of such a practice, however, despite the fact that the very term used to describe those other possible answers—the "distracters"—alerts us to the test maker's deliberate deception. (More modern texts describe distracters as "foils." Better public relations, perhaps, but the intent is the same.)

Just so we know what we are talking about, here are two multiple-choice questions from actual tests that provide plausible but incorrect answer options:

Using the metric system, you would measure the length of your classroom in

    a. grams
    b. kilometers
    c. meters
    d. liters

A requirement for a democratic government is that

    a. the people must have a voice in government
    b. government leaders must do what they think is best for the people
    c. judges must run for election rather than be appointed
    d. everyone must pay the same amount of taxes

In the first example, from a science test for middle school students, we can easily imagine that a student could be "distracted" by the word *kilometers,* since it contains the key word *meter.* (Would placing option b after option c change the number of students selecting it?) Though c is clearly the desired answer, "kilometers" is in fact acceptable—and might even be "best" in a particular context whose overall scale was immense. In the second question, the first two choices have been made almost equally enticing, given such phrases as "the people," "voice," and "is best for the people." But which answer is the "right" one?

Deception and ambiguity in assessment are not necessarily wrong. There are clearly times when the uncertainty generated in students by plausible, diverse answer options is essential for ferreting out real understanding.[16] But we *routinely* deceive young students by providing misleading answer options at their and our moral and intellectual peril. What is wanted are some guidelines for knowing when such deception is warranted and when it threatens students' respect for the assessor and, by implication, what is being assessed. (This demand is easily frustrated, however, by the secure and proprietary nature of such tests. Nonetheless, we must demand better professional and public oversight procedures and standards.)

Alas, we search in vain for any mention of the ethics of such deception in the psychometric literature. There is no mention of the problem of using distracters in the APA Standards, for example. In the most recent comprehensive analysis of large-scale test-construction principles and issues, distracter *analysis* is discussed ("Among high-scoring examinees, the keyed answer should be popular. . . . All foils should be chosen by a sufficient percentage of low-scoring examinees to warrant their use. . . . The discrimination value of the keyed answer should be positive, for the foils, negative"), but the *ethics* of the practice are not.[17]

Similarly, in most measurement textbooks, we find only technical advice on how to fashion the answer options: "Foils are designed to attract examinees who lack understanding of the content or who are unable to use the material in the desired way. Therefore, foils must be plausible responses for those examinees whose mastery of content is incomplete."[18] Leaving aside the obliqueness of the phrase "who are unable to use the material in the desired way," how are we to find and validate such foils? "The best way to create foils is to anticipate (predict) the kinds of misunderstandings or errors in knowledge that examinees are likely to experience." The authors even propose a field test for this: "A very objective method of creating foils for multiple-choice questions is to first write foils as completion items and try them out on students. If a wide range of student ability is represented in the field-test sample, a large number of plausible wrong answers will be obtained. These wrong answers will usually make good foils for multiple-choice versions of the items."[19] The authors note that "foils should *not* trick knowledgeable examinees into incorrect answers." They do not offer advice on how to determine whether that is occurring, however.

Another rule for composing effective distracters, found in an old text on test construction, is that the item writer "should max-imize the ratio of plausibility to correctness in his distracters."[20] Similarly, another theorist argues that "a portion of the art of item writing is the ability to conceive of distracters which are incorrect by any standard, and yet attractive to those not knowing the answer."[21] Still a third argues that "if an item distracter is obviously a wrong answer to everyone . . . this distracter probably should be replaced by a more plausible answer."[22]

Should we not be sure, before condoning trickery, that peo-ple are being tricked for the right reasons? If our reasons are in question, should we continue to assume that the use of such trickery is an appropriate tool if it has some technical value? Is the use of distracters so different from the use of inappropriately leading ques-tions or inappropriately gained evidence in law? It is tactless and perhaps morally objectionable to assess student understanding of an issue on the basis of a solitary tricky question; we could easily prevent this with more explicit design standards for the use of such test strategies.

To "maximize the ratio of plausibility to correctness" is clearly easier said than done, anyway—particularly when we see how easy it is to mislead students *simply by virtue of the fact that authorities are proposing the answers and the answers are plausible.* Although Binet, the father of modern testing, used distracters, he warned us of their perhaps excessive power to deceive. He devoted one of the set of intelligence tests to what he called "suggestibil-ity"—the force of a student's "judgment of a subject and his powers of resistance" to foils that were deliberately involved in the ques-tion. Each "test" was built upon deliberately disingenuous, impos-sible-to-honor instructions by the examiner: the student is asked to indicate the button when handed a thread, thimble, and cup; the instructor asks the student to find a "nitchevo" (or other nonsense word) in a picture; having already looked at pairs of unequal lines and designated the longer and shorter, the student is shown a pair of equal lines and asked "And here?" As Binet notes of this last prompt, "Led on by the former replies [the student] has a tendency, a required force," to succumb to what Binet calls a "snare."[23]

One wonders why Binet included such tests, then, particu-larly since he explicitly warns the reader that suggestibility is "by no means a test of intelligence, because very many people of superior intelligence are susceptible to suggestion through distraction, timidity, and fear of doing wrong."[24] In fact, in a later version of the test, Binet stressed that the child "falls into the trap because he allows himself to follow the lead of habit . . . [often due to] heedlessness, lack of attention."[25]

In another test, he rethought his original use of distracters. To test the student's ability to think logically, he made use of various logical absurdities, introduced into the test without warning. Examples included, "When a man plays marbles, why is he often decorated" and "When two men quarrel, why is there often near them a yellow dog?" Here too he noted that "very intelligent people sometimes fall into the trap. . . . [T]imidity, diffidence, confidence, and habit each plays its part." Binet thus notes the change in the test procedure: "Now instead of imposing an absurdity, we warn the child that it will come, and we ask him to discover it and refute it"; the examiner asks the student, "What is silly in this sentence?" Binet notes that "this experiment usually interests the children by its novelty."[26]

Piaget repeatedly stressed that the most difficult thing for all interviewers to avoid doing is eliciting what he called "suggested convictions." Especially important is the seductive power of the questioner's choice of words: "If one carelessly uses a word that is unexpected to the child, one risks stimulating . . . reactions which might then be mistaken for spontaneous." For example, "in asking 'what makes the sun move?' the suggestion of an outside agent occurs at once, thus provoking the creation of a myth."[27]

There is even a danger in the very method of testing, if one poses uniform questions under uniform conditions. The "essential failure of the test method" is that it "falsifies the natural mental inclination of the subject or risks doing so. . . . [I]t may well be that a child would never put the question to itself in such a form." The only way to avoid such difficulties is to "vary the questions, to make counter-suggestions, in short, to give up all idea of a fixed questionnaire." Since the "real problem is to know how he frames the question to himself or if he frames it at all," the skill of the assessor "consists not in making him answer questions . . . but encouraging the flow of spontaneous tendencies."[28] Piaget had some advice for those intending to use his methods to ascertain what the child *really* thinks: "[The questioning of a student] requires extremely delicate handling. . . . Play your part in a simple spirit and let the child feel a certain superiority."[29]

Consider how the following examples from a national standardized multiple-choice achievement test in mathematics violate Piaget's caution and advice:

1. In which numeral is there a 4 in both the hundred thousands and hundreds places?
   a. 140,426
   b. 410,642
   c. 416,402
   d. 414,602

2. How many faces does a cube have?
   a. 4
   b. 6
   c. 8
   d. 12

3. Which of these would you most likely measure in ounces?
   a. paint in a can
   b. gasoline in a car
   c. water in a bathtub
   d. medicine in a bottle

Leaving aside the apparent irrelevancy of such questions (these are clearly not questions that "one would likely pose to oneself" or even that would be posed in an arithmetic course), they (and others like them) are inherently "distracting."[30] And since "errors" might therefore be made for a variety of reasons having little to do with understanding of the concepts in question, it is unclear whether such questions can be adequately validated in a formal sense. What is wanted, in fact, are better guidelines for when distracters ought to be used and, when they are deemed apt, better guidelines for their validation.

Alan Shoenfeld has catalogued many "suggested convictions," one example of which, the army bus problem, I noted in Chapter Two. He also cites the work of a European researcher who came up with the following results to show how suggestion by the

tester and the habitual demands of the classroom can be stronger
than the student's judgment and knowledge:

> Reusser gave students a number of similar problems,
> for example: "There are 125 sheep and 5 dogs in a
> flock. How old is the shepherd?" The following quote
> from a fourth grade student working the problem out
> loud speaks for itself: "125 + 5 = 130 . . . this is too big,
> and 125 – 5 = 120 is still too big . . . while . . . 125/5
> = 25. That works. . . . I think the shepherd is 25 years
> old." Also, he asked 101 fourth and fifth grade stu-
> dents to work the following problem: "Yesterday 33
> boats sailed into the port and 54 boats left it. Yesterday
> at noon there were 40 boats left in the port. How many
> boats were still in the port yesterday evening?" He
> reports that all but one of the 101 students produced
> a numerical solution to the problem, and that only
> one student complained that the problem was un-
> solvable.[31]

We know from the work of Stanley Milgram, Ellen Langer,
and others in psychology that adults are all-too suggestible; they are
capable of induced thoughtlessness when commanded by "authorities" or situations to do odd or inappropriate things—none of
which bears any indication of what they might be shown to know
if the situation were less intimidating or less suggestive of the tester's "obvious" insights.

Recognition of human suggestibility and avoidance of test
deceit are more than issues of tact. The answers that result from
testing built upon trickery and suggestion may well be untrust-
worthy—invalid for making the kinds of inferences we want to
make. If the child is seduced into certain answers, if the child is not
"stimulated to any effort of adaptation" and produces answers at
random or as a kind of "romancing" (Piaget's term for the invention of an answer that the child does not really believe to be true),
then what have we learned? This has long been the position held
by teachers of young students, who often assert that standardized
tests are misleading and harmful to children and to their own work

as teachers. Their claim deserves to be better investigated and considered as a matter for policy.

Ambiguity and Equity

Note that the problem of unresponsive testing has little to do with whether the test is multiple-choice. In fact, many open-ended and performance tests use tasks and criteria of questionable merit and give students little opportunity to justify inherently ambiguous responses. For example, in a pilot of an open-ended mathematics test for third-graders in one southern state, the student is given two pictures, one of a cube and one of a pyramid, and asked, "How are these figures alike and how are they different?" The following scoring rubric is used:

0   Does not address the task, or no correct comparisons
1   Makes at least one comparison, but possibly only one category (alike or different) used
2   Makes at least 3 correct comparisons, with at least one in each category based on some geometrical property
3   Makes at least two correct comparisons in each category that are clearly stated and based on some geometrical property; no incorrect comparisons

Never mind the numerous questions about validity and score reliability that can be asked about such a question (I, for one, cannot fathom what this task is measuring or how the rubric can be validated as corresponding to genuine qualitative differences in performance); never mind the unfair secrecy in the student not having access to the judge's material. What about the *arbitrariness* of the rubric? From the wording of the question, why would the nine-year-old student imagine that the judges might reward for anything but the quality of her response? What validity can there be to a rubric that in fact discriminates answers on the basis of the number of a student's ideas only, not their quality? Or what about the fact that the scorers marked the following answer by a nine-year-old as wrong: "They are different because one is a square and one is a triangle"? That answer is correct if we go by the face of each shape (as the illustration invited: each face was highlighted).

We can understand the assessor's obligation to be more tactful in situations such as these by thinking about the legal principle of "equity." (I am using the word *equity* in its original philosophical meaning, which was then incorporated into the British and American legal systems in the courts of chancery or equity.) The idea is a commonsense one, captured in a surprisingly complex legal history: blanket laws are inherently unable to encompass the inevitable idiosyncratic cases to which we ought always to make "exceptions to the rule." Aristotle put it best: "The equitable is a correction of the law where it is defective owing to its universality."[32] A standardized test, unresponsive (by design) to the inevitable eccentricities of individual student thought and the inevitable ambiguities of the questions themselves, is thus intrinsically "inequitable."

Put in the context of testing, the principle of equity requires that we ensure that human judgment and the "test" of responsive dialogue are not overrun by an efficient mechanical scoring system. Tests that must be administered in a uniform, unidirectional way (and in which clarification of student answers is forbidden) are dangerously immune to the possibility that a student might legitimately require the opportunity to defend an unexpected or "incorrect" answer. How many times, for example, have *you* had to alter a judgment after your child, student, friend, or spouse explained an odd or "unacceptable" action or answer? Sometimes all a student needs is a rephrasing of the question to recall and use what he or she "knows." We rely on human judges in law, as in athletics, because the spirit of the law cannot be encompassed by the letter of the law; judgments cannot be reduced to algorithms. And because both questions and answers contain possible ambiguities, to gauge understanding we must explore an answer: there must be some possibility of dialogue between the assessor and the assessee to ensure that the student is fully examined.

The question that we must repeatedly ask is whether test makers are obligated to do a better job of probing a student's reasoning, particularly when the test format induces haste and efficiency in answering and when short answers are inherently ambiguous. Consider, as evidence of the problem, the following example from the NAEP "Learning by Doing" science test that was piloted a few years ago.[33] On one of the tasks, students were given three sets of statistics that supposedly derived from a mini-Olympics that some children put on. The introductory text noted that the children "decided to make each event of the same importance." No other information provided bears on the question. The test presented the students with the results of three "events" as follows:

Child's Name	Frisbee Toss	Weight Lift	50-Yard Dash
Joe	40 yards	205 lbs.	9.5 sec.
Jose	30 yards	170 lbs.	8.0 secs.
Kim	45 yards	130 lbs.	9.0 secs.
Sarah	28 yards	120 lbs.	7.6 secs.
Zabi	48 yards	140 lbs.	8.3 secs.

The first question asks the student, "Who would be the all-around winner?"
The scoring manual gives the following criteria for judging an answer:

> Score 4 points for accurate ranking of the children's performance on each event and citing Zabi as the overall winner. Score 3 points for using a ranking approach . . . but misinterpreting performance on the dash event . . . and therefore, citing the wrong winner. Score 2 points for a response which cites an overall winner or a tie with an explanation that demonstrates some recognition that a quantitative means of comparison is needed. Score 1 point if the student makes a selection of an overall winner with an irrelevant or non-quantitative account or without providing an explanation. Score 0 for no response.

Makes sense, right? But now ask yourself how you would score the following response given by a third-grader, using the given criteria:

a. *Who would be the all-around winner?*
No one.

b. *Explain how you decided who would be the all-around winner. Be sure to show your work.*
No one is the all-around winner.

The NAEP scorer gave the answer a 1. We see why, if we consider only the criteria: the student failed to give an explanation and any numerically related calculations to support the answer, and the answer appears incorrect since there was a winner. (The student, of course, did not have the rubric, which might have changed her answer.)

Suppose we assume, however, just as Piaget and Binet always warned us to assume, that an answer is usually apt in the mind of a student. Could it be that the nine-year-old deliberately and correctly answered "No one," thinking that "all-around" meant "winner of *all* events"? And, if looked at in this way, could it not be that the child was *more* thoughtful than most in deliberately not taking the "bait" of part b (which would have caused the child to pause in his or her answer, presumably). The full-sentence answer in part b—remember, this is a nine-year-old—is revealing to me: it is emphatic, as if to say, "No, your question suggests that I *should* have found one all-around winner, but I won't be fooled; I stick to my answer that no one was." (Note, by the way, that in the scorer's manual the word *all-around* has been changed to *overall*.) The student did not, of course, "explain" the answer, but it is conceivable that the instruction was confusing, given that there was no "work" needed to determine that "no one" was the all-around winner. One quick follow-up question would have settled the matter as to what the student's answer meant.

How ironic to learn that many of the tasks borrowed by ETS from the British Assessment Performance Unit (APU) were differently scored in the American version than in the original version. (APU scoring is discussed in a 1980 report on assessment prepared by the British Department of Science & Education.[34]) The APU considered in its scores the students' postexperimental voiced reflections on their work, seeing those reflections as being of great importance in determining what students understand. For example, in the six hands-on science tasks used to assess science skill in eleven-year-olds, the same question was asked each time, after the experimental work was over:[35]

> If you could do this experiment again, using the same
> things that you have here, would you do it in the same
> way or change some things that you did, to make the
> experiment better?

Responses were rated on a three-point scale as follows:

	Rating
shows awareness of variables which were not controlled, procedures which turned out to be ineffective, the need to repeat measurement, or criticizes other factors which are central, not peripheral, to the investigation	2
shows awareness of alternative procedures but unaware of particular deficiencies of those used (does not have very good reasons for suggesting changes)	1
uncritical of procedures used, can suggest neither deficiencies nor alternative procedures	0

At issue is a moral question with technical ramifications: to what extent is the tester responsible for ensuring that student answers are sufficiently explored or understood? To what extent is the assessor obliged to both excite the student's attention (so as to evoke all of what the student thinks and knows on a subject) and probe those answers that do not, on first glance, seem apt (but that may well be apt once we grasp the rationale at work)? And what does the constant failure to use such techniques teach the student about intellectual challenges and standards?

It is striking that in many of the APU test protocols, such as the science protocol cited above, the assessor is meant to probe, prompt, and even teach, if necessary, to be sure of the student's actual ability. In many of the APU tests, *the first answer (or lack of one) is not deemed a sufficient insight into the student's knowl-*

edge.[36] Consider, for example, the following sections from the assessor's manual in a mathematics test for fifteen-year-olds involving the ideas of perimeter, area, and circumference:[37]

1. *Ask:* "What is the perimeter of a rectangle?" [write student answer]
2. Present sheet with rectangle ABCD. *Ask:* "Could you show me the perimeter of this rectangle?"
3. *Ask:* "How would you measure the perimeter of the rectangle?" *If necessary, prompt for full procedure.*

As the APU report noted, these multiple opportunities to reveal knowledge were necessary, because many of the answers to the initial question were incorrect or confusing, while later answers revealed greater understanding: "About half the students [gave a satisfactory definition or formula for finding the perimeter.] Nearly all the testers commented on the inability of students to express themselves. . . . Many testers commented that there was some confusion between area and perimeter so that some pupils gave responses such as the 'area around the outside.' Looking at the results for the next two questions [, however,] over 80% could indicate the perimeter on the diagram."

A similar sequence of questions further illustrates the prompting allowed:[38]

10. "Estimate the length of the circumference of this circle." (answer: approx. 22 cm)
11. "What could you use to check your estimate?" *(string, rulers, etc. are on the table) If no response, prompt for string:* "Might you do something with the string?"
13. "Is there any other method?" *If student does not suggest using* $C = \pi\delta$, *prompt with* "Would it help to measure the diameter of the circle?"

If pupil does not suggest using formula, prompt:

> "Would it help to measure the diameter of the circle?"

It is of note that there was a 3 to 6 percent improvement in performance when students were prompted in these various offhand ways. As we shall see in Chapter Seven, this view of understanding—the view that we sometimes "forget" what we "know"—is more sound psychologically and philosophically than merely counting the first answer to a question.

This constant ability by the assessor to intervene, cue, or prompt in the APU assessments does not corrupt the test results, however, as revealed by the scoring system:[39]

1 Unaided success
2 Success following one prompt from the tester
3 Success following a series of prompts
4 Teaching by the tester; prompts unsuccessful
5 An unsuccessful response; tester did not prompt or teach
6 An unsuccessful response despite prompting and teaching
7 Question not given
8 Unaided success where student corrected an unsuccessful attempt without help

Successful responses were combined into 2 larger categories called "unaided success" and "unaided plus aided success" with percentages given for each.

The problem is not merely sloppy item writing nor poor rubrics; it is the inherent ambiguities in questions and answers that require some dialogue or follow-up. Consider the preliminary findings of Walt Haney and Laurie Scott in a study about ambiguity in test items. In an attempt to determine whether standardized test questions have inherent ambiguities that lead to misjudgments on the part of the assessor, Haney and Scott interviewed students on their responses. They often found, when students gave reasons for their answers, that "mistakes" and "correct answers" were not as they appeared. Consider the following example from a reading comprehension item:

> Jane Addams cared about people all her life. When she lived in Chicago, she saw many children who did not have a good place to play. They played in the streets. . . . Jane Addams was given a large lot. The lot had many old, unused houses on it. She had the houses torn down so that the lot would be empty.
>
> Jane Addams worked hard to clean up the lot. Then she bought swings and seesaws. This became the first playground in Chicago.
>
> Five comprehension questions were based on this passage. One of them, and the answer alternatives posed for it, was, "What did Jane Addams do with the swings and seesaws?
>
> > a.   cleaned them
> > b.   played with them
> > c.   had them put on the lot
> > d.   used them in the streets
>
> Six out of ten children marked the third answer, which was the intended correct answer. Two marked "played with them." . . . One girl marked the first answer alternative, . . . " 'Cause she doesn't want the kids to go on dirty things."

Haney and Scott note that the last child's inference is quite reasonable, given the comments about Addams's concern for cleanliness. The trouble is that this was not a test of "inference" but of "comprehension" from the test maker's point of view!

Haney and Scott catalogue dozens of similar examples and conclude that "ambiguity in children's interactions with test items is a phenomenon which occurs in a significant number of cases."[40] They recommend, as have other testing experts, that test makers routinely converse at length with students to probe these validity questions more carefully. They also warn that traditional notions of how to establish test validity are open to question as a result of their findings.

In sum, tact is not an option or a romantic demand. Any intellectual assessment is interpersonal—sensitive to different meanings and to context. One vital reason to safeguard the teacher's role as primary assessor is that the most accurate and equitable evaluation depends on relationships over time between examiner and student.[41] The teacher is the only one who knows what the student habitually can or cannot do, who has the ability to design completely contextualized and curricularly articulated assessments, and who has the ability and tact to follow up on confusing, glib, or ambiguous answers. In this country, we are so enamored of efficient testing that we overlook the feasible in-class alternatives to impersonal testing in use around the world. That is one reason why the German *abitur* (containing essay and oral questions) for graduation from the *Gymnasium* is still designed and scored by classroom teachers (who submit two possible tests to a state board for approval)—standards, but without standardization.

At the very least, we need to establish guidelines for the design of tests to ensure that the student's ability to justify or clarify a response is maximized. Tact is about responsiveness, after all. The relationship between test taker and tester must be made more morally balanced. In that relationship, as in all relationships, both responsiveness and equality are enhanced when each side has a say in the discussion. We can take that literally—"Let's have more oral examining"—or we can take it figuratively—"Let's ensure that the student has adequate opportunity to clarify both questions and answers." Either way, let us at *least* ensure that we "first, do no harm" to the student by testing; let us devise more rigorous procedures for determining and for counteracting the costs of tactless testing.

Notes

1. W. James, *Talks to Teachers* (New York: W. W. Norton, [1899] 1958), p. 24. For a thorough and illuminating discussion of tact and education, see M. Van Manen, *The Tact of*

Teaching: The Meaning of Pedagogical Thoughtfulness (New York: State University of New York Press, 1991).

2. J. Bruner, *The Process of Education* (Cambridge, Mass.: Harvard University Press, 1960/1977), p. 68.

3. A. Binet and T. Simon, "New Investigation upon the Measure of the Intellectual Level Among School Children," in *The Development of Intelligence in Children* (Salem, N.H.: Ayer, [1911] 1983), p. 295.

4. S. B. Nuland, "The Gentle Surgeon," in *Doctors: The Biography of Medicine* (New York: Vintage Books, 1988), p. 97.

5. Quoted in Nuland, *Doctors,* p. 98.

6. The aptness of the comparison between medical and educational theory and practice goes beyond this delicate relationship between client, practitioner, and knowledge. Consider, for example, the current work of the Carnegie Board on Professional Teaching Standards, which is attempting to professionalize education in the same way that Flexner (also Carnegie-commissioned) led to standards in medical certification at the turn of the century.

7. B. S. Bloom, G. F. Madaus, and J. T. Hastings, *Evaluation to Improve Learning* (New York: Mc-Graw Hill, 1981), p. 51.

8. H. Gardner, *The Unschooled Mind: How Children Think and How Schools Should Teach* (New York: Basic Books, 1991), p. 93.

9. J. I. Goodlad, *A Place Called School: Prospects for the Future* (New York: McGraw-Hill, 1984), pp. 114–115.

10. B. S. Bloom, ed., *Taxonomy of Educational Objectives,* Vol 1: *Cognitive Domain* (White Plains, N.Y.: Longman, 1956), pp. 163, 175. Serious would-be test designers would do well to reread the *text* of the Taxonomy, not just the appendix/list, as well as the follow-up handbook developed by Bloom, Madaus, and Hastings years later *(Evaluation to Improve Learning).*

11. As an indication of the failure to grasp Dewey's point, see P. H. Hirst, "The Logical and Psychological Aspects of Teaching a Subject," and D. W. Hamlyn, "The Logical and Psychological Aspects of Learning," both in R. S. Peters, ed.,

The Concept of Education (London: Routledge & Kegan Paul).

12. "There is next to no opportunity for each child to work out something specifically his own, which may contribute to the common stock, while he in turn participates in the productions of others. . . . All are set to do the same work and turn out the same results. The social spirit is not cultivated, in fact it gradually atrophies for lack of use." J. Dewey, "Moral Principles in Education," in J. A. Boydston, ed., *The Middle Works of John Dewey: 1899–1924* (Carbondale: Southern Illinois University Press, [1909] 1977), p. 275; *Democracy in Education* (New York: Macmillan, 1916), p. 156.

13. P. Burke, *You Can Lead Adolescents to a Test But You Can't Make Them Try* (Washington, D.C.: U.S. Office of Technology Assessment, U.S. Department of Commerce/National Technical Information Service, 1991).

14. D. R. Ravitch and C. E. Finn, Jr., *What Do Our 17-Year-Olds Know?* (New York: HarperCollins, 1987), pp. 41–42. It is also worth noting that the authors were dismayed to learn that open-ended questions of the essay and short-answer type were not going to be used: "We would prefer an essay examination that determined the depth of student understanding. We hope that testing agencies will soon develop additional ways to assess knowledge and not rely so exclusively on multiple-choice questions" (p. 21). And, NAEP personnel have, in fact, developed more open-ended and performance tasks in content-area tests since the book was written.

15. See R. Mitchell, *Testing for Learning* (New York: Free Press/Macmillan, 1992), for a full account of this and other new state hands-on tests.

16. See P. Elbow, *Embracing Contraries: Explorations in Learning and Teaching* (New York: Oxford University Press, 1986), for a thoughtful discussion of the difference between the "teaching" role and the "assessing" role and the necessity of detached and critical probing in the latter.

17. J. Millman and J. Greene, "The Specification and Development of Tests of Achievement and Ability," in R. Linn, ed.,

Educational Measurement, 3rd ed. (New York: American Council on Education/Macmillan, 1989), pp. 361–362.

18. G. H. Roid and T. M. Haladyna, *A Technology for Test-Item Writing* (Orlando, Fla.: Harcourt Brace Jovanovich, 1982), pp. 180–181.

19. Ibid., p. 105.

20. R. L. Ebel, *Measuring Educational Achievement* (Englewood Cliffs, N.J.: Prentice-Hall, 1965), p. 164. By the way, there appears to be confusion over how the word should be spelled: both *distractor* and *distracter* can be found in many books, and both spellings appear in this Ebel book.

21. A. Wessman, cited in W. Haney and L. Scott, "Talking with Children About Tests: An Exploratory Study of Test Item Ambiguity," in K. O. Freedle and R. P. Duran, eds., *Cognitive and Linguistic Analyses of Test Performance* (Norwood, N.J.: Ablex, 1987), p. 365.

22. S. Henrysson, cited in Haney and Scott, "Talking with Children About Tests," p. 365.

23. A. Binet and T. Simon, "New Methods for the Diagnosis of the Intellectual Level of Subnormals," in *The Development of Intelligence in Children.* (Salem, N.H.: Ayer, [1905] 1983), p. 57.

24. Ibid., pp. 56–57.

25. Binet and Simon, "New Investigation upon the Measure of the Intellectual Level Among School Children," p. 285.

26. A. Binet and T. Simon, "The Development of Intelligence in the Child," in *The Development of Intelligence in Children* (Salem, N.H.: Ayer, [1908] 1983), pp. 227–228.

27. J. Piaget, *The Child's Conception of the World,* trans. J. Tomlinson and A. Tomlinson (Totowa, N.J.: Rowman & Allanheld, [1929] 1983), pp. 10ff., 15 and 3.

28. Ibid., pp. 3–4.

29. J. Piaget, *The Language and Thought of the Child,* trans. M. Gabain (New York: New American Library, [1932] 1974), pp. 25–26.

30. The test company has the nerve to suggest that the first question is a valid test of the construct "concept of numbers."

31. As reported in A. H. Shoenfeld, "Problem Solving in Con-

text(s)," in R. Charles and E. Silver, eds., *The Teaching and Assessing of Mathematical Problem Solving* (Reston, Va.: National Council of Teachers of Mathematics/Erlbaum, 1988), pp. 83–84.

32. Aristotle, "Nichomachean Ethics," in J. Barnes, ed., *The Complete Works of Aristotle* (Princeton, N.J.: Princeton University Press, 1984), 1137b pp. 25–30. There is a lengthy and fascinating history to the concept of "equity."

33. National Assessment of Educational Progress, *Learning by Doing: A Manual for Teaching and Assessing Higher-Order Thinking in Science and Mathematics* (Princeton, N.J.: Educational Testing Service, 1987).

34. From Department of Education and Science, Assessment Performance Unit, *Mathematical Development*, Secondary Survey Report 1 (London: Her Majesty's Stationery Office, 1980), pp. 105–108.

35. From Department of Education and Science, Assessment Performance Unit, *Science in Schools: Age 11, Report No. 1* (London: Her Majesty's Stationery Office, 1981), p. 119.

36. Similar work on a research scale is being done in this country as part of what is called "diagnostic achievement assessment." See R. E. Snow, "Progress in Measurement, Cognitive Science, and Technology That Can Change the Relation Between Instruction and Assessment," in Educational Testing Service, ed., *Assessment in the Service of Learning*, Proceedings of the 1987 ETS Invitational Conference (Princeton, N.J.: Educational Testing Service, 1988), and J. S. Brown and R. R. Burton, "Diagnostic Models for Procedural Bugs in Basic Mathematical Skills," *Cognitive Science*, 1978, *2*, 155–192.

37. Department of Education and Science, *Mathematical Development*, pp. 105ff.

38. Ibid., pp. 106–107.

39. Department of Education and Science, *Science in Schools*, pp. 80–81.

40. Haney and Scott, "Talking with Children About Tests," p. 361.

41. See the research in language arts, for example, cited by Constance Weaver, in which the abilities that the standardized tests

purport to measure differ from the actual development of those abilities—and in which local assessments better support the construct. C. Weaver, *Understanding Whole Language* (Portsmouth, N.H.: Heinemann Educational Books, 1990).

5 | Incentives and Assessment

If "drive out fear" is a critical postulate in the modern quality-control movement, then school assessment is still rooted in the sweatshops of the industrial revolution. One-shot, high-stakes secure tests—be they national or local—are everywhere, and we are inured to their deleterious effect on student motivation. There are surely consequences to initiative if tests perpetually feel like a "gotcha!" kind of trap and if our early scores seem like self-fulfilling prophecies. In the interest of the relationship between test taker, test user, and assessor, we are at least obligated to consider whether our methods of determining scores inappropriately restrict a student's sense of the possible.

Students, like adults, do their best work when there is a clear opportunity for self-satisfaction—the feeling that comes from having mastered something or contributed something of obvious value. What if a test is composed of simplistic items with no opportunity to produce work of value? How does self-satisfaction grow then? Students, like adults, need the reinforcement that comes from getting better and better at difficult challenges. What if the assessment system provides only one-shot tests devoid of usable feedback? Students, again like adults, are far more inclined to risk failure if they have faith that the judge will thoughtfully and thoroughly consider their accomplishments. What if in test after test, the rationale for student work is never explored? We pay adults high wages and offer considerable perquisites and other tangible rewards for each job done well, yet we ask twelve-year-olds to accept the abstract (even questionable) idea that a naked score on a test is a sufficient reward and that that score will bear on their future goals. And what if student scores are perpetually low and seemingly resistant to change, in part due to deliberate psychometric strategies?

Worrying about whether the assessment process and its reporting supply the right kind of incentive is a different matter than worrying about the design of tasks, even though disincentives may well grow out of our reliance on dreary tasks and unpleasant methods of questioning, as we saw in the previous chapter. My main interest in this chapter is to consider the incentives and disincentives built into the tests, scoring procedures, and reporting processes that we devise. Rewards or sanctions are not our subject here, and they are not a tester's problem; whether the student is offered a risk that seems worth taking, a scoring system that encourages appropriate optimism rather than fatalism, a feedback system that provides user-friendly information and timely opportunities to use that feedback—all this is the tester's problem.

What Is an "Incentive"?

We cannot get deep into these matters without first clarifying the meaning of *incentive*. As the dictionary suggests, an incentive is "that which influences or encourages to action, a spur or stimulus." The implication is clear enough: sometimes we need a stimulus to do the right thing, human nature being what it is. Clever policy making has always understood this: since "all men are not angels," our founders justified the separation of powers in government; weight-loss clinics know of the need to counteract natural dysfunctional habits with various incentives and retraining; the tax code, salary schedules, and many family rituals honor the idea that sometimes we are not inclined, without a spur, to do what we should do.

One reason that a spur might be necessary, of course, is that the tasks assigned are onerous. But why do we implicitly assume that the only kinds of incentives to be called into play in assessment are necessarily *extrinsic*—as if the apparent value of the assessment tasks and scoring process need never be called into question? Alas, few test designers (be they classroom teachers or test companies) feel *obligated* to make their tests intellectually rich, stimulating, and seemingly worth mastering. Few teachers actively explore the negative effects on learning caused by their grading on a formal or de facto curve. Few administrators monitor the effect of testing practices on teachers' perception about the teacher's role in this or question why we assume that grades should fall along a curve for goal-directed behavior supported by effective teaching. (Why would administrators not work to overcome the teacher's use of a curve, since it has neither technical nor pedagogical value at the classroom level?)

       We still know too little about the conditions of assessment that are likely to induce student engagement or detachment. Why, for example, do students routinely report (and researchers confirm) that, of all school experiences, the challenges provided in the arts and physical education generate the greatest motivation in students?[1] Is Goodlad correct when he argues that students' enjoyment of the study of foreign language is rooted in "the slightly higher level of corrective feedback" that is provided? What of his speculation that the appeal to students of language, art, vocational education, and physical education can be found in what is common to all four: "They provide models against which to check one's own performance rather quickly"?[2] We need to know why Mihalyi Csikszentmihalyi and Reed Larson, University of Chicago psychologists, report that high school students exhibit the "curious anomaly" of extremely low motivation and affect but high concentration when taking a test. (They speculate that the concentration is "inspired by the fear of external punishment."[3]) John Raven goes further in arguing that motivation is an inseparable variable in the measurement of competence: "It is meaningless to attempt to assess a person's abilities except in relation to valued goals."[4] We need to discern to what extent the assessor is obligated to learn from such inquiries.

       Theodore Sizer is one of the few modern reformers to argue for assessment reform on the grounds of sensitivity to student psychology and the matter of fairness, rather than on the grounds of psychometrics alone. In line with that argument, he introduces the idea of the "exhibition of mastery" in *Horace's Compromise* in a chapter entitled "Incentives." The aim in all school reform should be to "get the incentives right, for students and for teachers. . . . For most adolescents, two incentives are dominant. They want the high school diploma, and they want to respect themselves and be respected. High schools will be effective to the extent that they design their policies and practices around these two powerful stimuli."[5]

The exhibition of mastery was initially proposed as a way to capitalize on the strong incentive provided in our culture by the diploma. "If a school awarded the diploma whenever a student reached the agreed-on level of mastery rather than after four years of attendance and credit accrual, the effect on student behavior would be dramatic." The aim of an exhibition of mastery was to stress the importance of an assessment that gives the student an "opportunity to show off" rather than be subjected to a "trial by question." And that opportunity was intended to be plural, since "not everyone shows off best on a single test." As a result, "a sensible school would have a variety of means for exhibition—timed tests, essays, oral exams, portfolios of work."[6] And Sizer placed implicit value on the high interest level of a more authentic test of one's ability, such as is often provided in schools by literary magazines, recitals, games, or debates—a value made explicit in his recent account of the unfolding work of the Coalition of Essential Schools.[7]

The reader should not infer (like educators seem to do—as I have observed from my discussions in workshops) that difficult tests, exacting standards, and dispassionate reporting of results per se provide the struggling student with disincentives to excel. On the contrary, self-improvement depends upon a heightened dissatisfaction with one's performance and accurate feedback about the gap between actual performance and the standard. (Putting it that way makes it clearer why the perceived value of the challenge becomes so important to spur the student on). A low score is not, by itself, a disincentive to further learning. The disincentive comes from having no opportunity to profit from the assessment, in the form of useful feedback and opportunities to try again. In fact, a low score on a *valued* test, with ample opportunity to get a higher score, is an incentive to harder work and better learning.

Incentives from Within the Assessment

My experience as a coach, more than that as a classroom teacher, revealed to me how important incentives from within the assessment process can be to student motivation. Years ago I coached girls' varsity cross-country. Because it was just becoming a regular offering in schools, we had teams made up of a wide range of athletes, including runners with little competitive experience. (Frankly, we took everyone who tried out, given the numbers.) Cross-country is not glamorous or pleasant; it is not a "game" to be "played" but a difficult course to be run while in pain. Workouts are grueling in both their difficulty and sameness, injuries are common, and there is little chance for public glory or fan interest (given that no one sees contestants for 80 or 90 percent of the race).

Leaving aside the question of what lures people to the sport, why do they stay? In particular, why did one girl, Robin, stay for four years, despite the fact that in those four seasons she never beat a soul on our team or on the opposing teams? (Think of how you would feel if you routinely came in dead last in front of the few remaining spectators but believed that you could not have run any faster.) The answer, as she told me, was to be found in the scoring and record-keeping systems of cross-country.

As anyone familiar with the sport knows, the scoring in cross-country gives points that correspond to each runner's place of finish: the first-place runner gets 1 point; the fourth-place runner gets 4 points; and so on—through each team's first five of seven runners. Thus the lowest score wins. A shutout of one team by another would yield a score of 15 to 40 (or more than 40, depending upon where the winning team's sixth and seventh runners finish).

There is thus a significant incentive provided for all runners to run their hardest, even when the leaders have long since passed the finish line. The scoring system, not just the "test" of the run itself, heightens everyone's effort. The fourth runner on a team would not expect to beat the first, second, or third runners on either team. But she would hope to beat the *other* team's fourth runner. This is especially significant in a close meet: often the performance of the least able runners decides which team wins or loses. In an evenly matched meet, if the order of finish moves back and forth from team to team, the meet will be won or lost by whether *your* fifth runner defeats *their* fifth runner—sometimes, in fact, whether your sixth runner defeats their fifth runner. (Even though the sixth runner does not figure in a team's total score, she can cause the other team's score to be increased by a point, since the fifth and final number making up the other team's total score is the place of finish of the fifth runner.) This always spurs on the less able. They naturally want to help their team win meets—and they often do so, even though they know themselves to be less talented than their teammates. (The failure to win or be the best, therefore, need not be the debilitating experience that many people perceive it to be— unless you expect to win or are expected to win by people whose judgment you trust.)

But Robin, you will recall, never had the experience of figuring in any team result. She never defeated anyone. Why, then, did she persist with the sport? What caused her to keep working hard in workouts and in meets? She persisted because we kept track of her times and her weight—and both steadily fell over the course of four years. In fact, by the end of her junior year and third season, she not only had the satisfaction of seeing measurable progress in her times and the feeling of being more fit; she also took quiet pleasure in the fact that her last race times for the year would have earned her fourth place in a race held back in her freshman year.

Any band director or special education teacher has many similar stories to tell. It is not merely the test itself that provides the incentive or disincentive (though we will want to look at how assessment tasks can be made more enticing and engaging). The form and manner in which we report the result, and the opportunity to improve through hard work, can provide crucial incentive for the student to give something difficult another go or work a little harder even when improvement does not seem possible.

Centuries before interscholastic racing, there was the "decurion" of Jesuit education—an academic team of ten students compelled to regularly compete in exercises and "disputations" with other decuria, using rules similar to those of cross-country. As Foucault notes, "The general form was that of war and rivalry; work apprenticeship and classification were carried out in the form of a joust; the contribution of each pupil . . . contributed to the victory or defeat of a whole camp; and the pupils were assigned a place [based on the individual's] value as a combatant in the unitary group of his decury."[8] Robert Slavin's recent work in "team learning" is a modern, less competitive version of the system.[9] Students in a classroom are placed on evenly matched, heterogeneous teams of five or six by the teacher. In addition to individual achievement and progress grades, students are assigned team achievement and progress grades. Nor is the measurement of such progress necessarily restricted to individual courses. As we shall see below, Great Britain has developed a national assessment system built upon longitudinal scales for each subject, providing students and teachers alike with feedback about progress against standards.

Student Motivation Versus Assessor Obligation to Provide Better Incentives

For far too long, we have assumed that all motivational issues are entirely the student's affair. Do students *need* a "spur," a sharp object to the side, to do what they "should" be doing? Or, as the cross-country story suggests, are there other, more intrinsic and useful motives that might be appealed to? We pay too little attention to the intrinsic incentives and disincentives that may be found in the assessment process itself. We pay too little attention in professional standards and design to the effect of assessment on the student's current and future motivation.

The trick in establishing more noble and effective incentives for mastering performance is to make the student dissatisfied with present effort and achievement but not overwhelmed or needlessly fatalistic. Too often we think that students are motivated only by immediate pleasure or fear of punishment or that we have to resort to heightened competition to appeal to such an interest. Robin's experience, and that of all athletes, musicians, and debaters, suggest otherwise. We should abolish systems of invidious comparisons, of course. Let us, however, *not* abolish incentives that cause students to be appropriately edified about and dissatisfied with their current performance. "Yes, I know you think I have made great progress, but how am I *doing?*" one student lamented when I encouraged him to ignore the lack of a grade on the paper—and that reaction was fair enough, I now think.

Robin, our runner friend, would have gained little had we been unwilling to keep both her times and place of finish, had we told her, in descriptive terms only, how much she had improved and accomplished. Common sense suggests that we will increase the number of successful student performers to the extent that we get the incentives right on a daily basis for the performer and the teacher of the performer (including *important* extrinsic incentives, such as a link between diplomas received, courses taken, and jobs available, as Albert Shanker and others have pointed out).[10]

It may seem odd to some readers that I am asking folks with responsibility for assessment and testing to worry about the problem of supplying adequate incentives to the student. Is this not the province of teachers—hence a separate question of what constitutes effective pedagogy? No. Because if we score on a curve, if we use one-event secure tests, if scores are meant to be stable over short periods of time, if we report results in an untimely fashion with minimally useful feedback, we make it far less likely that students (and teachers) will have the incentives that they need and that they might have with a measuring system sensitive to their gains. As Messick, Cronbach, Fredriksen, Collins, and Shepard, and others in the measurement field have been arguing for some time now, the test maker has an obligation to consider the effects of the testing on the test taker and the educational system the test is meant to serve: "The bottom line is that [test] validators have an obligation to review whether a practice has appropriate consequences for individuals and institutions, and especially to guard against adverse consequences. You . . . may prefer to exclude reflection on consequences from meanings of the word validation, but you cannot deny the obligation."[11]

A perceived obligation to the student causes us to see that one of the most adverse consequences of traditional testing is the disincentive provided by the methods of scoring and reporting systems that are designed to highlight differences and to keep rankings as stable as possible—methods that are often dependent upon psychometric tricks that keep the meaning of a score hidden. How we construct the report of results and communicate results can profoundly influence the student's ability to persist and to improve. And at the school level, one-event annual testing that takes no account of "value added" or local syllabi offers teachers little incentive to improve performance, although such tests are viewed as terribly important by others in the community. Lacking credibility, pedagogical usefulness, timeliness, and sensitivity to local curricula and small gains, mass testing encourages the deadly view that little can be done to change student performance.[12] (See Chapter Eight for a further discussion of the relationship between accountability and testing.)

Toward Better Incentive Through Better Measurement

Eight decades ago, Edward Thorndike, one of the fathers of modern educational measurement, called for an evaluation system similar to the system used in cross-country. His aim was to take what he considered our "natural" competitiveness and "redirect the rivalry into tendencies to go higher on an objective scale of absolute achievement, to surpass one's own past performance . . . and to compete cooperatively as one of a group in rivalry with another group."[13] We have yet to seriously take up the gauntlet of Thorndike's challenge to establish such a system in this country or to explore the psychology of motivation as it applies to student assessment.[14] More to the point, we have not begun to consider whether the assessor has an obligation to worry about student motivation, on either technical or ethical grounds.

The vice of the "old" system of scoring that Thorndike was critiquing and sought to change—our *current* system of letter grades, in fact—was not its detail but its "relativity and indefiniteness, the fact that a given mark did not mean any defined amount of knowledge or power or skill." Competing against "one's own past" or an "accepted standard" yields consistently greater motivation, according to Thorndike: "To be 17th instead of 18th does not approach in moving force the zeal to beat one's own record, to see one's practice curve rise week by week, and to get up to the standard which permits one to advance to a new feat." As in cross-country scoring, "in so far as excelling others would imply and emphasize making absolute progress upward on a scale of real achievement, even direct rivalry with others [and the motive power that comes from it] would be healthy."[15]

We rarely admit how difficult it is for even the best students to endure school without public and enticing standards and motivators, without a longitudinal system that measures progress over the years (as Thorndike recommended). Schooling offers few self-evident reasons for a student to persist or improve and many disincentives, including the demand that students accept a great deal of endlessly delayed gratification. To stick with a difficult assignment, to endure hours of perhaps dreary practice, and to overcome disastrous first efforts and acknowledge our mistakes—these are not natural instincts. Developing the self-discipline to sustain persistence in the face of abstract or far-off values requires tactful teachers (whom we must respect before we respect their standards), tasks that are more fulfilling, and scoring systems that reward progress and are built backward from worthy standards, in the way Thorndike described.

How quickly the priggish among us hear a concern for incentives as pandering. But tact is not coddling; ensuring that assessment is "in the students' interest" is not the same as calling for "fun" or immediately relevant tests. To strive to do our best on a difficult test, we must feel that the challenge is more engaging or ennobling than the possible failure (and perhaps humiliation) that can result. If the idea of "consequential validity" is to have any teeth to it, we must consider the most predictable consequence of all formal evaluation: the likelihood that all results will influence the learner's self-image and aspiration.

Call it a concern, then, for respect—respect for the student's intellectual pride and dignity—and the right to a fair chance at any test. This respect for the test taker (especially when the news is bad) was ironically most in evidence in the testing of OSS recruits during World War II. As the researchers who devised the many demanding simulations used to identify the best candidates for espionage wrote, "It seemed to us important to [talk with recruits] after all tests, but especially so after situations which were decidedly unpleasant or in which the candidates were made to endure extreme frustration. . . . [T]he success of the program depended on our ability to ensure their cooperation and their best efforts. . . . We made it a principle, after each upsetting test, to provide an opportunity for catharsis by having each candidate talk over the situation with a member of the staff, who tried to help him get over his feelings of failure and restore his self-confidence."[16] The researchers felt that this kind of catharsis was so important that they often encouraged a "playful expression of aggressions against the staff."

If this concern for the effect of a test was necessary for highly mature, intelligent, and well-motivated adults, why is it not mandatory when we deal with children? Why do most testing programs offer no such sensitivity, no such built-in incentives, but instead rely on scoring done by (invidious) personal comparisons only? Such systems provide profound disincentives to students; they are the equivalent of not keeping Robin's (or anyone else's) times or weight and reporting only place of finish each time. Ironically, everyone might be improving, yet no one would necessarily know it! (In norm-referenced testing, students are compared against each other in a way designed to keep individual scores stable over time, without reference to a clear, worthy performance standard such as the four-minute mile. And when tested only once, the student has even less incentive to improve, because the test system does not permit progress measures on separate criterion-referenced tests.)

To see progress and to *believe* it to be such requires something more than disembodied scores. The ideal assessment system is one in which the score or grade symbolizes *something we already know*. Our level of performance should be utterly transparent; like a player's statistics in a sport, the reporting system should simply convey, in shorthand, the results or consequence that we recognize to have occurred. I am not out at second base or batting .200 because of vague reasons that are known only through mysteriously gained scores or because I find out (too late) that the umpires do not like my style; I am out at second or batting .200 because the ball was seen to beat my foot to the base and I am getting a hit only one out of five times.

Criteria and standards inhere in the achievement, not in the judge's mind, and the sooner the student learns this through assessment, the sooner the criteria and standards can be both appreciated and internalized, as I argued in the previous chapter. Given a task and an objective, the judge should merely be ratifying what is there to be seen. (The fact that umpires can make mistakes does not make the criteria and standards any less objective—something that few students learn in the classroom. The fact that people argue with umpires *reinforces* this view of the objectivity of the criteria and standards, because we certainly could not argue with the umpire's taste.) That same objectivity should exist for essays or proofs as well: if I know that there are scoring rubrics and anchor papers against which I can compare my work, I can see for myself how I am doing.[17] I should be only minimally dependent upon "experts" to tell me how I am doing. Thus a key indicator of a sound scoring system is students' ability to both self-assess and self-adjust. And in such a scoring system, students should feel comfortable arguing with judges when they disagree with their judgment—that is, when in the students' view the judges misapplied the objective criteria and standards. (That is why the ongoing effort of some teachers to get rid of letter grading as part of reform is often so misguided: the problem is not with the symbols but with the absence of clear standards and criteria by which the symbols derive their meaning.)

This desirable transparency in assessment is not found in mere grades and scores, of course. Instead of seeing them as something earned or given for clear and obvious reasons, students see them as the semi-oracular, semimysterious judgments of adults— minus all apparent rationale. The consequences not only for performance but for students' views of what a standard is are profound. While a perception of standards as arbitrary is often due to test security, as was discussed in previous chapters, it is more often due in the classroom to a failure on the part of teachers to make standards and criteria obvious and manifestly appropriate.

Some Lessons from History

Our puritanism runs surprisingly deep when it comes to schooling and incentives. First, as I have noted, incentives have typically been viewed as extrinsic only. For example, in the *Cyclopedia of Education,* published in 1877, the authors define "school incentives" as "rewards of various kinds, offered to pupils for progress in study. . . . Besides these, various expedients are resorted to for the purpose of exciting emulation, such as giving public praise, awarding merit marks." The authors close by cautioning the reader to "always exercise care that their influence should not be so exerted as to impair the force of higher and more enduring motives to good conduct."[18] Alas, the authors provide no insight into what those higher and more enduring motives might be.

A concern with student motivation has in fact never seemed very—well, seemly or appropriate for the true scholar. Knowledge for its own sake! seems to be the battle cry of all pedants of yore. Consider something as simple as the question of whether to report the grade earned by the student to the student on the returned exam booklet. William James, like Thorndike, felt the need to argue (somewhat apologetically) for such a practice and against the then-common practice of keeping grades hidden from students.[19] One can better understand his apologetic tone when one reads the ever-increasing criticism of the formal examination system that began to dominate discussion of American schooling in the late 1800s: "The guiding question becomes not what is best for the pupil, but what will 'count.' . . . The best study is done where there is the freest play of natural motives, and the poorest study where there is the most absorbing interest in examination marks."[20] I have heard the same complaint in many workshops and conferences: grades are a nuisance and a disincentive to learning for its own sake. After all, a liberal arts education in the classic formulation is opposed to a (merely) utilitarian—a self-interested—education.

But no classroom teacher has the luxury of avoiding the dilemma. Most students do not, on a regular basis, seem willingly engaged in the hard work of mastering intellectual tasks. There needs to be obvious reasons and evidence for students to do so, but those reasons must somehow appeal to "higher" motives than immediate pleasure or tangible reward.

This tension can be seen in a venerable old text for the training of teachers written by David Page, a former New York State normal school principal, in 1847. While all "intelligent teachers" feel that *the* great question" is "How can I excite an interest among my pupils for their studies?" there is a constant danger that using "artificial excitement" for short-term gain of interest in lessons will cause long-term damage to the "pursuit of knowledge even after the living teacher has closed his labors." Page goes on to argue that all tangible extrinsic incentives—prizes and rewards—are in general harmful to educational aims, particularly when prizes are given to the same few predictable people. "Prizes stimulate the few, and the many become indifferent not only to prizes, but to other and better motives. That system of incentives only can be approved, which reaches all."[21] Page stresses that the ideal prize, modeled on "God's reward," honors noble intentions and hard work, not mere success.

Page does stress, however, in a section entitled "Proper Incentives," that there are "higher attributes, which, if called into exercise, will be sufficient to ensure the proper application of . . . pupils to their studies."[22] Those are (1) a desire to gain the approval of teachers and parents, (2) a desire for advancement, (3) a desire to be useful, (4) a desire to do right, and (5) the pleasure of acquisition of skill and knowledge. Not a bad list, all in all. But the bulk of the section is devoted to a careful analysis of the so-called desire for advancement and the difficult problem of what Page calls "emulation."

There are two kinds of emulation, one of which is laudable and worth promoting, the other of which is damaging (and "anti-Christian"), according to Page. The first kind of emulation is self-emulation, the sort of classic up-and-at-'em and I-can-do-better way of thinking that was so peculiar to nineteenth-century America: "An ardent wish to rise above one's present condition. . . . It presses the individual on to surpass himself. It compares his present condition with what it could be—with what it ought to be." (The "ought" here is not casual: Page reminds the reader that "this is the spirit which actuates all true Christians, as they wend their way heavenward.") The undesirable form of emulation is the mere "desire of surpassing others, for the sake of surpassing them." Such a motive is particularly to be avoided if this urge causes a student "to be satisfied with the higher place, whether he has risen above his fellows" on merit or whether they have "fallen below him by their neglect."[23] The harm of norm-referenced scoring and grading on a curve has never been more clearly, if quaintly, put!

In fact, Page's concern with win/lose, high-stakes assessment scoring systems was prescient. Horace Mann was soon after instrumental in moving schools away from idiosyncratic oral tests and exhibitions toward formal written examinations. And with the ad-

vent of social Darwinism as a respectable theory in the latter part
of the century (witness the growth of organized interscholastic athletics during this time as just one piece of evidence), there was an
increasing willingness for the first time to use scores as public accountability measures, in a harmful way familiar to us all. Note this
account from over 100 years ago: "No one familiar with graded
schools in cities need be told that these uses of the exam have been
the prolific source of bitter jealousies among teachers . . . and have
perverted the best efforts of teachers, and narrowed and grooved
their instruction."[24] Sound familiar?

The needs of students gave way to the needs of adult administrators, with unfortunate results. "It is the practice in some
schools to arrange the name of pupils in the order of their per cent
standings, and then publicly read the list, or post it in a conspic-
uous place." The perversion to student motivation was inevitable:
"I have never seen this done without feeling that the vanity of
certain pupils was unwisely flattered, and the feeling of other pupils
unjustly wounded."[25] Fear as the incentive underlay so much of this
system: "The tendency of teachers to use a coming examination as
a whip or spur to urge their pupils to greater application is one of
the most serious obstacles to be overcome. . . . [T]he desire to stand
creditably is reinforced by a fear of failure, and, as a result of these
intensified feelings, there is nervous excitement, morbid anxiety,
overstudy, cramming, and other evils."[26]

Forty years later, in an article in *Atlantic Monthly,* President
Lawrence Lowell of Harvard argued the case for working for good
grades as a proper incentive—but only where the grades stand for
something of clear value and validity: "To chide a tennis player for
training himself with a view to winning the match, instead of acquiring skill in the game, would be absurd. . . . [I]f marks are not
an adequate measure of what the course is intended to impart, then
the examination is defective." Lowell correctly observes that the
problems with both grades and tests arise only when our "natural"
concern for them perverts learning. If a student who, merely in the
interest of earning the highest grades, "devotes himself assiduously
to memorizing small, and comparatively unimportant points in a
course . . . and thereby makes a better showing than a classmate
with . . . perhaps a larger real command of the subject," then the

criticism of grades is apt. But if the questions "were so framed that mere diligence . . . would not earn the highest grade, then there would be no reason why the student should not work for marks, and good reason why he should."[27]

Lowell, Page, and Thorndike knew—as do the makers of Nintendo games, I might add—what few modern educators seem to grasp: namely, that clear and worthy standards, combined with the measuring of incremental progress, always provide incentives to the learner, even when the gap between present performance and the standard is great. "Mastery of a subject depends upon interest, but interest grows with mastery and with the personal exertion to acquire it, while both are aroused by the demand of the standard."[28] The National Assessment of Educational Progress (NAEP) results reveal the sad irony of what happens when we do not know where we stand in absolute terms. Black and Hispanic students have a higher regard for their math ability than their white counterparts, yet they perform more poorly.[29] Similarly, white students have a higher regard for their own achievement in mathemathics as compared with Asian American students, although the former perform more poorly. (The results in studies of the students' parents parallel the student results.) Anyone who is told time and time again that his or her work is okay will reach a performance plateau. Even good students easily become sloppy or cynical in such a norm-referenced feedback loop. However, when students perform in public, on stage, out on the field, or at the video arcade, they *never* receive "perfect" scores, no matter their talent or the performance. Yet they persist, often passionately.

Disincentives in Traditional Grading and Scoring

I noted above the value of the cross-country scoring process and systems like it. The general principle at work is clear: repeatedly assess with reference to progress against stable and compelling standards; in other words, conduct what is often called "value-added" assessment.[30] We need to consider more carefully the other side of the coin as well—namely, the disincentives provided by traditional one-shot testing and scoring schemes. We need especially to look at the harmful self-fulfilling prophecy of the grading curve.

Bloom and his colleagues have argued passionately for years against the use of the standard curve in testing and grading, on the grounds of the disincentives provided. This widely used yet poorly understood statistical artifact easily causes students to underestimate their potential to achieve and to overestimate the differences between them and other students: "There is nothing sacred about the normal curve. It is the distribution most appropriate to chance and random activity. Education is a purposeful activity, and we seek to have all students learn what we have to teach. If we are effective in our instruction, the distribution of achievement should be very different from the normal curve. In fact, we may even insist that our educational efforts have been unsuccessful to the extent that the distribution of achievement approximates the normal curve." The curve—especially when borrowed unthinkingly and ritualistically from the psychometricians by teachers—"reduces the aspirations of both teachers and students, it reduces motivation for learning in students, and it systemically destroys the ego and self-concept of a sizable group of students."[31]

Remember, this symmetrical spread of scores is an *intended* result in the design of test scoring, not some coincidental statistical result of mass testing. What an odd constraint: such testing operates under the assumption that teachers have only random effects (or none at all) on students. Nor is the curve a feature of overtly norm-referenced tests only: such achievement tests as the Advanced Placement exams, most college finals, and many tests related to job performance are *built* upon the premise that scores should be more or less distributed along the standard curve (as not just an examination of past results but also a discussion with technical advisers reveals).

What is often poorly understood is that test construction that assumes the outcome of the curve builds in a deliberate exaggeration of student performance differences to gain the most useful "spread" of scores.[32] This has implications for incentives and for future performance: curved scoring ensures that, *by design,* at least half of the student population is made to feel inept and discouraged about their work, while the upper half often has an illusory feeling of achievement. And how will we ever achieve our educational goals of universal mastery and achievement if our measurement system precludes uniformly excellent performance by the test takers?

There is thus a significant technical "secret" kept from the test taker when the standard curve is assumed. The student is led to believe that the test is measuring his or her accomplishments absolutely; the test is in fact *causing*, then measuring, the most observable differences across students that can be obtained and highlighted in relative comparisons. This practice is disingenuous and debilitating.

The harm becomes more apparent when we see that all low scores are resistant to change over time, again by design. Tests that assume a standard curve are constructed to ensure that there is maximum stability in the items—that is, that the rank order of student results would not change if other sets of items were used or another sitting of the exam taken. It is this property of tests that has led to some extraordinary incidents, such as the allegations of cheating made by ETS against Jaime Escalante's students (whose struggle to excel was depicted in the movie *Stand and Deliver*) and a recent court case in which a dramatic rise in SAT test scores by a student taking the test for the second time led ETS to assume that cheating had occurred. Leaving aside the question whether test companies can prove their case adequately when there are anomalies, the fact is that large gains are *designed* to be anomalies. Such tests are scored in such a way as to be resistant to dramatic change. What, then, of incentive? Of what value to the student, teacher, and school are such scores? And why should we assume that scores measuring education are meant to be stable? Clearly, we should not. That is why David McClelland argued so vigorously for achievement testing that defined achievement in terms of gains[33] and why mastery learning and competency-based education assume that achievement of standards is within reach of all students if the aims are clarified and the proper opportunities and incentives are supplied for meeting those standards—including first-rate feedback (see Chapter Six).

At the local level, use of the standard curve results in a self-fulfilling prophecy and test results that are technically invalid and educationally destructive. That the use of the curve in the classroom is statistically invalid and dysfunctional does not stop a majority of middle and high school teachers from using some crude form of it, however.

Each teacher begins a new term or course with the expectation that about a third of his students will

adequately learn what he has to teach. He expects
about a third to fail or to just "get by." Finally, he
expects another third to learn a good deal of what he
has to teach, but not enough to be regarded as "good
students." This set of expectations, supported by
school policies and grading, is transmitted to students
through [numerous school policies and practices].
This system creates a self-fulfilling prophecy such that
the final sorting of students through the grading process becomes approximately equivalent to the original
expectations.[34]

The use of the curve is thus misleading to successful as well
as unsuccessful students: the better students believe themselves to be
more objectively competent than they are (as we see when looking
at the same students over time in a criterion-referenced scoring system such as the NAEP scales). Perhaps as important, the use of the
curve allows teachers to continually bypass the harder but more
fruitful work of setting and teaching to performance criteria from
which better learning would follow.

Reporting systems are likewise culpable. Most grades given by
a teacher are a mysterious mix of student achievement, effort, and
demeanor in class, along with the teacher's hunch about whether
potential is being adequately realized. Valuing and assessing such
characteristics and traits is, of course, a wise idea; these are the intellectual virtues that ultimately outlast and outshine any particular
grasp of a course's content. But reducing these diverse and incommensurable traits to a single grade is capricious and misleading—
to students and parents alike. For how, then, do we distinguish
between two students, one of whom is working as hard as possible
and the other of whom is coasting, both of whom get B's for the
course? Such glib comparisons, whatever sense they might make to
the teacher struggling with a gradebook and a conscience, can easily
make students cynical about standards and their reasonableness.

Disaggregated reporting, based on a set of criteria that do
justice to all our objectives, clearly improves the incentives for everyone. No one is a standout at everything, but with particular

strengths more likely to be revealed in such reporting, most students can excel at something. Particular weaknesses are likewise more reliably identified so that improvement can be sought with a clearer focus on the problems to be solved, particularly if we do more longitudinal testing. As I noted in Chapter Two, colleges routinely seek this kind of disaggregated analysis in the letters provided by teacher-references. And the standards of the National Council of Teachers of Mathematics provide an example for how report systems might provide more subject-based information about performance. More diverse forms of information are in the interest of the student as well as the consumer for student performance data (such as colleges and employers). Especially important are judgments about a student's habits of work and thinking, irrespective of the difficulty of establishing reliable scores.

Toward an Ethic of "Getting the Incentives Right" in Assessment

Examining the consequences for students of testing, grading, and reporting is similar to pursuing the ethical dilemmas of the anthropologist. When does a supposedly neutral documentation process begin to have an effect on that which is supposedly being neutrally studied? In their new national assessment system, the British have explicitly taken a student-centered position on the matter.

The task force assigned the job of compiling recommendations for assessment in this new system was deliberately mindful of the potential harm of assessment to students (and also to teachers, parents, and schools). The national assessment plan was designed to anticipate moral and pedagogical, not just technical, problems. An explicit aim, for example, was to ensure that assessment results would be empowering to the student. Thus the need for "user-friendly" feedback was deemed essential to student motivation and the raising of standards: "Formative assessment must be in terms to which pupils can respond and which clearly indicate what has been and what remains to be achieved."[35]

A second aspect of student empowerment is to be provided by the actual method of reporting. The task-force report specifies the need for a public and common chart of what constitutes progress in meeting academic standards. These so-called "attainment targets" are being written for every subject in the curriculum, on a ten-band scale. The scoring scales themselves would provide better incentives for students to persist and improve. Students would now (in theory) be able to count on shared and stable methods of grading work and an assessment system in which primary value is placed on progress toward standards, not arbitrary and invidious comparisons of students to norms. Such scales, when "shared by teachers and pupils, appropriate to the current stage of the pupil's achievement and pointing the way forward to further progress, appear to play an important part in raising standards of achievement." As the report notes, "Many pupils seem to need short-term objectives which are clear and which they perceive to be obtainable. The possibility of achieving these builds enthusiasm for progress in learning. . . . Our proposals reflect these considerations and, we believe, can positively assist in children's development."[36]

By deliberately calling for a wider and more authentic array of modes of "presentation, operation and response," the task force also sought to "widen the range of pupil abilities" that are assessed and thereby to lessen the "discontinuity between teachers' own assessment of normal classroom work and . . . externally provided tests." How does this relate to incentives for the student? Student motivation is "enhanced when assessment and testing are carefully aligned to the curriculum." The design and implementation of assessment tasks is to be so unobtrusive that "pupils would not necessarily be aware of any departure from normal classroom work."[37]

The report also explicitly set out to honor a "widely-voiced fear that external tests will impose arbitrary restrictions on teachers' own work, and so limit and devalue their professional role." Four principles were adopted in light of this concern, by which all technical decisions were to be made, mindful of teacher and student interests. In a real sense, the "locus of control" in the national assessment was to be the teacher's classroom assessment:

- Teachers' assessments over time and in normal learning contexts play an important part.
- Externally-provided methods are broad in scope

and related to the curriculum attainment targets
all will share.

- These assessment methods may often be incorporated into normal classroom activities.
- The administration, marking, and moderation
  procedures rely on professional skills and mutual
  support of teachers.[38]

There exist assessment systems in this country too that honor
these ideas. Pittsburgh's portfolio process in writing, for example,
places a significant emphasis on student self-assessment. "Which
pieces were most satisfying? Why? Which pieces were least satisfying? Why?" are typical of the questions each student must answer.
Similarly, Vermont's portfolio process asks each student to submit
"best pieces" along with a letter explaining the choice.

A "multiple-levels-of success" system exists in South Bruns-
wick, New Jersey, to assess spelling progress. Based on the work of
Edmund Henderson (with the assistance of Ted Chittenden from
ETS), the assessment system charts the student's progress toward
correct spelling over a four-year period (K-3), using a Word Awareness Writing Activity (see Exhibit 5.1).[39] The different levels of
achievement are based on empirically sound criteria by which levels
of sophistication in spelling hunches are catalogued. In this assessment system, one's spelling is no longer "right" or "wrong"—information that tells the students too little about their progress and
the teacher too little about how to facilitate progress by understanding particular successes and errors.

A second example of a multilevel scoring system—this one
for foreign language students—is found in the American Council
on the Teaching of Foreign Languages (ACTFL) proficiency guidelines. Here too a concerted effort is made to provide the student with
a developmental scale of progress—to provide both incentive and
insight into the degree of progress being made toward fluency. A
third example can be found in the New York State School Music
Association (NYSSMA) assessment process. All pieces that might be
played by any student, either as a soloist or as a member of small
or large ensembles, are ranked by degree of difficulty on a scale of
1 to 6. Once the student or group has chosen the level of difficulty

Exhibit 5.1. Word Awareness Writing Activity.

This activity may be done with the whole class, small groups or individ-
ually. Introduce the task by saying something like, "I'd like you to try to
write some words that I will say. Even if you are not sure about what letters
to use, go ahead and try." Since the task could be threatening, reassure the
children that you do not expect them to know the correct spelling of the
words. . . .

Dictate the rest of the words, using each in the sentence given. You
may repeat each word as often as necessary. If a child seems overwhelmed
and upset, you may excuse him or her from the activity.

1.	bed	It's time to go to bed.
2.	truck	I see a dump truck.
3.	letter	The letter is in the mailbox.
4.	bumpy	The road is bumpy.
5.	dress	I bought a new dress.
6.	jail	The thief went to jail.
7.	feet	My feet hurt.
8.	shopping	Shopping at the mall is fun.
9.	monster	The monster is scary.
10.	raced	The car raced down the road.
11.	boat	I rode in a sailboat.
12.	hide	Let's play hide and seek.

Scoring the Word Awareness Writing Activity

A scoring chart is provided below to help you analyze the spelling. Before
going further, think about the features that you will look for at each
developmental level:

1. Precommunicative spelling is the "babbling" stage of spelling. Children
   use letters for writing words but the letters are strung together randomly.
   The letters in precommunicative spelling do not correspond to sounds.
2. Semiphonetic spellers know that letters represent sounds. They represent
   sounds with letters. Spellings are often abbreviated representing initial
   and/or final sounds. Example: E = eagle; A = eighty.

Exhibit 5.1. Word Awareness Writing Activity, Cont'd.

3. Phonetic spellers spell words like they sound. The speller perceives and represents all of the phonemes in a word, though spellings may be unconventional. Example: EGL = eagle; ATE = eighty.
4. Transitional spellers think about how words appear visually; a visual memory of spelling patterns is apparent. Spellings exhibit conventions of English orthography like vowels in every syllable and vowel diagram patterns, correctly spelled inflection endings, and frequent English letter sequences. Example: EGUL = eagle; EIGHTEE = eighty.
5. Correct spellers develop over years of word study and writing. Correct spelling can be categorized by instruction levels; for example, correct spelling for a body of words that can be spelled by the average fourth grader would be fourth-grade level correct spelling.

Look at the child's list. Were most of the child's spellings Precommunicative, Semiphonetic, Phonetic, Transitional, or Correct? This is the child's probable developmental level. You might feel that a child truly falls between two of the categories, but try to put in just one check mark per child.

| | 1 | 2 | 3 | 4 | 5 |
Words	Precommu-nicative	Semi-phonetic	Phonetic	Transi-tional	Correct
bed	random	b	bd	behd	bed
truck	random	tk	trk	truhk	truck
letter	random	lt	ldr	ledder	letter
bumpy	random	bp	bmp	bumpee	bumpy
dress	random	js	jrs	dres	dress
jail	random	jl	gal	jale	jail
feet	random	ft	fet	fete	feet
shopping	random	sp	spen	shoping	shopping
monster	random	m	mnstr	monstur	monster
raced	random	r	rast	raist	raced
boat	random	b	bot	bote	boat
hide	random	hi	hid	hied	hide

at which they wish to be judged, they are assessed in terms of various qualities of performance (as in many athletic contests, such as diving, figure skating, and gymnastics). Typically, however, we fail to separate quality of performance from the degree of difficulty of the task, and we thus deprive the student of insight into and incentive for meeting the highest standards.

Toward District and School Principles

These considerations suggest the need for explicit local policies to ensure that the matter of incentives does not fall through the cracks of a merely technical or logistical discussion of assessment. We would perhaps be wise to consider requiring the equivalent of an environmental impact statement when new forms of assessing, reporting, and use of the results are being considered locally thereby ensuring that we consider the effect on motivation, incentive, and instruction.

Researchers John Fredriksen and Allan Collins have identified some important principles by which such a statement might be developed.[40] In their quest for principles by which we might consider the impact of tests (what they wish to call "systemic validity"), they propose three different sets of criteria: components of testing systems, standards for the systems' operation, and methods for fostering improvement. We need cite here only those elements that relate directly to the issue of incentive.

They stress that test tasks ought ideally to be as authentic as possible. A "library of exemplars" of these tasks should be open to all teachers and, more important, to all students; by consulting this library, students "can learn to assess their own performance reliably and thus develop clear goals to strive for in their learning." Similarly, the test must be "transparent enough that students can assess themselves and others with almost the same reliability as the actual test evaluators achieve." The methods they cite as likely to improve performance over time include many that we have considered thus far: practice in self-assessment, feedback on performance, and multiple levels of success "so that students can strive for higher levels of performance in repeated testing. The landmarks or levels might include such labels as 'beginner,' intermediate,' or advanced,' to motivate attempts to do better."[41]

We at least must begin to ensure that there are explicit principles for the ethics of assessment obtrusiveness, along the lines of the British manifesto, as well as principles that aim to safeguard student (and teacher) motivation.

Incentives and the Ethics of Intellectual Access

Our assessments must do more than reveal whether the learner has mastered what one isolated teacher happened to just finish teaching. The examining of students at *each* stage must embody and point toward the tasks, criteria, and standards that represent the future goals of the entire K-12 system. Assessment must always be constructed out of "enabling" forms of those tasks, in Glaser's sense of that phrase.[42] Only then does assessment itself provide the most incentive possible for the student.

The method of honoring this idea—so-called outcomes-based education—could not be simpler: design curricula backward around the achievements that you wish from all graduating students. Then design assessment procedures that help you know whether your intentions are being realized.[43] But what is too rare in the districts and schools where this work on outcomes takes place is a careful look at the validation of local standards. Do our exit-level standards actually mesh with real-world assessments and standards? Part of justifying outcomes, standards, and measures is ensuring that the assessments that the school uses articulate with the specific achievements most demanded by the "institutional clients" of schools—the desirable colleges, professions, and civic roles.

The ultimate intellectual challenge of all formal schooling is the dissertation and its defense (or, to say it more generally, the rigorous development and full account of one's own ideas and arguments). The case can be made, therefore, that to maximally enable students to graduate from a graduate or professional program, we should anchor our K-G system by this "standard-setting" task, where personal knowledge creation and its justification is the focus. Not because all or even most students will become Ph.D.'s (heaven forbid!) but because "teaching to" the ultimate task causes students to continually practice and be tested on that task (even if in simplified form) from the beginning of learning.

Such pointing toward culminating challenges in the lower grades is not as farfetched as it might seem. A K-5 school in Littleton, Colorado, for example, requires all of its students to satisfactorily complete a week-long research and presentation assessment for "graduation." As I mentioned earlier, in the Advanced Placement art portfolio exam, students submit evidence of their choosing that reveals their breadth of control over important genres and studies, and they also submit an in-depth project focused on one problem, theme, or style. In effect, they are judged on the effectiveness of the realization of their intentions (as with the dissertation), not someone else's view of what subject matter they should "know." The instructions to students and judges makes this clear: the assessors look for pieces that "work in their own way." Illinois, in a modest way, honors the same principle by scoring sixth- and eighth-grade papers together, against the same standard, in its statewide writing assessment.

This concern with exit-level influences on earlier assessment (what Sizer often calls "casting a shadow back on prior teaching and learning") is a problem of student incentive. The failure to assess the student with reference to culminating tasks of value seduces test designers (as well as curriculum writers) into developing stultifying and inauthentic assessments that reduce complex performance to a set of simple parts. (As I shall argue in Chapter Seven, the epistemological assumptions about mastery and its development that cause testers to devise a range of "items" instead of a range of scaffolded performances are outmoded. My aim in this chapter, however, is to consider the problem of encouraging incentives to flourish in a world of such atomistic testing and mastery by accretion.)

There is no novelty to the idea of assessing with reference to culminating tasks in the performance world, of course. Look at Little League, ballet, and chess instruction at the lowest levels: they either involve or point to the ultimate tasks and standards daily. If our aim is to have students performing, then we must get them performing as soon as possible. As Lowell put it years ago, "That a standard, known to the student, is as important in education as in every other form of training will hardly be denied. One would not train an athlete for a mile run without having him speed over the track, giving him the time he has made and the records for that distance. To be proficient in anything a man must have a standard and occasionally measure himself thereby."[44] This requires the use of ultimate assessments, adapted to the knowledge and skill level of the student at each prior level (as in music, foreign language, and sports). We vary our expectations based on the student's age or experience, *but the standard must come from exemplary performance at the exit or even the professional level.* Imagine persisting with baseball or music lessons if we had to wait years to play an entire game or piece or see models of excellent performance; consider the loss of interest in academic work that is precipitated by tests that seek no original or sustained thinking or production by the student. How rare it is for middle school teachers to see our best high school papers and tests to know how to maximally equip their students for success! (One can successfully use good rubrics across many grade levels since the criteria of tasks done well is invariant across experience: a good persuasive essay meets the same criteria for persuasiveness irrespective of the student's age. Thus one sixth-grade team is using Advanced Placement English composition rubrics and samples to help their students know what is expected.) How rare it is for isolated high school teachers to see how dysfunctional excessively-didactic "content coverage" teaching and testing is for their *former* students.

Access to Real-World Tasks and Standards as an Equity Issue

This call for more use of exit-level and professional-level tasks and standards, backed down through the entire K-12 assessment experience, can be put in moral language. The challenge is to maximize incentive by improving the educational equity that comes from ensuring that all students have regular access to real-world standards and repeated opportunities to master them. If we are ever to educate all our students—that is, maximally qualify them for worthy intellectual performance (and thus open the door to a more meaningful and rewarding adulthood)—we must require that *all* tests and grading procedures educate with respect to college and professional standards. Assessment must be more than valid and reliable; it must be enabling, forward-looking, standard-revealing. Why is this an *equity* issue? Because testing that is conducted without explicit reference to real-world standards for performance, in the name of "low-level" students needing a different kind of teaching, learning and testing, deprives students of the knowledge and preparation needed for admission to the most desirable institutions and jobs.

Let us look at some freshman exams at Harvard to show what one good-college-as-customer wants. The following is an excerpt from a recent final exam in European history:

1. *(30 minutes)* The student must choose eight of 16 sets of items and explain why one of the items in each set does not belong. [I have included only three sets here.]
   a. Waterloo, Trafalgar, Austerlitz
   b. Night of August 4, General Will, terror
   c. Montesquieu, Madison, Calhoun

2. *(45 minutes)* Choose one question.
   a. Imagine yourself Jean-Jacques Rousseau, but living in the early 20th century. Write a brief review and evaluation of Freud's work in light of your own theories of society.
   b. Imagine yourself Karl Marx, living half a century later. Write a brief evaluation of the programs of the Fabian socialists and the American reformers such as T. Roosevelt to present to the Socialist International.
   c. "Women's history can only be understood as part of general historical development." Do you agree? Why or why not?

3. *(45 minutes)* Choose one.
   a. "Both Germany and the U.S. fought decisive wars of unification in the 1860's, but in Germany the landlords retained great power after the war, while in America the landlord classes lost decisively." Discuss.
   b. Compare and contrast the causes of the two world wars.
   c. Would the European economies have developed differently without the role of the non-European peoples?

4. *(60 minutes)* Choose one.
   a. Is the history of Western society in the last 350 years or so a history of progress? (Make sure you define "progress.")
   b. "Until 1945, the history of Europe is a history of warfare: preparing for it, conducting it, concluding it. This was the price of a continent of nation states, and democracy did not improve the situation." Discuss.

Clearly, something more than mastery of dates and names is wanted here. Rigorous and creative analysis is required—but a good amount of style in answering is also desirable. Observe too that students have significant choice, which is true of most good college exams. Incentives abound for tackling this challenge. But as in most exams at elite colleges, there is an implicit barrier to success for ill-prepared students. The *unspecified* standards and criteria of performance expected—a paradox of upper-level education—make it unlikely that a student without previous exposure to questions of this kind will succeed. We (by and large correctly) *assume* that students in good colleges ought to understand, by the time of their admission, the kind and quality of the answers that are required here. In an excellent college preparatory experience, where students have long practiced the construction and refinement of historical analyses, such vague instructions as "discuss" or "compare" are (or ought to be) sufficient. A good precollegiate education prepares students for genuine "examinations" in which knowledge is compared, critiqued, extended, or verified—not merely cited.

But how prepared are students who graduate from the Content-Coverage and Multiple-Choice School District? Not well prepared, given our nonsystem of educational tribalism, where local syllabi and tests rely on provincial or eccentric tastes about what learnings really matter. The graduates of Recall and Regurgitate High School are in for a rude shock—an *immoral* shock: the realization that our "system" is no system at all. Why are high school teachers not *obligated* to know the kinds of tasks and grading standards that are required for success in good colleges? Why are national achievement tests not more closely linked to the kinds of performance-based exams found in good colleges? What untold harm is done to students who find out *too late* that they are unprepared for their future aspirations because their schools felt no need to go beyond simplistic tests? "But we don't send any kids to Harvard!" many teachers and principals have argued in workshops. "Maybe you would if they knew for a number of years what Harvard wants," I invariably reply.

The issue is *maximally qualifying* students for admission to the most worthy programs, not ensuring their admittance to any particular place.[45] Nor should we be dissuaded from this task by the red herring of what is tested in college admissions tests such as the SATs and ACTs. At issue is better protection of younger students from the harm that results when people believe that what is tested

on simplistic, indirect proxy tests is all that good colleges demand
and desire of their students.

For that matter, few students are fully prepared even for the
admissions process—and I am not thinking of the standardized
tests. How many students in the poorest high schools of America
realize (in time to develop skills) that these are the kinds of essay
questions they must write on when applying to college:

> What is the single invention the world would be better off
> without and why?
> What is your philosophy of closet organization?
> Describe a risk and the impact it has had on your life.
> Describe yourself playing the part of a renaissance man or
> woman.
> Construct an encyclopedia entry.
> Describe an interview with three fictitious characters.
> What does your room say about you?

At the very least, every student has a right to validated criteria
and standards against which his or her work will be judged, as well
as prior knowledge of those criteria and standards. One Canadian
district near Ottawa, Carleton, goes further. That district publishes
an "Exemplar Booklet" in which students can find not only all the
scoring rubrics and analysis of the descriptors used and their meaning but also a dozen student papers, previously marked and exten-
sively analyzed, from which they can learn in detail the standards
they must meet when they are later examined. The "Exemplar Booklet" also contains ungraded student papers to be evaluated in class
by students so that they can develop the skill of reliably grading
papers; with that skill, students are better able to self-assess and self-
adjust. (We will return to this vital pair of capacities in Chapter Six,
on the subject of feedback.)

Our student knowledge-workers need what adults in the
workplace require to routinely produce quality work. They require
not merely knowledge of which tasks they must perform and how
well, but functional knowledge of the standards that will be applied
in judging the work—that is, the *inspector's* knowledge. We have
(slowly) begun to learn this lesson through quality-control pro-

grams borrowed from the Japanese, in which workers are equipped with statistical and systems-control knowledge formerly reserved for managers.

The issue behind quality-control programs is not primarily one of techniques; it is an issue of moral equality. The worker is given not only the skill but the right (formerly reserved for "superiors") to judge how to produce quality and avoid defects. Instead of just "doing the job" without really thinking about the consequences of individual work, labor participates with management in *preventing* substandard work and shoddy service to the customer. How better can workers learn to raise their standards—and derive the motivation that comes from being able to do so? And how can we similarly empower our students so that they can enjoy the heightened motivation that inevitably comes with empowerment?

The consequences of years of norm-referenced testing and grading on a curve go deeper than we imagine. Two generations of relentless norm-referenced testing have caused many teachers to believe in the inevitability of vast differences in student achievement and in the inevitability of *current* levels of total performance. We have an educational system built upon an increasing "prejudice," in the literal sense of a sweeping "prejudging": teachers and administrators assume that they can predict all future results on past performance. Harmful tracking (not to be confused with appropriate and helpful placement) is the *inevitable* result of such thinking and of grading on a curve. The school ends up institutionalizing the test-fabricated fixed student range: as the very word *track* implies, the standards never converge. Students in the lower tracks end up being assessed and taught under the assumption that they cannot be expected to produce quality work.[46] Faculty members then never have to establish a justification for their grading policies or "cut scores." (A "cut score" is the one chosen to distinguish minimal success from failure—a 60 for most schools, for example.) More to the point, no one feels obligated to close the gap between our best and worst students. And no one believes that comparisons with other, "better" schools are therefore credible or useful.

The many recently established district mission statements—most asserting that "all children can learn"—will not solve this deeply rooted fatalism. We need an assessment system that simultaneously maintains high standards, provides multiple opportunities for teachers to meet student performance standards (as opposed to one-shot tests), allows flexible schedules for meeting those standards, and supports diverse instructional and assessment strategies. Such a system, now in use in many districts, assumes more than that "all children can learn." It builds in the tests, structures, incentives, and opportunities—for teachers as well as students—that make it likely that all children *will* learn.

Kentucky has done so, in its sweeping new set of reforms. Its new school accountability system is based on the logic of self-emulation described by our nineteenth-century professor friend, Dr. Page (although it parallels business's very modern quality-control system of "continuous progress"). In Kentucky, schools are no longer compared to other schools at one point in time in reference to a common test. They are compared against themselves, over time, in terms of the *increase in the percentage of students, over time, who meet performance standards,* as determined by more credible and teacher-involved performance and portfolio assessments. Kentucky has also instituted rewards and sanctions for relative success and failure, over time, in school self-improvement.[47] This new system will make it impossible for Kentucky schools to do what is now universally done around the country—namely, to assume that a school's reputation is a function of one's best students only (which enables the faculty to write off the failure of the worst students as "not our problem").

By contrast, New York State, up until its recent reforms, had a considerable built-in disincentive for faculties to maximize the performance of all students—a disincentive engendered by the reporting and accountability system: by reporting only the *percentage* of students passing Regents exams (and offering no incentive for schools to place students in Regents courses), the state provided an unwitting incentive to keep marginal students out of the more demanding Regents program. Why? Because what is reported in the newspapers and in over-the-fence conversations are Regents exam scores, all New York schools have a great incentive to *reduce* the number of marginal students in Regents courses to improve the passing rate for those courses.[48]

Some Recommendations

I have proposed that the assessor always has an obligation to consider the effects of testing on student motivation to learn, with a particular emphasis on the scoring system and how performance is reported. Here are some practical suggestions for honoring these ideas:[49]

• *Assess the student's accomplishments and progress, not merely the total score that results from points subtracted from a collection of items. In other words, score "longitudinally" toward exemplary performance at exemplary tasks, not by subtraction from "perfection" on simplistic and isolated tests.* Until we design scoring systems based on models of exemplary performance, students will lack a system for charting progress. Without such a system, we end up scoring what is easy to score, and we subtract points without justifying the criteria and standards that went into the making of the test. Let us try to undo a time-honored habit: instead of subtracting points from a fixed total signifying "perfection," let us add up or note the important *successes.* The scoring criteria should isolate the essential features being sought in the student's overall work over time and be designed to assist the scorer in recognizing *patterns* of relative success (or their absence), so that the scorer is not distracted by more obvious (but trivial) errors.

At the very least, we should require all teachers and testers to justify the use of cut scores, so that a 61 is something more than two points better than a 59. There should be a validated cut score, based on studies that show a qualitative difference in the levels of performance of people who "pass" and those who "fail."

Implicit in these proposals is the "radical" idea that every student has a right to be proud of work done. Remember Sizer's words, quoted earlier: tests should allow the students to "show off what they are able to do, not be a trial by question," with arbitrary question selection and time limits. The task in test design and scoring for instruction is to ferret out the most discernible effects of teaching and learning on each student.

That would also mean not rewarding the merely intelligent or lucky for right answers or simple articulateness, as is so often the case now. Rather, we would get better at isolating aptitude and achievement and ensuring that grades reflected and revealed the *differences* as well as the connections between the two. For some reason, teachers are squeamish about assessing students on the basis of potential; coaches, of course, do it all the time: the good musician or athlete is not allowed to "dog it" simply because he or she happens to be relatively more able than his or her peers. Why can we not be more honest and up-front about assessing *actual* achievement, given excellent or poor native ability and prior background? Why should we not hold more able students to higher standards?

- *Devise a "sliding" grading system wherein the proportions of what is counted in scoring vary over time: initially weight effort and progress heavily, but move toward increased emphasis on achievement.* How can we devise a grading and feedback system that sets all students a clear and worthy performance standard target while providing better incentives for those who start out at a disadvantage?

Imagine a three-level system that encourages the less able by initially rewarding effort and progress to a large extent. "Mastery" (judged as pure achievement) might count for only one-third of their grade at this first, "novice" level; effort and progress toward various "milepost" standards over the course of the year would determine the other two-thirds of the grade. At the "apprentice" level, the ratio of mastery/effort/progress might be 50/25/25 percent; and at the "veteran" level, the grade might be 80/10/10 percent—the percentages varying depending upon the course or the faculty's judgment about its standards. The students' grades in the gradebook could be followed by the appropriate letter (N, A, V, indicating the level of the grading) as a way to help colleges and employers read the transcript and judge student performance more fairly and effectively.

Teachers and departments could then devise tests and assignments that offered either different tasks for each level or different criteria for the same tasks given to all students. And students could be given the option of choosing which level they wanted to be assessed on. (Central Park East Secondary School is now using a teaching, testing, and grading system that provides for two levels:

"competent" and "advanced." All syllabi lay out the performance standards for each level in every course.)

This is the *opposite* of tracking; it is fair grouping: students are expected (or explicitly required) to move up. I call this the City Softball League grading plan: let the N-league students initially perform at a less-competitive level. But build in required movement upward to the next level: once students have earned a certain GPA at a lower level, they move up to the middle and top levels, where more "objective" mastery is required—just as the top two teams at one level of a league must move up to the next higher level the next year. (Perhaps by a certain time in a student's career, he or she is moved up irrespective of preference or prior performance.)

Implicit in this multileveled grading scheme is a curricular philosophy that allows all students access to the highest-level tasks but judges their work with regard to their experience and ability. Putting it this way suggests a variant in assessing and scoring work:

- *Give* all *students the "same" demanding work but differently scaffolded assessments, based on equitable expectations.* I call this the tee-ball approach to learning: just as pre–Little Leaguers now learn to play baseball by hitting off a batting tee (since good pitching overwhelms them), we could expose less able students to the most difficult questions without holding them to the highest standards of performance. This way they learn what "real" work is while being treated fairly. Instead of falling further behind their more able peers (and then typically being given the less engaging coursework),[50] these students would know the kind of work required of *all* serious students.

For example, younger or less able students might be given a difficult essay assignment but be judged on fewer or less demanding criteria, such as "thoroughness of research" or "creative arguing." The operant metaphor: *provide students with training wheels; don't condemn them to ride a tricycle forever.*

A simple example of how this can be done: make *all* teachers at the high school level work from either Advanced Placement syllabi in their subject or from the syllabi for "gifted and talented" students. Then supply the necessary materials and appropriate grading schemes based on a careful assessment of need and ability levels (with the understanding that the levels of difficulty might very well increase, as proposed in the above plans).

The implication in all of this is that we need to dramatically rethink what we mean by "fairness" to students and "standards" to the community. We do not ask 110-pound wrestlers to wrestle heavyweights; we do not allow varsity teams to compete against junior-varsity teams unless we are assured of rough equality in ability or physical size; chess, bridge, tennis, and other individual sports use a ranking system to enable individuals to be matched fairly in competition. At the heart of these stipulations is the belief that improvement occurs *only* when competitors are evenly (or closely) matched.

In tracking that "dummies down" coursework, we guarantee low standards by mandating low expectations. Not so with the tee-ball approach: although we make it easier for less able students to handle the more difficult tasks, we nonetheless hold them to the "standard" syllabus. How else can we ensure that the student is making authentic intellectual progress and provide our clients with a clear sense that the quality of the work we assign, as well as the quality of work we receive, truly matters?

Fair instruction and assessment designed to help the student make progress both attempt to do two things: (1) ensure that everyone is learning to play the "same" game so that everyone can improve at it and (2) group players fairly, through an equitable judging system, enabling them to gain from the kind of assessment and competition that properly balances challenge and possible success.

States and districts can also do a great deal better with extrinsic incentives, even allowing for proper concern with such approaches. Professionals need and are often given tangible rewards to better themselves: Tom Peters and others who write on effective businesses have documented how the best companies are constantly rewarding the successful meeting of specific performance goals. Albert Shanker, citing the work of John Bishop at Cornell, has written tirelessly on the topic of how rare it is for school achievement to matter in terms of jobs and scholarships for more than a tiny handful of students.[51] Unlike Canada, Japan, and other countries, where the high school transcript and leaving exams have a direct bearing on job placement and scholarship possibilities, this country provides practically no incentives for those between the ages of ten and seventeen to see a direct, palpable connection between school performance and life's opportunities.

Teachers and administrators (local, district, and state) also need incentives. The noble intentions of educators cannot overcome a system filled with disincentives to take risks or admit error—the preconditions of improved performance. If our attempts to alter teaching and assessment practices are subtly discouraged, we will rationalize our existing habits. This danger of rationalization is increased if we further isolate and empower "assessors" as distinct from "teachers" and "curriculum specialists." By divorcing assessment from all other facets of the educational system, we make it far more likely that not only students but teachers and administrators will take little responsibility for their poor performance. It was not *their* test, *their* standards, *their* fault.

• *Devise a scheme that assigns degree-of-difficulty points to assignments and test questions, thereby distinguishing the quality of performance from the degree of difficulty of the task, and let students choose the degree of difficulty they feel comfortable with.* Students would earn final grades by amassing total scores within set ranges. Devising a greater number of test questions (so that varying degrees of difficulty are represented) and having to assign difficulty-points to them would likely help teachers be clearer about which tasks and traits were most essential and which were most difficult (since the two might not be the same).

One aim here is to build an *appropriate* element of student choice into assessment. The example of diving is helpful: some dives are required, but there are also "optionals" that give the diver some flexibility in designing a program for competition. It would not be necessary to assume that all student assessment plans ought to be equal: the more able students might be *required* to tackle more difficult questions graded on the usual scale. The transcript and report card might then reflect the fact that some work is more demanding than other work and that an A on an easier task might well be a less outstanding performance than a B on a very demanding task. This might also help us solve the horrible dilemmas that so many teachers encounter as to how to fairly but honestly give grades to a diverse class of students. Why, after all, should a more novice (less skilled) student be compared to a highly skilled student in the grading of work? If our systems of staffing place kids in a heterogeneous grouping, that is our arbitrariness, which does not necessarily serve the students' best interests.

To see how this might work in practice, assume that each classroom becomes something analogous to a one-room school-house where people are working at different levels of difficulty—in effect, working in different classes within the same classroom. Thus, instead of French I, II, and III being in different rooms, they are all, in effect, in the same room. The teacher might then note on the transcript, "I [level], B [performance quality]" and "II, A" to distinguish the difficulty from the performance quality. This makes the transcript more reliable and fair; students get rewarded for the quality of work they do, but readers of the transcript are not mislead (as they currently are) into thinking that a letter grade stands for both a fixed level of performance and degree of achievement. It avoids the evils of tracking while clarifying the quality and level of work done, particularly if students can regularly choose the degree of difficulty they feel ready to handle.

Notes

1. It is *not* because art, sports, debates, recitals, and science fairs are more fun. It has to do with the feedback and the potential for felt competence (as an individual and group member) provided by these activities. See my Chapter Six on feedback in M. Csikszentmihalyi and R. Larson, *Being Adolescent: Conflict and Growth in the Teenage Years* (New York: Basic Books, 1984), and J. I. Goodlad, *A Place Called School: Prospects for the Future* (New York: McGraw-Hill, 1984), on the evidence about student motivation and performance that supports this claim.
2. Goodlad, *A Place Called School*, pp. 114–115.
3. Csikszentmihalyi and Larson, *Being Adolescent*, p. 207.
4. J. Raven, "A Model of Competence, Motivation, and Behavior, and a Paradigm for Assessment," in H. Berlak and others,

Toward a New Science of Educational Testing and Assessment (New York: State University of New York Press, 1992), p. 89.

5. T. Sizer, *Horace's Compromise: The Dilemma of the American High School* (Boston: Houghton Mifflin, 1984), pp. 214, 59. See also T. Sizer, *Horace's School: Redesigning the American High School* (Boston: Houghton-Mifflin, 1992), pp. 23–27, 98–101.

6. Sizer, *Horace's Compromise*, pp. 68, 64, 68.

7. Sizer, *Horace's School.*

8. M. Foucault, *Discipline and Punish* (New York: Vintage Books, 1979), p. 146.

9. R. E. Slavin, ed., *Using Student Team Learning*, 3rd ed. (Baltimore, Md.: Johns Hopkins University Press, 1986). Alas, Slavin notes that the scoring of team achievement per se was dropped in favor of team progress over the objection of teachers who disliked the overly competitive nature of the assessments.

10. A. Shanker, "A Good Job for Good Grades" (in his Where We Stand column), *New York Times*, March 5, 1989. See also J. Bishop "Why the Apathy in American High Schools?" *Educational Researcher* 18 (1989): 6–10.

11. L. J. Cronbach, *Essentials of Psychological Testing*, 5th ed. (New York: HarperCollins, 1989), p. 6. See, for example, J. R. Fredriksen and A. Collins, "A Systems Approach to Educational Testing," *Educational Researcher* 18 (Dec. 1989): 27–32; S. Messick, "Meaning and Values in Test Validation: The Science and Ethics of Assessment," *Educational Researcher* 18 (1989a): 5–11; and L. Shepard, "Why We Need Better Assessments," *Educational Leadership* 46 (1989): 4–9.

12. See R. Linn, "Educational Assessment: Expanded Expectations and Challenges," *Educational Evaluation and Policy Analysis* 15 (1993): 1–16, on the motivational importance of performance assessment.

13. E. Thorndike, *Educational Psychology*, Vol. 1. (New York: Teachers College Press, 1913), p. 288.

14. The National Assessment of Educational Progress (NAEP), often called "the nation's report card," does in fact use such

a scale for reporting results, but the complex (and controversial) method used to derive the scores and the sampling nature of the test make it useless as a feedback loop for students and teachers. See the various NAEP reports for more information. National Assessment of Educational Progress, *Learning by Doing: A Manual for Teaching and Assessing Higher-Order Thinking in Science and Mathematics* (Princeton, N.J.: Educational Testing Service, 1987).

15. Thorndike, *Educational Psychology,* pp. 288–289.

16. Office of Strategic Services, *Assessment of Men: Selection of Personnel for the Office of Strategic Services* (Troy, Mo.: Holt, Rinehart & Winston, 1948), p. 93.

17. It is certainly true, however, that I can disagree with both the criteria being applied and the standards used to anchor the system. In fact, as I will argue in Chapter Seven, many of the current scoring rubrics in use are deficient, in that we are scoring what is easy and uncontroversial to score, not what is essential to exemplary performance.

18. H. Kiddle and A. J. Schem, *The Cyclopaedia of Education* (New York: E. Steiger, 1877), p. 455.

19. W. James, *Talks to Teachers* (New York: W. W. Norton, [1899] 1958).

20. In I. Kandel, *Examinations and Their Substitutes in the United States* (reprinted from *American Education,* Men, Ideas, and Institutions Series II) (New York: Arno Press, [1936] (1971), p. 31. The quote is from a Cincinnati superintendent during the 1930s.

21. D. P. Page, in *Theory and Practice of Teaching: or The Motives and Methods of Good School-Keeping* (Savage, Md.: Barnes & Noble, [1847] 1953), p. 119ff.

22. Ibid., p. 139.

23. Ibid., p. 131.

24. E. E. White, *Elements of Pedagogy* (New York: Van Antwerp, Bragg, 1886), pp. 199–200.

25. Ibid., p. 204.

26. Ibid., pp. 204–205. White argues, as the solution to this, that the exam "should be permitted to come unheralded."

27. A. L. Lowell, "The Art of Examination," *Atlantic Monthly* 137 (1926): 58–66, p. 61.

28. Ibid., p. 66.

29. NAEP, J. A. Dossey, I.V.S. Mullis, M. M. Lindquist, and D. L. Chambers. *The Mathematics Report Card: Are We Measuring Up?*, Report no. 17-M-01 (Princeton, N.J.: Educational Testing Service, 1988).

30. See Chapter Eight and the work of A. W. Astin, *Assessment for Excellence: The Philosophy and Practice of Assessment and Evaluation in Higher Education* (New York: American Council on Education/Macmillan, 1991), for example. The practice of pre- and posttesting is a familiar example of value-added assessment.

31. B. S. Bloom, G. F. Madaus, and J. T. Hastings, *Evaluation to Improve Learning* (New York: McGraw-Hill, 1981), pp. 52–53, 50.

32. See J. Oakes, *Keeping Track: How Schools Structure Inequality,* (New Haven, Conn.: Yale University Press, 1985), pp. 10–12. The procedure typically involves piloting test items and throwing out those items that everyone gets right or wrong.

33. D. McClelland, "Testing for Competence Rather Than for 'Intelligence,'" *American Psychologist* 28 (1973): 1–14.

34. Bloom, Madaus, and Hastings, *Evaluation to Improve Learning,* p. 50. Ironically, this is a direct quote from the substantially different 1971 edition of the book, which the authors introduce with "Let us begin with a statement of ours that has been widely quoted." *Plus ça change. . . .*

35. Department of Education and Science, Assessment Performance Unit, *Task Group on Assessment and Testing (TGAT) Report* (London: Her Majesty's Stationery Office, 1988), par. 37.

36. Ibid., pars. 37, 14.

37. Ibid., pars. 48–49, 14, 49.

38. Ibid., par. 16.

39. See E. H. Henderson, *Teaching Spelling,* 2nd ed. (Boston: Houghton Mifflin, 1990), pp. 194–199.

40. Fredriksen and Collins, "A Systems Approach to Educational Testing."

41.   Ibid., p. 31.
42.   See R. Glaser, "Cognitive and Environmental Perspectives on Assessing Achievement," in Educational Testing Service, ed., *Assessment in the Service of Learning,* Proceedings of the 1987 ETS Invitational Conference (Princeton, N.J.: Educational Testing Service, 1988).
43.   Alas, too much OBE and mastery learning has been built around easy-to-measure instead of essential-but-difficult-to-measure outcomes.
44.   Lowell, "The Art of Examination," p. 65.
45.   We know the bad news: Harvard, Stanford, Howard, Swarthmore, and the others are running Offices of Rejection. The 8:1 (or worse) ratio of application to acceptance is irrelevant, however, to the moral obligation of all lower-schooling faculties to equip students to be maximally prepared, should the fat envelope arrive in the mailbox on April 16.
46.   See Oakes, *Keeping Track,* on the inequities of curricula in the different tracks. The British plan calls for a grading system of 1 to 10 for the *career* of the student, obligating teachers across ages to establish progressive performance criteria. (Note too that Binet's original intention was to identify students needing more intensive and effective teaching and then to bring them up to speed by helping them learn how to learn.) See S. J. Gould, *The Mismeasure of Man* (New York: W. W. Norton, 1981), p. 154.
47.   I was one of five consultants who helped design the new Kentucky performance assessment system according to the broad guidelines laid out in the law (Kentucky General Assembly, *Kentucky Education Reform Act [KERA],* House Bill 940, 1990). While I stand behind the design of our assessment process, I (along with the other four consultants) specifically questioned the law's provision that rewards and sanctions be given on the basis of very tight parameters for success and failure. We believed then, and I still believe, that the law calls for greater precision in the measurement than is possible when dealing with small schools. In fact, in our final report to the state board of education, we requested that the board seek an amendment to the law with respect to the calculation of the

rewards and sanctions. (We saw and acknowledged the theoretical value of such rewards and sanctions, however.)

48. The state reporting system has been recently modified so that each school accountability report now lists the percentage of students eligible to take such courses and exams. Whether the mere addition of such a category provides a new incentive for faculties to entice more students into Regents courses (without the provision of other incentives linked to rewards and/or sanctions) remains to be seen.

49. Many of these ideas first appeared in G. Wiggins, "Rational Numbers: Scoring and Grading That Helps Rather Than Hurts Learning," *American Educator* (Winter 1988): 20–48.

50. Oakes, *Keeping Track*.

51. See, for example, Shanker, "A Good Job for Good Grades," and Bishop, "Why the Apathy in American High Schools?"

6 | Feedback

Test scores are often referred to as *feedback*. This is only one of many indications that we do not understand in the least what feedback is and the role it should play as a feature of the test itself. A score on a test is encoded information; feedback is information that provides the performer with direct, usable insights into current performance, based on tangible differences between current performance and hoped-for performance. "Arcane feedback" is thus a contradiction in terms, though this is what test companies and teachers often provide. Yet as Walt Haney notes, "Common sense, theories of learning, and research on intrinsic motivation . . . all of these clearly indicate that the sort of standardized testing now commonly employed in schools and via which students do not get rapid or specific feedback on their work . . . is simply not conducive to learning."[1]

Classroom teachers are rarely much better at providing useful feedback than test manufacturers are. Many still believe that a grade and a short series of comments constitute feedback. Most of the time, the comments involve praise and/or blame or "code" phrases for mistakes (such as "sent. frag.")' in the margin. Code is not feedback; praise and blame are not feedback. What is wanted is user-friendly information on how I am doing and how, *specifically,* I might improve what I am doing. If we take those criteria seriously, Management consultant and researcher Thomas Gilbert's sweeping dismay seems apt: "In years of looking at schools and jobs, I have almost never seen an ideal confirmation [feedback] system. Managers, teachers, employees, and students seldom have adequate information about how well they are performing."[2]

The best story I know for illuminating these ideas about feedback works better orally, alas, but I offer it anyway. Our friend from an earlier chapter, the student teacher who had her students decide on possible final exam questions, had the following exchange with a student after teaching English for a year. It seems that Mike, a young man who had been in her tenth-grade class, came up to her on the last day of the year to say thanks. After wishing her well, he added, a little sheepishly, "Oh, by the way. You kept writing one word over and over on my papers, but I don't know what the word means." "What's the word?" asked Sharon. "Vagoo," was the sound the boy made. (Think about the sound as a too-literal phonetic reading of a printed word!)

Having been a secondary English teacher, and having often written that word in the margins of student papers (the word, of course, was *vague*), I couldn't help but laugh and wince at the same time. How much we try to give helpful feedback in the little time we have, given our duties! How little, though, we understand what constitutes usable, helpful feedback—and how much time we end up wasting, then, despite our good intentions.

I have told the story many times in workshops and conferences, to good effect, and have followed it up with this exercise: Spend a few minutes talking with your neighbor about what exemplary feedback would be in this case. Discuss what you should write in the margin to *ensure* that the student gets the message and profits from it. Surprisingly, many teachers do not do well at this task. (Peter Elbow noted this phenomenon: "Many teachers are incapable of commenting in *any way* on a student performance such as a paper except by saying how it measures up or doesn't."[3]) Most tend to want to "teach" the student—in this case, how to write a better sentence. Few teachers, and even fewer tests, ever provide what students most need: information designed to enable them to accurately self-assess and self-correct—so that assessment becomes "an episode of learning," as Dennie Wolf and her colleagues put it.[4] In this chapter, we explore the student's need and the student's right to better feedback than testers now provide.

Feedback and Guidance

The teachers who want to "teach" the writer how to write better sentences in response to an error confuse guidance with feedback. Feedback is information about the effect of our actions. The environment or other people "feed back" to us the impact or upshot of our behavior, be that impact intended or unintended. Guidance gives direction; feedback tells me whether I am on course. Guidance tells me the most likely ways to achieve my goal; feedback tells me whether I am on track or off track in a way that enables me to self-adjust. Why, then, is guidance not the same as feedback? (Why, in other words, is teaching never adequate to cause successful learning?) Because no matter how well you "guide" me in advance, I still need to determine whether I am successfully doing what you asked me to do and told me to accomplish, and make adjustments as necessary based on the feedback.

Here is a simple analogy that highlights the difference between guidance and feedback and shows why good feedback from assessment is essential to learning. Suppose I want to drive from New York City to Sacramento, having never done so and knowing little about appropriate routes. My goal is to get to Sacramento in the shortest period of time, by a safe route. I certainly need guidance; where will I find it? Other people who have driven the route might provide it. But I may not be easily able to find such folks. Ah, there are maps! Maps provide thorough and portable guidance. Better yet are the personally annotated maps provided by AAA and other travel services. These Triptiks divide my journey up into map pieces, strung together in a binder. Not only do I have a customized map to guide me on the journey; an AAA employee has taken a yellow marker and traced out the route on the map so that there is no confusion at tricky intersections.

But maps are never enough. Guidance, even expert guidance made portable, as in the Triptik—is insufficient. As a traveler, I need to obtain and use feedback to ensure that I am correctly following the map or—in more difficult cases, where the map is not reliable or the route involves unexpected detours due to, say, accidents or construction—that I am at least heading in the right direction. What supplies the feedback? Discernible landmarks and especially roadsigns. Without these, the guidance—the map—is useless. (Teaching without good assessment and feedback is similarly useless.) I will be forced to stop and ask for directions every few minutes unless there are roadsigns to provide feedback as to the correctness or incorrectness of my turns. "Roadsigns provide the feedback? Don't they provide guidance?" Yes and yes. In the absence of maps, we can use the signs for guidance to know what routes to take. That's why roadsigns usually say things such as, "Route 90 to Buffalo, 2 miles ahead." But signs provide crucial feedback too. For they tell us whether we are correctly following the map or not. (If I start to see signs saying, "Cape Cod 184 miles," I realize that I turned in the wrong direction back near where I saw the sign for Buffalo.)

In the more formal language of systems theory, feedback is evidence that confirms or disconfirms the correctness of my actions. Think of it this way: How would I ever be sure I was on the road to Sacramento in the absence of the confirming or disconfirming evidence that comes from roadsigns? What happens, for instance, should I come to a fork in the road that is confusing because, although the map seems to imply "bear right," the only options in fact seem to be going straight ahead and going left? How can I be sure of what the guidance means, even assuming it to be correct, without signs at the intersection and then other signs or landmarks that confirm or disconfirm the correctness of my move?

What the travel example reveals is that feedback must be continuous, or almost so, if I am to achieve my goal with maximal efficiency and *minimal reliance on ongoing guidance*. If there are only one or two roadsigns along the way, if I get feedback miles after I need it, if I am dependent upon other people instead of environmental feedback, it is far less likely that I will succeed. This *system* of feedback loops (in which I constantly confirm or disconfirm the results of my actions by attending to the visible effects of *prior* feedback) is a central aspect of successful performance. Or, as Peter Senge put it in his recent book on organizational management, to get feedback is not to "gather opinions about an act we have undertaken. . . . [Rather,] in systems thinking, feedback is a broader concept. It means any reciprocal flow of influence."[5] In education, that means that an educational "system" is one in which not just the teaching but also the testing adapts to my failing just as I adapt to it to succeed. (It may also mean that I should receive the feedback I need until I get the task done properly: this is the heart of competency-based education.)

Here we see at once how conventional testing and its artificially imposed limits on immediate and ongoing feedback seriously fail to serve the interests of the student performer. We habitually assume that to "test" the student's knowledge, our only obligation is to supply a well-designed stimulus to which the student must successfully respond. But "understanding" is not demonstrated by responding once to simple cues. Complex intellectual performance (like all performance: see Chapter Seven) is achievable only through my working within a feedback system to complete the task. I do not just "know" navigation, in this example; I know it in context. And you test me by my ability to seek and use the feedback *that the situation provides* to assess my mastery at navigation. If, in your constant testing of me through the use of mere stimulus-response items, you provide me with no feedback other than my score, how will I learn how I am really doing on the use of knowledge in context? Try getting to Sacramento without roadsigns, your only help being a score given by the guy at the gas station; or try getting to Sacramento armed only with norm-referenced data on how other drivers do in trying to get there. And if the class has to move on through the syllabus after a test is over, the likelihood of my mastery and insight of a given lesson is further impeded. Similarly, good luck getting to Sacramento if the highway folks do not have time to put up roadsigns because they are too busy building new roads.

The complete absence of adequate performance "roadsigns" is the norm in most classrooms. This is indicated by constant student questions such as, "Is this right?" "Is this what you want?" "Am I doing it right?" When the student receives a mere score on indirect, proxy forms of testing, we make it very unlikely that the student is both prepared for performance and knowledgeable as to what performance entails. (Try getting to Sacramento after only a multiple-choice test in your stationary car on driving, navigation, and the scenery on the way to California. Or try getting to Sacramento with no roadsigns, armed only with expert-trucker adjectives labeling your successes and errors.) Some of the teachers I have worked with on this problem argue that the best way to give feedback is to engage students in a Socratic conversation about their work, in hopes of getting them to see their errors. (But imagine a Socratic gas station attendant trying to get you to better explain what your mistake was as his or her solution to your being lost.)

This constant failure to receive good feedback is a legacy of defining education as "teaching" and assessment as "testing" after teaching. Our inability to give good feedback and our inability to find the time to give feedback of any quality indicates that we fail to understand the *inherent limits* of "teaching" (guidance) as a means of achieving mastery. We must come to see that the successful performance of complex tasks is possible only if students learn through the effective use of more timely, frequent, and helpful feedback.

Writing teachers perhaps understand this problem better than most teachers, given the nature of their work (and the fine assistance that has been provided by the Writing Projects). They typically structure their use of time to ensure that both thorough guidance and feedback are provided. But even they can be too eager to merely guide—for example, when they tell students to have a punchy opening sentence, avoid run-on sentences, get better at knowing their audience, and so on. This is all useful and important—but it is not feedback, and it is not adequate for assisting a successful writer. Feedback is the result of our (or peer editors') reading of students' work and then playing back to students their attempt to honor the guidelines and our intentions. The best feedback helps the student understand that a paper "worked" (or failed to), why a paper "worked," or why a mistake *is* a mistake.

Thus, as Elbow argues so well, sometimes good feedback is not "criterion-based" but "reader-based": the reader simply reacts to the effectiveness of the piece (an instance of what we considered more generally in Chapter Three as "consequential" aspects of contextual performance).[6] While it is true that peer editing can amount to pooled ignorance, that negative aspect is avoidable if we train peers to read papers while mindful of models, mindful of the author's intent, and mindful of their own visceral reactions as readers. Students certainly profit from being told how to write a better sentence if they have made a mistake—but only if they understand that they did not, in fact, accomplish their purpose in the sentence as written.

Let us then consider answers to my earlier question about "vagoo": What comment in the margin would help Mike realize not only that he had made a particular kind of mistake teachers call "vagueness" but what vagueness is and why it is a mistake by the writer. Whatever the specific answer, the principle is now clearer: the key is to show Mike that he has failed to achieve his intent. Mike must come to see his error as an error so that he can *self*-correct it (if he chooses). It was not Mike's intention to be vague: his aim was not to describe the characters' views; it was his intent to describe his own change of mind about the hero's character. We nowhere have to say on the paper that Mike "made a mistake." Real feedback tells Mike that he is off track without labeling or judging his effort.

Feedback is purely *descriptive*, in other words. Any value judgments are an outgrowth of the feedback—namely, a value being placed on the importance of the gap between intent and effect as described. As the description of an error is "fed back" to me, revealing that my effect does not match my intent, I am now in a position to improve. I need that description more than I need an evaluation of the error's importance. Feedback has to do with seeing more clearly and usefully the consequences of our actions and thus obtaining enough information to regularly realize our intentions. Elbow has no doubt put this better than anyone in his discussions of feedback to students, especially feedback on their writing. He argues that feedback is commentary, not measurement. The mixing up of the two ideas "tends to keep people from noticing that they could get by with far less measurement. . . . The unspoken premise that permeates much of education is that every performance must be measured and that the most important response to a performance is to measure it. The claim need only be stated to be seen through. . . . When an individual teacher, a department, or a whole faculty sits down and asks, 'At what point and for what purposes do we need measurement?' they will invariably see that they engage in too much of it."[7]

Years ago, Gilbert summed up the principles of good feedback in his delightful and informative book entitled *Human Com-*

petence. In it, he catalogued the requirements of any information system "designed to give maximum support to performance." The requirements involve eight steps:

1. Identify the expected accomplishments. . . .
2. State the requirements of each accomplishment. If there is any doubt that people understand the reason why an accomplishment and its requirements are important, explain this.
3. Describe how performance will be measured and why.
4. Set exemplary standards, preferably in measurement terms.
5. Identify exemplary performers and any available resources that people can use to become exemplary performers.
6. Provide frequent and unequivocal feedback about how well each person is performing. This confirmation should be expressed as a comparison with an exemplary standard. Consequences of good and poor performance should also be made clear.
7. Supply as much backup information as needed to help people troubleshoot their own performance. . . .
8. Relate various aspects of poor performance to specific remedial actions.[8]

Gilbert sardonically adds that "these steps are far too simple to be called a 'technology,' but it may be that their simplicity helps explain why they are so rarely followed." I see steps 4 through 7 as particularly vital for improving student performance immediately. Note, in particular, that feedback must be given in reference to an "exemplary standard," an idea that has important implications for how teachers give grades and comments and distinguish between standards and expectations while specifying both (see Chapter Eight). This is also an idea at the heart of the argument for viewing learning as "cognitive apprenticeship."[9]

These principles suggest how we should solve Mike's "vagoo" problem. The key, as Gilbert's points 5 and 6 suggest, is in "feeding back" to him the consequences of his vagueness as felt by a reader, to help him see that he is unintentionally off course as a writer. We might therefore write in the margin next to the sentences in question, "When you say, 'The hero was not what he was expected to be,' you could mean *either* (1) the hero was not as you expected or (2) the hero was not as the other characters expected. Which do you mean? This is *vague,* in other words." We describe his performance, we describe or allude to exemplary performance, and we suggest or state why his performance is not exemplary, in a way designed to be understood by him.

Concurrent Feedback

The professional measurement folks who are reading this may be getting impatient. "What has this pedagogical advice got to do with us?" A good deal, actually. Because the deeper meaning of Elbow's ideas, Gilbert's list, and the competency-based movement is that feedback should not occur only once *after* assessment but often and *during* it. Concurrent feedback is information that comes to us *as we perform*; it serves as the basis for intelligent adjustment en route and as learning for later attempts. Mastery, in other words, is not answering inert questions correctly but *solving a complex problem by responding to the feedback provided within the problem and situation itself.*

A simple example from my recent exploits as a first-time gardener makes clearer the role of feedback in performance and the need to evaluate the learner's use of feedback in validly assessing the total performance. This past summer, in my first vegetable garden, I planted lettuce, carrots, snow peas, and green beans. A good amount of helpful guidance was provided by the seed packets and by various Sunday newspaper columns on gardening. But no mere instruction could have prepared me for the problem of recognizing healthy and unhealthy growth in my plants. Once the seeds yielded plants, I needed feedback on whether my plants were healthy and my vegetables ripe. The snow peas and lettuce were simple: the critical information was right there in front of me, easy to discern, since all the growing was above ground. I did self-adjust on the basis of some feedback from the growing snow peas: "common sense" told me that the growing pods should not be allowed to lie on the ground, so I built little trellises for them, and many good stir-fries resulted from my efforts.

But what about carrots, which grow underground? How does one know when they are ready to be picked? My only information was the guidance provided by the packet: ready to pick in sixty-five days. On day sixty-five, I started picking—only to see the saddest little one-inch stubs of carrot—despite the fact that the green growth above ground looked about as long as what I had seen on fresh carrots at the store. A week later, I tried again. Again the only available feedback was the green stem: it was high and flourishing. "Must be time," I thought. Wrong again: stubs again. This happened three more times. I clearly failed the test—not because I was a novice gardener and my first carrot was too short, but because I did not use the feedback that I *did* receive effectively; I kept employing a method that was unlikely to work.

I had similar problems with the tomatoes: the plants all drooped badly and by midsummer looked more limp than even this novice thought they ought to be. Water did not help; in fact, it seemed to hurt. I dutifully staked and staked. At the time when the seed packet told me I should be having bright red beauties for my salad and salsa, I had dozens of little green things that had me wondering if I had somehow gotten the wrong seeds. As it turned out, the culprit this time was the weather: the coldest summer in western New York in a century; even the experts had bad tomatoes. But without adequate confirming or disconfirming evidence, I did not know if I was on the road to success or not. I did the best I could with the feedback I received.

How does this aside into the vagaries of gardening help us grapple with issues of student assessment? First, my experience as a tomato grower is the experience of almost every student: like me, students follow directions and do the work, but they typically have no way of knowing whether they are "on the road" to success *until it is too late*. Waiting until the test to find out how you are doing is as ineffective as having to wait until the fall to learn whether you will have garden produce for the winter. Both the traveling and gardening examples show us that teaching and testing alone are *never* enough to assure successful performance at complex tasks, nor do single "responses" to our one "stimulus" tell us whether someone has "learned." Second, as the carrot-growing example suggests, knowing everything there is to know about carrots and spitting it back on a 200-item test will not reveal whether I can successfully grow carrots or keep them in the ground for the right amount of time. My mastery is dependent upon my use of situational feedback. Testing my mastery is dependent upon seeing me use or fail to use situational feedback intelligently.

Successful performance depends upon concurrent feedback that enables the learner to self-assess and self-adjust with maximal correctness. If mastery typically involves whether a performer makes intelligent adjustments based on available feedback, a valid assessment of mastery would require us to see whether the student can use feedback to complete a complex task successfully. That is what we mean, after all, by "accurate self-assessment"; it was also a key aspect of what the OSS termed "effective intelligence" (see Chapter Seven). All "performance" invariably requires numerous "trials" (and thus the correcting of many "errors" through feedback) if standards are to be met. Does it not follow, then, that an authentic test of ability would require the learner to use feedback *during* the test? And is there not something hopelessly inauthentic and alienating about performing dozens of tasks without human or situational concurrent or immediate feedback, as happens with every conventional test?

The link between the issues of incentive raised in Chapter Four and the arguments here become clearer now. Concurrent feedback provides better incentives for the student and makes it more likely that we will learn the limits of a student's abilities. Haney notes that this idea is as old as Thorndike's psychology (as in the "law of effect, which holds essentially that learning is enhanced when people see the effects from what they try") and buttressed by years of learning theory: "A meta-analysis of forty previous studies on the instructional effects of feedback in test-like events showed that relatively rapid feedback (i.e. immediately after a test was completed) is more effective than feedback after a day or more. Also, feedback providing guidance to, or identification of, correct answers is more instructionally effective than feedback that simply tells learners whether their answers are right or wrong."[10]

From the vantage point of defining mastery, using a test composed of simplistic and unambiguous items, with no feedback built in (either in the form of materials to respond to or judges' judgments to react to), ensures that we will not be assessing for higher-order capacities. Again let the hoary Taxonomy be our guide. A synthesizing product or performance is, as I have noted, essentially a "unique communication. Usually the author is trying to communicate certain ideas and experiences to others. . . . Usually, too, he tries to communicate for one or more of the following purposes—to inform, to persuade, to impress, or to entertain. Ultimately he wishes to achieve a given effect (response) in some audience."[11] Dewey made a similar point in criticizing most so-called problems, which "call at best for a kind of mechanical dexterity in applying set rules. . . . [T]here is only a challenge to understanding when there is a desired consequence for which means have to be found by inquiry, or things are presented under conditions where reflection is required to see what consequences can be effected by their use."[12] All genuine problems that lead to understanding involve a testing, in other words, by the student, whereby suggestions or hunches are refined in light of concurrent feedback: the student "confronted with the situation that has to be thought through returns upon, revises, extends, analyzes, and makes more precise and definite the facts of the case."[13]

What, then, of testing methodologies that give students no feedback as they work, or deliberately use only those questions that are simple exercises? (Again, recall that I do not mean by this question that the feedback should be provided by testers in words; I mean all kinds of situational feedback, such as that provided by roadsigns and tomato plants.) What, then, of large-scale tests or final exams that give feedback on a June test in September? There are in fact two essential and separate issues here—one relating to a better understanding of test validity, the other relating to the ineffectiveness (hence disincentives) of tests that offer no concurrent or ex post facto feedback.

The potential harm to performer effectiveness and incentive is more easily grasped. Of what value to the performer is a test where the feedback occurs days, weeks, or months later—and even then, in a form rarely usable by the student (in the case of standardized tests)? This is why conventional testing programs, in which we use one-shot summative tests at the very end of a course of study, are so dysfunctional: if testing is what you do only after teaching and learning are *over*, then testing cannot, *in principle*, improve complex student performance. Feedback must be timely, and the recipient must have opportunities to employ it, if it is to be effective. User-friendly feedback must occur within the assessment; the curriculum must make the consideration and use of feedback the next lesson.

Consider, as an example of useful concurrent feedback, the following welding test devised by a vocational teacher I have worked with for the past two years. Ralph has practiced much of what is preached in this book and serves as an inspiration as to what is possible. For example, he routinely works from industry specifications, taught to each student. Real inspectors are often brought in to conduct tests on the student welds. But the best lesson I have learned from his teaching is the power of models to provide feedback and improve performance *within the assessment itself*.

In an early exercise, for example, Ralph teaches his students about corner welds. Their task is then to produce a ninety-degree weld that is "up to standard." The test is conducted as follows: When the student welder thinks that a given weld may be acceptable, he or she is to bring it to a table on which are many completed welds, each with the name of a former student on it. In addition, there is a marking pen. The student is to write his or her name on the weld and place it down with the others.

What happens, of course, is that minds are changed en route. I watched a boy jauntily come forth—ready, apparently, to put his product on the table. He picked up a marker, but then he was moved to inspect the other welds. On looking at one particular weld, his whole countenance changed. What had been a smile became a worried frown. His glance went back and forth between his weld and the one that had been on the table—one that was clearly superior to his own. A moment later, he quietly placed the exemplary weld back down on the table and went back to his station, with a bit of a furtive glance (as if he hoped not to be seen having prematurely come forward with his piece) to work further.

One could cite this story as telling about many things: the importance of teaching self-assessment, the need for exemplars, the ability of performance tests to be self-sustaining. In light of this chapter's discussion, however, the reader should reflect on the role that feedback plays here (and perhaps ought to play in every test as a part of the test)—namely, providing us with a clear measure of both the student's ability and willingness to produce quality work, in light of the obvious feedback about the standards to be met.

What would have happened had there been no table of other welds? It is likely, of course, that the overall quality of the welds would have been lower and that the range of performance would have increased—results of value to the psychometrician, perhaps, but decidedly harmful to student and teacher objectives and enthusiasm. What if the test, criteria, and standards had been secure, allowing no feedback at all? A greater range of performance, no doubt. But why would we deliberately design such a test if our aim was to design assessment *in the learner's interest?*

It should be noted that in the welding case, the feedback was not a function of human but of situational interaction—as it is in all the best feedback systems. Perhaps the greatest obstacle to making feedback a part of testing is the inaccurate assumption made by teachers and test designers that feedback has to be dialogical. On the contrary, as the roadsign discussion illustrates, we optimize student performance and autonomy by depersonalizing the feedback—by making students less and less dependent upon "experts" for feedback. Because if feedback comes only from experts, and comes in the form of evaluative language only, it is very unlikely that the student will develop insight into standards (and thereby autonomy). Worse, the student will come to think that standards and criteria are subjective, *since no feedback loop makes clear their objective value and appropriateness.*

Concurrent confirming and disconfirming information, as the travel and garden examples imply (and Gilbert's eight points illustrate), are provided by a system of models, criteria, and indicators. I need to be able to "confirm," as I go, that I am on the right path. But that confirmation is possible only when I have a known destination or measurable goal, when I have a plan that maps out the exemplary route, and when I know the key landmarks en route and/or constant access to timely indicators (roadsigns) of success or failure. Without such a system, I am completely dependent upon experts at every turn; without such a system, I must perpetually ask, as so many students do, "Is this right?"

In education, the "destination" is a standard: exemplary performance. The concurrent confirmation or disconfirmation is therefore provided either by models and criteria or by human response. Elbow, in speaking of "criterion-based feedback" and "reader-based feedback" (noted above), generalizable to "audience-based feedback" or "client-based feedback," remarks that the former in effect asks "What is its quality?" while the latter asks, "How does it work?"[14] These questions become part of an ongoing assessment process whereby we honor the truth that writing is revision: we do not ask students to write a complete paper in one silent sitting; we assess students' ability to seek and profit from feedback (and from further reflection, by which they distance from their thinking and provide *themselves* with more disinterested feedback when their minds are not so clouded by their intentions).

As Elbow's latter question ("How does it work for the reader?") implies, gauging the effect of our intentions is at the heart of what he terms "commentary" (as opposed to "measurement"). Determining what to *do* with "subjective" feedback en route becomes as much a part of the challenge as the writing task itself. One teacher I know accomplishes Elbow's aim in the following way. He requires that students staple a preface to each paper they write, stating their intent as authors: What were they trying to accomplish here? What response were they hoping to generate? What problem were they trying to explore (as when an artist engages in a study of color or form)? Two or three peer editors then read each paper through the "lens" of that intent: How did the paper strike them? In light of their response, what was the relation between the author's intent and the (diverse!) effects? Each student then determines how—or whether—to use the feedback in improving the paper. The second phase of the peer editing process focuses on the most basic aspect of whether a paper "works" or not: peer editors are asked to mark the place in the paper where they lost interest. Then, in the next phase of editing, more formal and criterion-referenced criteria are brought to bear on the editing by the peers, as directed by the teacher. And often the weaknesses identified by the initial peer responses are now seen in more formal terms, giving the student a better grasp of why the formal criteria make a difference in the quality of writing. Only when this multipart process is completed does the paper go to the teacher—who employs the same process in his review.

"What teacher has the time to give intensive one-on-one feedback?" is a common lament when I raise these issues in workshops. Another misconception about feedback. Remember, the best feedback systems minimize human intervention, as the system of roadsigns reminds us. What is the equivalent in writing to the roadsigns? Model papers and performances, scoring rubrics, and performance troubleshooting guides, to be used by individuals or in peer review, can go a long way toward providing good feedback. (You will recall, from Chapter Five, the Canadian district that publishes all such material in an "Exemplar Booklet" for students.) After all, the performance is meant to "work" or accomplish a goal. Even a novice can provide feedback under those conditions.

"Nice idea, but how can this happen on a large scale?" Well, the approaches described are similar to what the Advanced Placement art portfolio exam (described earlier) entails. In assessment, judges determine whether student pieces "work in their own way." To that end, students are asked to attach a one-page summary of their intent, and the judges judge accordingly. (I might add that this makes the scoring more reliable, not less, since the criteria are not about individual aesthetic tastes.) And Jefferson County, Kentucky (greater Louisville), one of the largest districts in the country, uses a four-day writing assessment that requires students to submit drafts and final versions for evaluation, with the soliciting of feedback thus a part of the process. Most European countries use interactive oral examinations as a major part of their secondary system for many of the reasons suggested in this chapter: we do not know what students really know until we examine their answers with them and see how they respond to our responses.

Providing *some* on-going feedback would thus seem to be a moral obligation of any test. I need to know, as a student, if I am heading in the direction of an excellent paper, lab report, or debate presentation. (It is no longer clear to me why "formative" and "summative" assessments are thought of as different, in other words. The student is *always* entitled to information about how to improve performance.)

It may be useful to summarize some of these points in a list that compares and contrasts effective and ineffective feedback:

Effective Feedback	*Ineffective Feedback*
Provides guidance and confirming (or disconfirming) evidence. For the traveler, a map offers guidance while roadsigns offer feedback.	*Provides praise or blame, and non-situation-specific advice or exhortations.* "Try harder" offers no specific assistance.
Compares current performance and trend against successful result. In other words, the taste and appearance of the food, not the recipe alone, guarantee the meal as described.	*Naively assumes that instructions and hard work will bring people to their goal.* Planting seeds according to directions and watering with care does not ensure a successful garden.
Is timely and immediately usable.	*Is not timely: suffers from excessive delay in usability or arrives too late to use at all.*
Measures in terms of absolute progress; assesses the accomplishment; specifies degree of conformance with the exemplar, goal, or standard.	*Measures in terms of relative change or growth; assesses student behaviors or attitudes; relative to the self or norms, tells students how far they have come (not how far they have left), what direction they must go to get there, and how close people generally get.*
Is characterized by descriptive language. For example, "You made a left turn instead of a right turn onto Main Street."	*Is characterized by evaluative or comparative language.* For example, "You made many correct turns and one incorrect turn. Your navigating is greatly improved and better than that of most of your peers."

Is useful to a novice; offers specific, salient diagnoses and prescriptions for each mistake. A teacher might supply an explanation of why something is a mistake, illustrate how it compares to exemplary performance, and explain how to correct it—as in good coaching.

Is not useful to a novice; offers only a general summary of strengths and weaknesses; criticism uses language only experts can "decode." Such feedback might, for example, use one word to explain a mistake ("vague," "illogical"), as if the labeling of the mistake were enough to let a student know how to correct it.

Allows the performer to perceive a specific, tangible effect of his or her efforts, symbolized by an apt score. The grade or score confirms what was apparent to the performer about the quality of the performance.

Obscures any tangible effect so that none (beyond a score) is visible to the performer. The evaluation process remains mysterious or arbitrary to the performer, no matter how valid and reliable the test and score are to the expert.

Measures essential traits. The criteria represent the key qualities found in diverse, exemplary performance; they enable the judge to validly discriminate between excellent and other kinds of performance.

Measures only easy-to-score variables. The qualities of merely competent performance are used to assess performance; feedback offers insight into formal errors only, although avoiding only those errors does not guarantee excellence.

Derives the result sought from analysis of exit-level or adult accomplishment. For example, first-grade evaluation of reading is linked to the capacities of successful adult readers; feedback is offered in terms of the goal—specific accomplishments of those who effectively read to learn.

Derives the result sought from an arbitrarily mandated or simplistic goal statement. For example, the feedback to first-grade readers relates only to first-grade objectives. As a result, there is too much feedback in terms of learning to read and not enough in terms of reading to learn.

Feedback, Consequences, and Validity

Regardless of whether there is a moral obligation to supply better feedback to the student during and after testing, is there a technical obligation to do so? The validity questions are murky and provocative. The question to consider is this: Can I infer what I need to from a score on a test that provides no concurrent feedback, whether or not the student can complete the task? Secure paper-and-pencil tests almost never provide concurrent feedback; students have no idea whether their answers are apt and on the right track. Yet in any real-life situation, we get some feedback, either from the environment or from the client, to gauge whether we are on track. Are the test makers' inferences valid, then, if the student is operating in the intellectual equivalent of a sensory deprivation tank?

The reason that tests do not routinely build in concurrent feedback (and the rich contextual detail such feedback requires) no doubt has to do with efficiency and test security. But if it is possible to provide such feedback without compromising the test or our budget—and it is, as all simulator tests reveal—should we not feel bound to do so? A simple example: we would learn a great deal more from students about their ability in history if they were allowed access to history reference material and their own notes while writing essay questions on the Advanced Placement exam—but only *after* they had sketched out some *general* answers in the first hour. And what more might we learn about the performer if we required (and considered in our evaluation) self-assessment as such a multipart task unfolded?—something possible only if there is a model and a set of criteria (as in the welding example earlier in this chapter and in the m&m's problem in Chapter Four). Perhaps we cannot make valid inferences about the student's *memory* of weld specifications or volume formulas, but was that what we were testing in the first place? Of course not. Even the test manufacturer of multiple-choice volume problems describes such problems as testing for understanding of the "concept" of volume and how to "apply" it. That is why a dissertation is insufficient and a defense is crucial to assessing graduate-level mastery: the student must respond to expert reaction; our judgment as to the student's expertise will in large part be due to the student's ability to handle our feedback.

William James helps us see why validity issues are raised by the denial feedback. He notes that the student who tells us, "'I know the answer, but I can't say what it is,' we treat as practically identical with him who knows absolutely nothing about the answer." James argues that this is a mistake, because "the vaguer memory of a subject . . . and of where we may go again to recover it again, constitutes in most men and women the chief fruit of their education."[15] How is this related to feedback? Because memory and mastery depend upon situational cues that enable us to locate what we "know" but have "forgotten"—a contradiction only to test makers.

We do not so much "know" things as reconfirm and verify to others what we know situationally; or we reveal to the tester *and ourselves* that indeed we do *not* know it. Recall the example in Chapter Four from the British APU math interview: if students seemed not to know the formulas for area and perimeter, the feedback given *merely by the reframing of the question and the availability of manipulatives* provided a context that enabled some students to "remember" what they "knew." (This attention to reframing and contextual detail is especially important when we consider the role of context in understanding, as we shall see in the next chapter.) Feedback thus enables me, as well as an assessor, to distinguish between what I know and what I *think* I know—an essential element of an education, a trustworthy assessment process, and a distinction perpetually blurred by conventional testing.

Teacher Resistance to Giving Feedback

As remarkable as it seems, I have met teachers who are unwilling to give feedback. Generally, though, these teachers perceive feedback to be value-laden comments such as "poorly said" or "not good enough." In an effort to avoid negativity, they resist putting any grades or comments on student work. But this confuses feedback with a "judgmental" evaluation of performance; it confuses standards with expectations; it confuses progress with growth. Whether or not I am on or off track is a matter of *fact*; whether you praise or blame me for my journey and destination has nothing to do with whether you supply me with usable information about my journey.

Similarly, I have heard many teachers say that it is unwise to present students with models of the task you want accomplished, since that will "stifle creativity." But this is simply false—*if* the task is a worthy one. All we have to do is think of music or drama: How can a person learn to play pieces or scenes properly without access to (diverse) samples of model performance (and feedback in terms of those models)? How would I ever have learned to play a Chopin prelude when I was ten had I not heard both my teacher and Rubenstein play it beautifully? Again, as Gilbert noted, feedback can be accurate only if it is given in reference to the models or standards of exemplary performance. "But then the students will be intimidated by perfection or depressed by how poorly they are doing!" But the retort should be obvious: How will they ever get better otherwise? (Using *multiple* models limits mechanical imitation.)

William James offered a simple, if quaint, description of the essential role of feedback in learning. We should "receive sensible news of our behavior and its results. We hear the words we have spoken, feel our own blow as we give it, or read in the bystander's eyes the success or failure of our conduct. Now this return wave . . . pertains to the completeness of the whole experience."[16] But to honor this notion in schooling, the feedback must be supplied by models, criteria, and standards—standards that are not arbitrary tastes or whims but that inhere in the particular job done well, standards that have been validated against wider-world standards.

Leaving aside the issue of whether grades and comments are adequate feedback, to my dismay many teachers completely balk at the idea of telling students where they stand in terms of standards. They seem convinced that feedback provided in reference to standards—that is, in reference to the desired destination of the educational "journey"—will likely be debilitating, especially for the less able students. But without such feedback, how will the less able become more able? How can a student ever master an inherently difficult task without disinterested feedback about the quality and progress of the mastery?

In fact, what the fear often reveals is that teachers tend to confuse "standards" with "expectations." For developmental reasons, they correctly fear arbitrary, time-linked expectations of performance. But this is no reason to deny students helpful feedback about how their work compares to exemplary work (as I noted in discussing the longitudinal spelling assessment in Chapter Five). The teachers' fear is no doubt due to our culture of testing, but as I argued in Chapter One, we then have a sadly ironic situation: teachers learn to fear giving feedback, yet feedback is the thing that makes it most likely that students will improve later performance effectively and efficiently.

The most effective forms of feedback thus do more than confirm or disconfirm. Feedback should enable you to recognize your errors and successes as particular errors and successes on the way to a performance goal. Assessment feedback must therefore be more than the children's game of "hot and cold." Good feedback tells you not only *that* you are straying from your "guidance" and your goal; it tells you more than *what kind* of straying off course you made. Feedback gives you sufficient information about the error and its relation to your goal that you can likely see how to correct the mistake yourself.

Many educators cannot imagine how assessment reform will ever work if they must give one-on-one guidance and feedback to each student all the time, but they have given too little thought to the classroom equivalent of maps and roadsigns. If we are clear on our "destinations," then feedback can often be objectified. Consider, for example, troubleshooting guides for electronics products. The writer anticipates our likely errors—as does the positioner of roadsigns—and catalogues a series of descriptors and recommendations whereby we might self-correct. Teachers and test makers would greatly help their students if they provided the equivalent for what is being learned. (Indeed, it is worth noting that Bloom and his colleagues did just this: the Taxonomy describes the typical errors made at each level. Their account is inadequate, however, and we would profit by a more substantial research base on intellectual performance errors and diagnostic advice linked to the tasks and scoring rubrics we will be using.)

At the very least, let us begin to have more dynamic and adaptive forms of testing that allow students to self-assess and self-adjust more frequently as part of the assessment. We will never dis-

tinguish between thoughtless, superficial knowledge and thoughtful error unless we do so.

Notes

1. W. Haney, "We Must Take Care: Fitting Assessment to Func-
    tions," in V. Perrone, ed., *Expanding Student Assessment for
    Supervision and Curriculum Development* (Alexandria, Va.:
    Association for Supervision and Curriculum Development,
    1991), p. 155.
2. T. F. Gilbert, *Human Competence* (New York: McGraw-Hill,
    1978), p. 178.
3. P. Elbow, *Embracing Contraries: Explorations in Learning
    and Teaching* (New York: Oxford University Press, 1986),
    p. 232.
4. D. Wolf, J. Bixby, J. Glen III, and H. Gardner, "To Use Their
    Minds Well: Investigating New Forms of Student Assess-
    ment," in G. Grant, ed., *Review of Research in Education*
    (Washington, D.C.: American Educational Research Associa-
    tion, 1991.
5. P. M. Senge, *The Fifth Discipline: The Art and Practice of the
    Learning Organization* (New York: Doubleday, 1990), p. 79.
6. P. Elbow, *Writing with Power: Techniques for Mastering the
    Writing Process* (New York: Oxford University Press, 1981).
7. Elbow, *Embracing Contraries and Explorations in Learning
    and Teaching*, pp. 231–232.
8. Gilbert, *Human Competence*, pp. 178-179.
9. See, for example, A. Collins, J. S. Brown, and S. E. Newman,
    "Cognitive Apprenticeship: Teaching the Crafts of Reading,
    Writing, and Mathematics," in L. B. Resnick, ed., *Knowing,
    Learning, and Instruction: Essays in Honor of Robert Glaser*
    (Hillsdale, N.J.: Erlbaum, 1989), for a discussion of how self-
    monitoring and self-correction work in cognition.
10. This is the research of R. Bangert-Drowns, C. Kulik, J. Kulik,
    and M. Morgan, as cited in Haney, "We Must Take Care,"
    p. 155.
11. B. S. Bloom, ed., *Taxonomy of Educational Objectives,* Vol. 1:

Cognitive Domain (White Plains, N.Y.: Longman, 1956), p. 163.

12. J. Dewey, *How We Think: A Restatement of the Relation of Reflective Thinking to the Educative Process* (Lexington, Mass.: Heath, 1933), p. 147.

13. Ibid., p. 169.

14. Elbow, *Writing with Power*, p. 241.

15. W. James, *Talks to Teachers* (New York: W. W. Norton, [1899] 1958), p. 101.

16. Ibid., p. 41.

7 | Authenticity, Context, and Validity

A chapter on validity in testing is inherently more technical than the others. I say this to alert readers, not to scare them off. Those readers with a limited understanding of test design and validation will profit from the analysis because there is too much confusion at the local level about the relationship between *authenticity* and *validity*. And professional developers of performance tests will benefit because they are now working with inadequate guidelines as to what constitutes appropriate scoring criteria and tasks. Our ability to improve performance through assessment will be stymied unless *everyone* considers issues of validation more thoughtfully.

Since the book is not a technical treatise but an attempt to articulate a new philosophy of assessment, however, I will not revisit such traditional test-design and test-use topics as how to establish construct validity, how validity coefficients are devised, and the problem of generalizability. A variety of recent as well as time-honored accounts of those problems exist in the technical literature.[1] Rather, what we need to consider here are questions of validation that are newly raised or practices that are rendered newly problematic by a student-centered view of assessment. We will want especially to examine the limits of the traditional test format, whereby simple, indirect tasks are routinely used to measure complex performance, and to consider what obligation testers might have to use more direct ("authentic") measures.

Because some elemental conceptual clarification is necessary, we will also consider these questions: What is *authenticity*, why is it more than face validity, and why should it be a test-design value— irrespective of any correlations that might exist between proposed tests and preexisting tests? What do we mean by *performance* and how will an understanding of it change our conception of *competency* (and hence *validity*)? To what extent is validity inseparable from the context in which tests are used? These questions deserve a better airing than they now receive.

The point of this chapter is to make clear that there is an inescapable tension between the challenges presented by contextualized performance and conventional, large-scale, generic testing. The construct of "understanding," which we are measuring gains with respect to, is in need of overhaul, to put it simply. Understanding is not cued knowledge: performance is never the sum of drills; problems are not exercises; mastery is not achieved by the unthinking use of algorithms. We cannot be said to "understand" something, in other words, unless we can employ it wisely, fluently, flexibly, and aptly in particular and diverse contexts. As Lauren Resnick has put it, the two key assumptions of conventional test design—the decomposability of knowledge into elements and the decontextualization of knowing (whereby it is assumed that if we know something we know it in any context)—are false.[2] It may in fact make better sense to think of understanding as being more like good judgment or a disposition than a possession of information, implying that assessments should test for *habits*; and habits, by their repetitive nature, are not something that can ever be tested by a one-shot test.

Something more than face validity is at stake, in other words. (Many current *performance* tests and scoring criteria are in fact invalid, as we shall see in looking at examples of tasks and scoring rubrics.) The simplest way to sum up the potential harm of our current tests is to say that we are not preparing students for real, "messy" uses of knowledge in context—the "doing" of a subject. Or, as one teacher put it to me a few years ago, "The trouble with kids today is that they don't know what to do when they don't know what to do." That is largely because all of our testing is based on a simplistic stimulus-response view of learning and evidence of learning.

Two key words in this chapter are *context* and *judgment*. Competent performance requires both. It makes no intellectual sense to test for "knowledge" as if mastery were an unvarying response to unambiguous stimuli. That would be like evaluating court judges on their knowledge of law only or doctors on their memory of biochemistry lectures. Rather, what we should be assessing is the student's ability to prepare for and master the various "roles" and situations that competent professionals encounter in their work. But we should keep the test maker's dilemma in mind: fidelity to the criterion situations maximizes the complexity and ambiguity of the task requirements and the freedom to respond as one sees fit—conditions that work *against* maximizing standardization and reliability. This validity-versus-reliability dilemma must never be construed as an either-or choice, however, but as a design problem to be carefully negotiated on the basis of better guidelines for balancing the concerns.

We fail to negotiate the dilemma at present. Modern professionally designed tests intended for national and state use tend to sacrifice validity for reliability in the design. In other words, test makers generally end up being more concerned with the precision of the resulting scores than with the intellectual value and contextual grounding of the challenge. As a result, the forms of testing and scoring used are indirect and generic, designed to minimize the ambiguity of tasks and answers (including those within performance measures). But such forms of testing simply do not tell us what we need to know—namely, whether students have the capacity to use wisely what knowledge they have. This is a judgment that we can make only through tasks that require students to "perform" in highly contextualized situations that are as faithful as possible to "criterion situations." Answers are not so much correct or incorrect in real life as apt or inappropriate, justified or unjustified—*in context*. Deprived of the opportunity to have perspective, to explain an answer, or to self-assess en route through contextual cues and feedback, students are invariably tested on verbal knowledge and cultural savvy as opposed to competence.

Deeper educational issues lie under these concerns. To *as-*

sume that tests should assess whether all students everywhere have the same "knowledge" (especially in the absence of a highly specific national curriculum) is to short-circuit a vital educational dialogue in a pluralistic and diverse modern society. Genuine intellectual performance, like other kinds of performance, is inherently personalized. And the meanings, strengths, and aspirations that we derive from an education are inherently idiosyncratic. Common knowledge is *not* the aim of any robust education for lifelong learning. To use only uniform tasks that are insensitive to the syllabi and cultures of each local curriculum is to limit tested knowledge to simple truisms, definitions, or easily verifiable but random facts. (The situation is even worse than that implies, since in the absence of common syllabi, we cannot even include questions about texts read and course-content-related achievements.) If competence is more like contextual insight and good judgment than inert knowledge, if ability is more due to disposition than to the possession and plugging in of information, we will need to rethink our reliance on short-answer, unambiguous items and one-event tests.

What is wanted is a more robust and authentic construct of "understanding" and a more rigorous validation of tests against that construct. We can begin by keeping in mind that the aim of education is to help the individual become a competent intellectual performer, not a passive "selector" of orthodox and prefabricated answers.

What Is "Performance"?

The word *perform*, as Webster's unabridged dictionary reminds us, comes from root words meaning "consummate" or "accomplish." When we "perform," we try to "execute a task or process and to bring it to completion." Our ability to *perform* with knowledge can therefore be assessed only as we produce some work of our own, using a *repertoire* of knowledge and skills and being responsive to the particular tasks and contexts at hand. (The use of the plural [tasks, contexts] is important: we assess "performance" through many different "performances" in diverse settings and situations, whether we are considering professional athletes or doctors.)

One way to illustrate the difference between drilled skills and performance ability is with an anecdote from my soccer-coaching career. As you may know, it is common practice in soccer and other sports to do practice drills related to gaining numerical advantage on offense (since, if one can execute the moves, that is a surefire way to score). Every coach routinely does what are called "2 on 1," "3 on 2," or "4 on 3" drills—drills in which the offense has the ball and a numerical advantage to exploit. But mastery of these drills does not translate into game mastery, as the following tale reveals. One time, during a game early in a season, one of my better players had a series of opportunities to exploit such a numerical advantage. I yelled from the sidelines, "2 on 1!" She actually stopped dribbling the ball and yelled back at me, "I can't *see* it!"

That incident sums up in a nutshell the problem with testing by indirect items. Items are the equivalent of drills: deliberately simplified and decontextualized events designed for isolating and practicing discrete skills. But the sum of the drills is never equal to fluid, effective, and responsive performance—no matter how complex or varied the items. As all good athletes and coaches know, judgment and "anticipation" (perception of the unfolding situation) are essential elements of competence—so much so that players who are able to "read" the game can often compensate for skill deficiency. Yet almost every major test (or set of problems in the back of textbooks) is a *drill* test, not a performance test.

What we must keep asking, then, is, What is the equivalent of the game in each subject matter? In other words, how is each subject "performed"? What does the "doing" of mathematics, history, science, art, and language use look and feel like in context, and how can our tests better replicate authentic challenges and conditions instead of isolated drill exercises? Nor should this argument for authenticity be seen as applying only to older or more advanced students. If we want later competent performance, we need to introduce novices to that performance from day one. We see this in language learning and skiing; only a deep and ancient prejudice about academic learning keeps us thinking that intellectual competence is achieved by accretion of knowledge and movement through simple logical elements to the complex whole—instead of movement from a *crude* grasp of the whole to a *sophisticated* grasp of the whole.

Consider Exhibit 7.1, a test given in a U.S. history course after a unit on the Revolutionary War period. It illustrates how a performance for understanding differs from a test of knowledge.

Leaving aside the feasibility of using tasks such as those shown in Exhibit 7.1 in large-scale assessment (though this is done in other countries and is being pursued in a modified way in research conducted by the Center on Evaluation and Testing, CRESST[3]), the question raised by the task is, Isn't this what we mean by *performance?* It can be easily seen here that students must "do" history to master the task. Mere control over what was in the textbook would neither prepare students adequately for doing such a task nor adequately represent the "criterion situation" of "doing" history. This task makes it clear that to merely "understand" what the textbook said is neither to understand the events themselves nor to understand what it means to do historical research on such events. In fact, when I have used this task in some fine suburban high school classes, many students have been stunned to discover that textbooks disagree—a sure indication that they have not "understood" or "done" history.

Put differently, all tests, even of novices, must always point toward and be "enabling" of adult performance, in the sense suggested by Robert Glaser. "To place tests in the service of learning in a marriage of cognitive and psychometric theory, we must consider assessment . . . as measures of skills and dispositions that are essential to further learning. Once mastered, the skills and knowledge of a domain can become enabling competencies for the future."[4] We will thus need a better understanding of how understanding develops in a subject, as modeled by Harvard University psychologist William Perry's more general scheme for intellectual development in college.[5] Or, as Glaser has put it, "Modern learning theory is taking on the characteristics of a developmental psychology of performance changes. . . . In the future, achievement measurement will be designed to assess these changes."[6] (This has implications for our development of criterion-referenced scoring rubrics, as we shall see below.)

We must begin to do a better job of testing for emerging competence by moving backward from the ultimate criterion performance, even when the current knowledge is rudimentary. We

Exhibit 7.1. Testing Understanding, Not Knowledge.

You are a prosecutor or a defense attorney in a trial brought by a parent group seeking to forbid purchase by your high school of a U.S. history textbook, excerpted below. (The book would be used as a *required supplement* to your current text, not in place of it.) You will present a ten-minute oral case, in pairs, to a jury, taking either side of the question, Is the book appropriate for school adoption and required reading? (supported by a written summary of your argument). You will be assessed on how well you support your claim about the accounts in the text, in response to the question, Are the accounts biased, inaccurate or merely different from our usual viewpoint?

On the American Revolution

As a result of the ceaseless struggle of the colonial people for their political rights, the 13 colonies practiced bourgeois representative government by setting up their own local legislatures.[7] As electoral rights were restricted in many ways in every colony, those elected to the colonial legislatures were mostly landlords, gentry, and agents of the bourgeoisie, without any representation whatsoever from the working people. There were struggles between the Governors and the legislatures. These struggles reflected the contradictions between the colonies and their suzerain state. . . .

The British administration of the colonies was completely in the interests of the bourgeoisie in Britain. . . . The British colonial rule impeded development of the national economy in North America. It forced certain businesses into bankruptcy. As a consequence, contradictions became increasingly acute between the ruling clique in Britain and the rising bourgeoisie and broad masses of the people in the colonies. . . .

Heretofore [prior to the Boston Massacre], the struggle of the colonial people had been scattered and regional. In the course of the struggle, however, they summed up their experience and came to feel it necessary to stand together for united action. Thus in November 1772, a town meeting held in Boston adopted a proposal made by Samuel Adams to create a Committee of Correspondence to exchange information with other areas, act in unison, and propagate revolutionary ideas. . . . In less than 2 months, a Committee of Correspondence was formed by more than 80 cities and towns in Massachusetts, and later became the organs of revolutionary power. . . .

The Declaration of Independence was a declaration of the bourgeois revolution. The political principles enun-

Exhibit 7.1. Testing Understanding, Not Knowledge, Cont'd.

ciated in it were aimed at protecting the system of capitalist exploitation, legitimizing the interests of the bourgeoisie. In practice, the "people" referred to in the Declaration only meant the bourgeoisie, and the "right of the pursuit of happiness" was deduced from the "right of property" and intended to stamp the mark of legitimacy on the system of bourgeois exploitation. The Declaration was signed by 56 persons, of whom 28 were bourgeois lawyers, 13 were big merchants, 8 were plantation slave owners and 7 were members of the free professions, but there was not one representative of the working people.

During the time of the war, America began its westward expansion on a large scale. From the first, the colonies had been founded on the corpses of the Indians. . . . In 1779 George Washington sent John Sullivan with a force of soldiers to "annihilate" the Iroquois tribe settled in northern New York. In his instructions he wrote: "The present aim is to completely smash and flatten their settlement, take as many prisoners as possible, the more the better, whether they are men or women. . . . You must not only mop up their settlement but destroy it." Thus at the time of its founding, America had already nakedly exposed its aggressive character. . . .

During the war patriotic women also played a big role. While men went to the front, they took over the tasks of production. They tilled fields and wove cloth, and sent food, garments, and other articles to the front. When Washington was in a precarious situation retreating into Pennsylvania with his army, the women of Philadelphia raised a huge fund to procure winter clothes for the revolutionary army. This event deeply moved the fighters. Under fire on the battlefields, women risked their lives to bring ammunition, transmit intelligence, and rescue the wounded. Some even served as artillery gunners. . . .

After the outbreak of the war, America not only failed to organize the enslaved Negroes but guarded them even more closely, thus intensifying their oppression. This seriously impeded their participation in the war and was one reason why the war for Independence was slow in achieving victory. . . .

The American people are a great people. They have a revolutionary tradition. At present [1970], they are in a period of new awakening. We believe that the American people will make still greater contributions to the cause of human progress in the future.

Exhibit 7.1. Testing Understanding, Not Knowledge, Cont'd.

Questions to Consider in Your Research and Presentation

1. What can be said to be the most likely political influences on the authors' point of view? What evidence is there of those influences? How do they affect the authors' choice of language? Does the language reflect bias or an acceptable (but different) point of view? Explain your reasoning.
2. Why does it make sense, given the authors' perspective, that they pay particular attention to (a) the Committee of Correspondence, (b) the contribution of women, and (c) the plight of "Indians" and "Negroes"? Are the facts accurate? Do they warrant that much attention in your view, or does such selective emphasis suggest a biased treatment? (How are these topics treated in the current text, and is the treatment there less biased or selective?)
3. You will be judged on the accuracy, aptness, and convincing qualities of your documentation, and the rhetorical effectiveness of *your* case. Be fair, but be an effective speaker and writer! A six-point scoring scale will be used for each dimension to be assessed: persuasiveness of evidence, persuasiveness of argument, rhetorical effectiveness of speech, and support material.

---

need to generalize from such approaches as those of Berlitz and other immersion language courses, which get the learner speaking and listening in context immediately, and working toward the ultimate criterion of fluid, contextual, fluent performance. As a simple illustration of what this might mean for testing, we might want to give the m&m's volume problem (see Chapter Four) to both sixth-grade math students and high school calculus students, to assess the development of insight.

But to make tests truly enabling we must do more than couch test tasks in more authentic performance contexts. We must construct tests that assess whether students are learning how to learn, given what they know. Instead of testing whether students have learned to read, we should test their ability to read to learn; instead of finding out whether they "know" formulas we should find out whether they can use formulas to find other formulas, and so on. As Glaser notes, "Knowledge at every level should be assessed in ways that allow students to see how they can use it to gather further information, evaluate evidence, weigh alternative courses for action, and articulate reasoned arguments."[8]

The kinds of tasks necessary for testing competent understanding, if we are to assess emerging performance, must therefore *always* be "higher-order." We must come to recognize that what we now call tests are really only exercises (or quizzes, in the common language of teachers). They are diagnostic, incapable of being valid as achievement or aptitude tests because they do not measure directly for effective competence. We might do well, then, to use Lauren Resnick's criteria in designing tests. She argues that higher-order thinking

- Is *non-algorithmic*. That is, the path of action is not fully specified in advance.
- Is *complex*. The total path is not "visible" from any single vantage point.
- Often *yields multiple solutions*, each with costs and benefits.
- Involves *nuanced judgment* and interpretation.
- Involves the *application of multiple criteria*, which sometimes conflict with one another.
- Often involves *uncertainty*. Not everything that bears on the task is known.
- Involves *self-regulation* of the thinking process. (One is not coached at each step.)
- Involves *imposing meaning*, finding structure in apparent disorder.
- Is *effortful*. There is considerable mental work involved.[9]

As I noted in Chapter One, Bloom and his colleagues were quite clear about this in the Taxonomy. In synthesis, "the student must draw upon elements from many sources and put these together into a structure or pattern not clearly there before. His efforts should yield a product." And as they stressed repeatedly, higher-order production was therefore to be thought of as a *creative* act, requiring "conditions favorable to creative work . . . Perhaps the most important condition [being] that of freedom."[10]

Not all hands-on work involves performance, therefore.
Doing simplistic tasks that merely "cue" us for the desired
knowledge-bit is not a creative employment of knowledge and skill
but drill or exercise out of context.[11] Consider, for example, a task
on the original hands-on science test given a few years ago to all
fourth-graders in New York, mentioned in Chapter Four. In the
first of five "stations," the student is given a cup, water, a ther-
mometer, and other instruments. The student is expected, among
other things, to accurately measure the temperature of the water.
Toward what end? To what degree of precision? No one measures
in general. Are we simulating the measuring of body temperature
or roasts in the oven? Are we making gravy or medicine? Purpose
and context *matter* in our assessment of skill. The test requires that
the answer must be correct within two degrees above or below the
"actual" water temperature. But why two degrees? Why such gener-
osity? (And why is the student not told of this tolerance margin?)
With no consequence or purpose to the measuring, there can be no
appropriate margin of error. The particular substance to be measured and the purpose to which the substance and measure will be
put determine how precise we need to be and how precise we are
judged to be. (A better form of this task would be to choose a recipe
that requires just the right temperature of a liquid for a result to
occur. At the very least, we need to use far more adaptive testing to
ensure that we know the limits of a student's performance ability.[12])

Understanding and Habits of Mind

Another way to see how contextual understanding might be better
tested is to consider the idea that understanding is inseparable from
certain habits of mind.

Habit is a word rarely used to describe academic mastery. We
tend to reserve it now for the more pressing and oppressing concerns
of affective issues or personal addictions (to drugs, alcohol, food, or
dysfunctional relationships). That is a pity, because a case can be
made that academic learning and our assessment of it cannot be
understood unless we see our aim as the formation of good habits
of mind in each subject.[13] We then continue to do large-scale testing
in a one-event format—a format *inherently* incapable of revealing

whether the student is in the *habit* of performing up to standards—at our students' peril.[14]

Through the work of Piaget, David Hawkins, Eleanor Duckworth, and the naive misconception literature in science education (all well summed up and extended by Howard Gardner in his recent book *The Unschooled Mind*), we are reminded that many "obvious" adult ideas are counterintuitive.[15] As Dewey put it, "Old ideas give way slowly; for they are more than abstract logical forms and categories. They are habits."[16] A new concept, especially an odd or counterintuitive one, can be said to be a difficultly learned habit. In the same way, imagining a world without friction from which to derive laws of motion, the idea of "negative space" in art, and the concept of skating *at* the defender when one has both the hockey puck and a numerical advantage over the defenders are odd and hard-to-master habits.

The word *habit* is revealing, I think, of what assessment needs to be to become directed toward thoughtful and effective understanding.[17] A higher-order habit is an intelligent *proneness*, not a reflex. To say that academic learning aims ultimately to develop the habit of employing knowledge effectively alerts us to the fact that we need more than an assessment of *learnedness;* we need to assess for intellectual *character,* as I mentioned in Chapter Two. A person with character has autonomy (literally, self-rule). Any test of understanding should therefore make it possible for us to know whether the student can accurately and *willingly* adapt knowledge to varying situations.[18] The "disposition" to be critical and effective in ill-structured situations requires forms of testing that evoke and require such dispositions for success. (Think back to the m&m's volume problem mentioned in Chapter Four; or such open-ended prompts such as this one in the recent twelfth-grade performance-based tests in Connecticut: "How much does it cost to take a shower?") Instead of artificial distracters there should be *realistic distracters,* in other words.

It is instructive that we speak of mathematics or history as a "discipline," related in some way to the "discipline" expected in classroom behavior. The dictionary reminds us of the root link: discipline is a "training that develops self-control, character, or orderliness and efficiency." The implication is clear: students need more than *someone else's* discipline and knowledge; they need to develop their own. That self-discipline may be reflected in something as simple as a student's double-checking work by consulting texts that are available. But how, given our present system of testing, can we assess that sort of discipline? The assessment of control—over oneself and over the theories, methods, and standards of a field of study—requires a very different kind of testing than the present one, relying on instruments that make it clear that the aim is to identify circumspect thinkers and intellectual leaders, not people who can glibly and facilely employ borrowed ideas.

To become progressively self-disciplined, as a thinker or active agent, one needs more than an imposed rigor and the fruits of someone else's studies. One needs to learn how to be in the habit of inquiring and engaging in discourse with care and thoroughness. What follows for assessment should be clear to anyone who grasps such an objective. How can I have evidence as to whether students have "discipline" in a discipline without asking them to *inquire* and *present* during the test? How can I assess their learning unless I see whether they have *learned how to learn* in the subject in question? How can I assess their understanding without assessing their ability to ask and *persist* with the right questions? It is clear, then, why a predominance of ill-structured tasks is essential for assessment of understanding: the lack of structure to the answering process is the only way I can discern whether a student has the necessary intellectual habits. If that focus on *understanding* is our goal, then secure, one-event, well-structured tasks with arbitrary criteria are dysfunctional, at the very least.

In short, it is one thing to learn how to respond to an unambiguous stimulus; it is another to become disposed to invoke the right habit in a fluid performance context—in other words, to have a *repertoire*. Good teacher-coaches have students constantly moving back and forth between drill and a "whole" performance; that way, students can learn what it feels like to be in the habit of skillful performing and can see the value of developing the newer, more difficult habits. We develop a repertoire by continually practicing strategies in performance contexts, by using our judgment as to what works (and when and why), and by being constantly tested (through real or simulated performances). We assess for repertoire by making test tasks ill-structured and multistaged—faithful to performance demands and responsive to the student's actions.

Understanding as Revealed Through Good Judgment

If performance requires a larger purpose, a rich context, and a repertoire wisely used, then effective performance is impossible without good judgment. Thus competence is testable only through tasks that demand good judgment in the use of knowledge. To test for understanding is to see if knowledge can be thoughtfully adapted: "Acquiring information can never develop the power of judgment. Development of judgment is in spite of, not because of, methods of instruction that emphasize simple learning. . . . [The student] cannot get power of judgment excepting as he is continually exercised in forming and testing judgments."[19] Rather than merely having knowledge of general principles to which unambiguous cases are somehow clearly applied, "to be a good judge is to have a sense of the relative values of the various features of a *perplexing* situation."[20]

Judgment involves effective adaptation to *specific* (adult) roles and situations; that is what we mean by *competence.*[21] We should recall that Binet defined intelligence as good judgment, "practical sense, initiative, the faculty of adapting one's self to circumstances"—what the French call *bon sens,* or good sense.[22] To develop a thoughtful control over performance, therefore, depends not so much on learning and employing "knowledge and skills" but on having our judgment awakened and empowered through problems that *demand* judgment. This is how learned material becomes a repertoire.

Judgment certainly does not involve the unthinking application of rules or algorithms—the stock in trade of all conventional tests. Dewey uses the words "knack, tact, cleverness, insight, and discernment" to remind us that judgment concerns "horse sense"; someone with good judgment is someone with the capacity to "estimate, appraise and evaluate." (Dewey adds, not coincidentally, "with tact and discernment.") The effective performer, like the good judge, never loses sight of either relative importance or the difference between the "spirit" and the "letter" of the law or rules that apply. Neither ability is testable by one-dimensional items, because to use judgment one must ask questions of foreground and background as well as perceive the limits of what one "knows."

All performers must be judges, in other words. In a unique or new case, how do we know which rules to apply? The performer, like the judge, "has to innovate, and where he innovates he is not operating from habit."[23] That is precisely what the soccer player mentioned above could *not* do: discern when and where her "2 on 1" knowledge should be applied. Nor can many students who first do the m&m's problem cope with the inherent ambiguity of the task—despite their mathematical knowledge. I watched one boy become paralyzed when he looked up from his construction of a tetrahedron to see a dozen differently shaped containers around the classroom—each thought by its maker to maximize the volume. Dismayed, he did not know how to proceed; he was not even able to use his textbook formulas to get a handle on possibilities—yet he was a B+ student in the geometry class. Unending drill tests prevent the development of the perception and adaptive intelligence needed for that sort of challenge. Can that boy be said to understand volume and its relation to surface area if he is incapable of developing a line of attack—even if he knows all his formulas for volume when cued by specific items? I don't believe so.

Consider a different perspective on good judgment in the employment of skills—the account by the OSS staff of what they called behavior "of the highest order of effectiveness." In the view of the OSS, effective use of knowledge and skill requires someone to "perceive and interpret properly the whole situation that confronts him . . . and his ability to coordinate his acts and direct them in proper sequence. . . . [T]hey all require organization. . . . Consequently, [a test for effectiveness requires] tasks and situations which cannot be properly solved without organization." The OSS staff elsewhere describe these tasks as requiring "mental operations on a higher integrative level; and since there is a difference between 'know-how' and 'can-do' we made the candidates actually attempt the tasks with their muscles or spoken words."[24]

Put in modern testing language, *any* test of intellectual competence requires that we give the student "ill-structured" tasks, in authentic settings, in which nonroutine uses of knowledge and skill are required; in other words, *any* test must be judgment-based. After all, when asked to evaluate the correctness of an answer in real-world settings, we typically respond, "Well, it depends on . . . " But this is the antithesis of testing as we know it, where the aim is to use well-defined, unambiguous problems with one apparent variable and one correct answer, to ensure reliability and cost-effectiveness.

Let us now consider two tests—both designed for use in a general science course for middle school students, both from published texts/curricula. The first, an ill-structured test that requires thoughtful performance, is known as "the Sludge." In an introductory physical science course, it is one of the major events. In this multiday test, students have to chemically analyze a sludgelike mixture of unknown solids and liquids. (In fact, in one New Jersey district, South Orange–Maplewood, the Sludge takes up the last two weeks of class in June, serving as a very elaborate performance test of the year's work.) This is an ill-structured, authentic task par excellence: though the procedures and criteria are quite clear to all students in the course, there are no pat routines, procedures, or recipes for solving the problem. And because of that, the test faithfully simulates a wide range of real-world "tests" of chemical analysis.

By contrast, consider the brief selection of traditional items that follows, from a summative test of 200 items out of a science textbook, to be given in a ninety-minute period at the end of the eighth grade:

2. A general statement based on a hypothesis that has been tested many times is
   a. a conclusion   b. scientific law   c. scientific   d. a theory
                                              knowledge

125. Green plants and algae are
   a. omnivores   b. herbivores   c. consumers   d. producers

191. The level in the classification that is broader than species but narrower than family is
   a. class   b. order   c. genus   d. phylum

Such exhaustiveness may well provide a certain superficial "content" validity, but the test bears little relationship to the practice of science and the ultimate "test" of one's knowledge.

Norman Frederiksen made this point a decade ago in his paper about the "real bias" that exists in testing, as noted in Chapter One.[25] His point was that the "tests" of life are more like the "sludge" or cost-of-the-shower problems than any neat and clean multiple-choice item. The "real bias" in testing is that tests that are inherently restricted to unambiguous items by their design end up influencing what is taught and what is thought to be a problem.

The critic might respond, "But surely before students can perform, we must give them first drills and then tests concerning their mastery of the drills." This logical fallacy has probably done more harm than any other operant principle in American education. Look how Bloom's Taxonomy was and still is improperly construed as a chronology, though its authors warned against that. Look how often syllabi unendingly postpone the student's exposure to genuine performance with knowledge, in the name of "lessons" whose meaning is opaque and whose interest value (without the context of performance) is minimal. All one has to do to see the fallacy of this way of thinking is to look at the adult performance world: musicians, athletes, architects, and doctors learn how to "perform with knowledge" by practicing the criterion performance. The Little Leaguer gets to play baseball; the medical student makes hospital rounds; the young artist starts by drawing. Any drill testing for these young performers is a means to an end; it is certainly not to be confused with the important performance itself. The whole point of an *educative* assessment system would be to introduce the students as soon as possible to criterion performances so that they will know what they ultimately face. Students would then see why certain drills are necessary for competence—a key aspect of motivation, as we saw in Chapter Five.

Some roles and situations that might serve as possible "templates" for better test design (perhaps as part of a more comprehensive and nonsecure "bank" in a school district or state agency) are presented in Exhibit 7.2. These roles and situational challenges are common to professional life.

The roles and situational challenges shown in Exhibit 7.2 might be generalized into a more sophisticated and feasible classification system (or set of *representative* tasks), linked to documents such as the SCANS report or to role-based research such as that by

**Exhibit 7.2. Professional Roles and Situations Through
Which Students Can "Perform with Knowledge."**

Roles

Museum curator: design museum exhibits on a given topic; compete for
"grant" money with other designers.

Engineering designer.
1. Bid and meet "specs": largest-volume oil container, MIT egg drop,
   and so on.
2. Apply theory: design and build a working roller coaster, a catapult,
   a herbarium, or anything else that requires application of theory
   studied.
3. Map/survey: focus on a region around school or school buildings,
   perhaps.

U.N. representative: design model U.N. tasks and activities, particularly
those that require a careful analysis of the interplay of "knowledge" and
culture.

Characters in historical reenactments.
1. Trials: Socrates, Scopes, *Brown* v. *Board of Education,* the Pied Piper.
2. "Meeting of the Minds": on a shared event or theme.
3. Diaries: made up as if by a historical person present from another era.
4. "What if . . . ?": writing/acting out a historical scenario.

Ad agency director: design advertising campaigns, book jackets, blurbs, and
so on for the book(s) read in class.

Tour organizer/cultural exchange facilitator: design travel, logistics, and
cultural guides for a world tour—within a specific budget and time frame
and for a particular purpose.

Psychologist/sociologist: conduct surveys and statistical analysis, graph
results, write newspaper article on the meaning of the results.

Bank manager: structure budgeting exercises needed in running a bank.

Document archaeologist: "From what text/culture/time frame is this
fragment?"

Person archaeologist: "Who Am I?" (given clues).

Essayist/philosopher, student of essential questions. "History: evolution or
revolution?" "When is a generalization a stereotype and when not?" "Is a
mathematical system an invention or a discovery?" "Does the 'heart know
things the mind cannot'?" "Does history repeat itself?" "Are there Great
Books, and if so by what criteria?" Consider these (and similar) questions
through research and debate products; present conclusions in writing.

Newspaper editor and writer.
1. Research and write articles as if set in the studied historical time.
2. Make complex ideas and/or facts accessible to readers (magnitude of
   the Kuwait oil spill, Middle East background history, and so on).

**Exhibit 7.2. Professional Roles and Situations Through
Which Students Can "Perform with Knowledge," Cont'd.**

3. Attempt to address a single issue from multiple perspectives: for example, write an editorial, a straightforward article, and letters to the editor from a wide variety of readers.

Historian.
1. "Biased, or just different?" Analyze and assess *controversial* accounts of historical events.
2. Conduct an oral history.
3. Review accounts of an event in three different textbooks for accuracy.
4. Outline the design of a "meaningful" textbook on U.S. history for kids.
5. Predict a future event (simulate CIA or State Department analysis) in an existing country.

Product designer: Conduct research, design an ad campaign, run focus groups, and present a proposal to a panel.

Job applicant: Prepare a portfolio with which to attempt to get hired for a specific job related to skills of the current course (with an interview by other students or the teacher).

Teacher: "If you understand it, you should be able to teach it." Teach younger children something you "know."

Expert witness: Give expert testimony to "Congress" on such issues as, Are all aspirin alike? Are advertising claims accurate? Should children's television viewing be regulated?

Speaker-listener: successfully communicate directions.

Debug expert: address problems with a car engine, an experimental design, an incomplete or garbled "text" (fragment of a book, radio transmission, incomplete translation, and so on).

Reviewer: "The medium is the message." Compare and contrast two presentations of one work—a book and its movie, a poem and song, play and musical, and so on.

Commercial designer: propose artwork for public buildings.

Situational Challenges

Discern a pattern.
Adapt to and reach an audience.
Empathize with the odd.
Pursue alternative answers.
Achieve an intended aesthetic effect.
Exhibit findings effectively.
Polish a performance.

Infer a relationship.
Facilitate a process and result.
Create an insightful model.
Disprove a common notion.
Reveal the limits of an important theory.
Successfully mediate a dispute.
Thoroughly rethink an issue.

**Exhibit 7.2. Professional Roles and Situations Through
Which Students Can "Perform with Knowledge," Cont'd.**

Lead a group to closure.	Shift perspective.
Develop and effectively implement a plan.	Imaginatively and persuasively simulate a condition or event.
Design, execute, and debug an experiment.	Thoughtfully evaluate and accurately analyze a performance.
Make a novice understand what you deeply know.	Judge the adequacy of a superficially appealing idea.
Induce a theorem or principle.	Accurately self-assess and self-correct.
Explore and report fairly on a controversy.	Communicate in an appropriate variety of media or languages.
Assess the quality of a product.	Complete a cost-benefit analysis.
Graphically display and effectively illuminate complex ideas.	Question the obvious or familiar.
Rate proposals or candidates.	Analyze common elements of diverse products.
Make the strange familiar.	Test for accuracy.
Make the familiar strange.	Negotiate a dilemma.
	Establish principles

Robert Gagné.[26] Many school districts are now developing sets of learner-outcome criteria and standards that point in the same direction. The Aurora, Colorado, schools, for example, use the following criteria (which are meant to be logically prior to subject-area goals and methods): self-directed learner, complex thinker, quality producer, community contributor, and collaborative worker. These criteria are instantly suggestive of performance-based tasks, devisable within the context of traditional courses of study.

Situational accuracy depends upon the kind of "job analysis" mentioned in the APA Standards (and of which we spoke in Chapter One) but rarely applied to K-12 education. Yet this kind of role analysis is at the heart of competency-based education: "The competency-based approach begins with the definition of the knowledge, skills, and attitudes required for successful performance in a particular role."[27] Or, as Gerald Grant put it in a book thoroughly analyzing competency-based education at the collegiate level, "Competence-based education . . . derives a curriculum from an analysis of a prospective or actual role in modern society."[28]

Distinguished psychometricians have been making these points for years. As Samuel Messick has argued, we fail to serve the demands of validity if we try only to correlate simplistic tests with other tests (even other performance tests). We cannot use content validity procedures alone, if the aim is to capture the essential "doing" of the ultimate performance and the most valid, contextual discriminators for assessing that "doing." In describing the typical validation procedures that involve mere correlation between test scores and criterion scores, he notes that "criterion scores are measures to be evaluated like all measures. They too may be deficient in capturing the criterion domain of interest." The solution, he argues, is "to evaluate the criterion measures, as well as the tests, in relation to construct theories of the criterion domain."[29] A similar concern with inattention to construct validity through reference to the criterion performances in adult job testing was recently noted by Lloyd Bond: "The measurement community has for various reasons not insisted on the necessity for evidence of construct validity in licensure and certification. . . . But I believe even small-scale studies comparing highly accomplished practitioners with novices or journeymen . . . are essential if we are to understand at some deeper level the kinds of tasks critical to safe and effective practice."[30] And consider E. F. Lindquist's remarks of forty years ago: "It should always be the fundamental goal of the achievement test constructor to make the elements of his test series as nearly equivalent to . . . the elements of the criterion series as considerations of efficiency, comparability, economy and expedience will permit."[31] (But the last clause gives away too much: there is excessive concern at present with "efficiency, comparability, economy, and expedience." We need a countervailing set of principles or oversight procedures to ensure that the educational benefits of authentic testing clearly justify the greater costs.)

Unending unwillingness to blueprint K-12 tests in reference to ultimate criterion situations was at the heart of David McClelland's influential critique of standardized testing twenty years ago. He argued that validity coefficients for tests were too often derived from other indirect tests or from predictors such as college grades, which are still not the real measure. The best testing, he argued, is "criterion sampling. . . . [T]here are almost no occupations that require a person to do word analogies. The point is so obvious that it would scarcely be worth mentioning, if it had not been obscured so often by psychologists." The solution? "Criterion sampling means that testers have to get out of their offices . . . and into the field where they actually analyze performance into its components. If you want to test who will be a good policeman, go find what a policeman does." He knew well the difficulty of getting testers to honor his concern, however: "The task will not be easy. It will require psychological skills not ordinarily in the repertoire of the traditional tester. What is called for is nothing less than a revision of the role itself—moving it away from word games and statistics toward behavioral analysis."[32]

Frederiksen made the same point a decade ago: "We need a much broader conception of what a test is if we are to use test information in improving educational outcomes," and he argues for more simulation-like forms of testing. In so doing, he quotes a 1962 article: "Neither the objective test, nor the essay examination . . . much resemble[s] the situation in which the student will use his training in professional or daily life." Vernon recommended then, as I do now, that "we employ techniques that will resemble as closely as possible the ways in which understandings will ultimately be expressed."[33]

As the OSS staff put it, anticipating all the discussion well: "The best that can be done [given the limits of predictive testing] is to expose a man to a variety of situations of the same type as those he will find in the field. . . . All we are affirming here is that the "real" test of a football player is playing in a real football game, or, if you choose, a real season of games. This assumption, a commonplace to laymen, is not without novelty in the field of psychological testing."[34] As William Neumann points out in his history of the competency-based movement, one of the recommendations growing out of the commissions established after World War II by the American Council on Education to examine the educational implications of military training was this: "It is important to note that the armed services used actual tests of performance of the required skills whenever practicable. . . . Possibly a similar type of practical testing could be used far more widely in liberal and professional education than is now the case."[35]

The OSS staff noted particularly that traditional forms of paper-and-pencil tests failed to test for "effective intelligence"—the ability to select goals, the best means in context for attaining them, and quick resourceful thinking or good judgment. They were "prompted to introduce realistic tests of ability" when they observed inconsistencies between paper-and-pencil tests of real-world abilities and performance in the world on problems of the same sort. (They also noted that, while tests are given in isolation, all real problems involve social interaction variables and complexities.) They ruefully added, however, that few of their colleagues "seem to have been disquieted by the fact that taking a paper-and-pencil test is very different from solving a problem in everyday life."[36]

In fact, my claim about the tendency in testing to sacrifice validity for reliability was assumed presciently by the OSS team of researchers to be a problem: "In retrospect it seems a little peculiar that we psychologists should have devoted so much time to improving the reliability of our tests and so little time to improve their validity. . . . Surely the essential criterion of a good test is its congruence with reality; its coherence with other tests is a matter of secondary concern." They went so far as to recommend that we *reverse* typical validation procedure: "Tests that are being developed should be administered only to persons who have been thoroughly studied, persons about whose activities sufficient data have already been collected."[37]

Finally, Lee Cronbach notes, in a review of these issues, that "a bad criterion may make inappropriate tests look good. Tests that predict training criteria differ from those that best predict job performance."[38] Our school-based tests are inauthentic and inappropriate as predictors for the same reason. It is time that test makers were held more accountable for their methods of validation and required to do more careful trait and job analysis to justify both the form and content of tests they design.

Authenticity

What we require, therefore, are more general design criteria that can be useful for framing challenges that are psychometrically useful but also more "authentic"—that is, that require performance faithful to criterion situations. But first we need to be clear about what we mean by *authenticity*. Here is my latest version of a much-revised set of criteria for judging the authenticity of a test.[39] Authentic tests of intellectual performance involve the following:

1. Engaging and worthy problems or questions of importance, in which students must use knowledge to fashion performances effectively and creatively. The tasks are either replicas of or analogous to the kinds of problems faced by adult citizens and consumers or professionals in the field.

2. Faithful representation of the contexts facing workers in a field of study or in the real-life "tests" of adult life. The formal *options, constraints, and access to resources* are apt as opposed to arbitrary. In particular, the use of excessive secrecy, limits on methods, the imposition of arbitrary deadlines or restraints on the use of resources to rethink, consult, revise, and so on—all with the aim of making testing more efficient—should be minimized and evaluated.

3. Nonroutine and multistage tasks—in other words, *real* problems. Recall or "plugging in" is insufficient or irrelevant. Problems require a repertoire of knowledge, good judgment in determining which knowledge is apt when and where, and skill in prioritizing and organizing the phases of problem clarification and solution.

4. Tasks that require the student to produce a *quality* product and/or performance.

5. Transparent or demystified criteria and standards. The test allows for *thorough* preparation as well as accurate self-assessment and self-adjustment by the student; questions and tasks may be discussed, clarified, and even appropriately modified, through discussion with the assessor and/or one's colleagues.

6. Interactions between assessor and assessee. Tests ask the student to *justify* answers or choices and often to respond to follow-up or probing questions.

7. Involve response-contingent challenges where the *effect* of both process and product/performance (sensitivity to audience, situation, and context) determines the quality of the result. Thus there is concurrent feedback and the possibility of self-adjustment during the test.

8.   *Trained* assessor judgment, in reference to clear and appropriate criteria. An oversight or audit function exists: there is always the possibility of questioning and perhaps altering a result, given the open and fallible nature of the formal judgment.
9.   The search for *patterns* of response in diverse settings. Emphasis is on the consistency of student work—the assessment of *habits* of mind in performance.

We might summarize these points by using the perhaps oxymoronic term "authentic simulations" to describe what we should be after in educative test design. Or, as Robert Fitzpatrick and Edward Morrison put it twenty years ago in their comprehensive review of performance testing issues, we seek two things in authentic simulations: the "fidelity" (or degree of realism) of a simulation and the "comprehensiveness" with which the many different aspects of situations are replicated. Any simulation, like any test, "involves choices and compromises." Both the fidelity and the comprehensiveness of either admit of degrees, and the purposes and budgetary or logistical constraints under which we test may cause us to settle for a lesser degree of each than is optimal. But the problems are more than practical. As Fitzpatrick and Morrison put it, "The dilemma of simulation is that increasing fidelity and comprehensiveness appear [to increase] validity but on the other hand with decreasing control [over the situation and possible responses] and thus reliability."[40] Tests are simplified of contextual "noise" and "surround" to make scores more reliable. Yet we need to maximize the fidelity and comprehensiveness of the simulation for validity reasons.

We can thus learn to negotiate the dilemma in a way that is educationally sound only by gaining better insight into what it is we must be more faithful to: the setting in which the challenge is embedded and the constraints under which the student is expected to operate. If "generic performance" is a contradiction in terms and if judgment-based performance should be a major part of testing, then testers are going to have to think through the role of context in testing.

Context, Constraints, and Authenticity

In real life, we use our intellect and acquired knowledge and skill in particular contexts to solve particular problems: as Arthur Chickering and Charles Claxton, researchers of competency-based learning, put it, "Competence is . . . situational and personal. This is the most critical principle. Competence levels and qualities are dependent upon situations and contexts. Particular contexts and situations interact with particular clusters of predispositions and abilities brought by the person. The outcomes depend upon these complex interactions . . . A person who is 'literate' in one culture can at the same time be 'illiterate' in another."[41]

Over the past few years of thinking these matters through, I have come to believe that this claim is so true that testers should pay most attention to the second of my nine criteria of authenticity (mentioned above)—that is, replicating or simulating the diverse and rich contexts of performance.

As I noted in talking about judgment, competency requires contextual sensitivity. For example, the doctor is not expert merely because he or she possesses a set of general rules and propositions in the brain or habits in the muscles—rules and habits called "medicine"; the doctor knows (or does not know) how to adapt relatively abstract guidelines of pathology and technique to this individual patient and that one, with their unique case histories. The architect does not design "structure"; the architectural student is never assessed on the design of buildings in general—whatever that is. The "test" is to design a particular building that solves a particular design problem on a particular building site for a particular client. The ability to meet that test is then transferred to new settings, scenarios, and problems—perhaps idiosyncratic ones. ("Thoughtless mastery" is possible, however, and many overly technical professionals are guilty of it: they lose their tact for the oddities and idiosyncrasies in front of them because their theories, models, and dispositions seem to work adequately when only "applied.")

Support for heightened attention to contextual detail can be found in a variety of research sources. As the OSS staff put it, a "large proportion of the determinants of the direction and efficiency of a person's behavior consists of components of the environmental situation; therefore, the more precise *and complete* the definition of the environment, the more accurate will be the predictions of behavior."[42] Bloom and his colleagues noted that synthesis as an aim is always context-sensitive: "The nature of the audience to whom the student addresses himself or his work is often crucial in determining what he does."[43] The competency-based model used in higher education, especially at Alverno College, makes "contextual validity" an essential part of the design problem.[44] And John Brown, Allan Collins, and Paul Duguid have argued the more comprehensive point that all cognition is "situated" in cultures and contexts, rendering decontextualized learning and assessment invalid and dysfunctional—"not fully productive of useful learning." (In fact, they define "authentic activity" as purposeful work embedded in the "ordinary practices" of a subject-area practice.) Since schoolwork is "very different from what authentic practitioners do" and because learning and testing tend to reflect the culture of school and not the culture represented by the field of study, "contrary to the aim of schooling, success within this culture often has little bearing on performance elsewhere."[45]

A test may always be a contrivance, then, but it should not *feel* like one or be perceived as one. Consider the best professional training and testing. Doctors and pilots are confronted with situations that replicate the challenges to be later faced, including vital human interaction complexities. (For example, many of the simulations used for recertification of professional airline pilots involve the need to work effectively as a crew; no one crew member has all the necessary information.) A context is thus realistic to the extent that we so accept the premises, constraints, and "feel" of the challenge that our desire to master it makes us lose sight of any extrinsic or contrived factors at stake—factors such as the reality that someone is evaluating us—in the same way that Outward Bound exercises and the publishing of a school newspaper for a journalism course do not feel contrived. Researchers doing competency-based research during the last few decades have consistently found that this verisimilitude and the chance to feel and be efficacious are essential not only to producing one's best performance but to student motivation.[46]

Here is a simple example of one high school teacher's initial attempt to design a performance task, and how it evolved as a concern for context was introduced. The original task (in a global studies course) required students to design a trip to China or Japan—the purpose being to determine if they knew the most important things about either country, based on the reading. But what kind of trip should be designed? For what customers? With what constraints of budget or time? The teacher then refined the task: each student had a $10,000 budget to design a one-month cultural-exchange trip for students their age. Okay, but the purpose is still too abstract: What must the tour designers accomplish? Are they trying to design a tour in the abstract or to really attract tour takers? The students were finally charged to be travel agents who would develop an extensive brochure, fully researching the cost and logistical information using the SABRE computer-reservations system (available through the school computers). One student asked during the project: "Boy, this is hard. Is this what real life is like?"

Paradoxically, the complexity of context is made manageable by contextual clues. For the student to have a clear sense of what kind of answer (with what degree of precision) fits the problem at hand, detail is essential: it clarifies the desired result, hence the criteria and standards, as we saw in the previous example. Think how difficult it would have been for students to "design a trip" with no parameters or contextual clues. Put differently, in the best case studies, the problem is solvable only within the framework of the contextual information provided. This is why business and law school cases are so difficult to write: they must be as faithful as possible to the important and unimportant situational facts. "A case typically is a record of a business issue which actually has been faced by business executives, together with surrounding facts, opinions, and prejudices upon which executive decisions depend."[47] Any criteria and standards required by a performance task should be clear and natural to the situation, in other words. (Thus there were two important oversights by the teacher of the global studies class: she failed to supply the students with model tour brochures by which standards and criteria would have been more clear and to specify an intended market for the tour so that students could match the tour and brochure content with the audience's needs.[48])

The Authenticity of Contextual Constraints

The most vital aspect of contextual fidelity has to do with the authenticity of the constraints put on performance by the demands of (mass) testing. We are effective or able to accomplish a set task to the degree that we negotiate realistic constraints. But most educational testing involves constraints that have little to do with fidelity to the criterion situation and everything to do with maintaining standardization of task and procedure. It is time that we looked at the validity questions raised by this imbalanced trade-off.

There are typically four kinds of constraints facing any performer. There are demands placed upon us by others, whether or not we would make such demands of ourselves; there are limits on the time available to complete the task;[49] there are limits, sometimes due to the situation and sometimes due to the time limits, on the human and material resources at our disposal; and there are limits on our ability to get guidance and feedback as we proceed. We can pose this as a set of design questions, then: What are *appropriate* limits on the availability of time (including time to prepare, rethink, and revise), reference materials, other people (including peers, experts, the test designer and/or the "judge"), and prior knowledge of the tasks, criteria, and standards to be mastered (often rendered problematic by the issue of test security)? I am certainly not arguing that the student should have unlimited access to resources in testing. But let us ask, What kinds of constraints authentically simulate or replicate the constraints and opportunities facing the performer in context? When are constraints authentic, and when are they inauthentic? It is often a matter of degree, but the principle needs to be maintained and defended.

Consider the following guidelines from Benjamin Bloom, George Madaus, and Thomas Hastings for testing for synthesis: "The student may attack the problem with a variety of references or other available materials as they are needed. Thus, synthesis problems may be open-book examinations, in which the student may use notes, references, the library, and other resources as appropriate. *Ideally synthesis problems should be as close as possible to the situation in which a scholar (or artist, or engineer, etc.) attacks a problem he or she is interested in. The time allowed, conditions of work, and other stipulations should be as far from the typical, controlled examination situation as possible.''*[50]

Whatever assessors are testing in a twenty-minute essay (such as found on the NAEP), therefore, most certainly is *not* the ability to write. As those of us who write for a living know, writing is revision, a constant return to the basic questions of audience and purpose—a process that is missing from standard writing tests (where there is no audience, no opportunity to reflect on each draft, and no *real* purpose).

The amount of time (in absolute terms) allowed for performing is not always what determines whether time constraints are reasonable or unreasonable; sometimes the issue is how that time is allotted. Is the limiting of a test to *one sitting* authentic? If writing is indeed revision, for example, why not allow the writing assessment to occur over three or four days, with each draft graded? Many districts now do so, including such large districts as Jefferson County, Kentucky, and Cherry Creek, Colorado.[51]

Restrictions on access to texts and human resources, on time for revision and reflection, and on opportunity to ensure that one's answer is apt and understood would seem to change what a test is measuring. What are we really testing in, say, the Advanced Placement exams, when we deny the student access to reference material and human resources—despite the obvious availability of such things in almost all criterion situations that could be imagined in the particular subject matters (such as history or mathematics)? What can the exam results possibly tell us about the student's ability to bring research to fruition, sift through facts to discern the significant from the insignificant, or use knowledge to good effect?

We do not need to keep all textbooks and other materials from students if the task is genuinely authentic. For example, in many of Connecticut's performance tasks in mathematics, the key formulas are given to the student as background to the problem. And why not allow the student to bring notes to an exam? Is this not precisely the sort of thing we really want to find out about students—whether they are organized, well-prepared, and effective at using what they know? Is that not what a test of either aptitude or achievement entails? (The test makers' defense—that I am seeking to measure something different than they claim to be measuring—is a dodge: what they are measuring is inappropriate if our aim is to see what students understand.)

Authenticity in testing, then, might well be thought of as an obligation to make the student experience questions and tasks under constraints as they typically and "naturally" occur, with access to the tools that are usually available for solving such problems.

The Relationship Between Authenticity and Validity

Attention to the authenticity of purposes and constraints in context and to the perhaps dispositional nature of understanding makes clear why a performance-based *task* is not necessarily a valid or authentic *test*. Have we sampled the performance domain fairly or comprehensively? Would scores be different if we used different prompts or different genres? Have we gathered sufficient evidence, using diverse forms and diverse settings, of the *pattern* of responses that indicates competence? These are questions that demand every test maker's attention.

And the problem is not limited to the selection of tasks. Most of the scoring rubrics that I have encountered seem invalid to me. We are scoring what is easy, uncontroversial, and typical in English classes, not necessarily what is apt for identifying exemplary writing or apt for the situational demands of real-world writing. (This is thus a more subtle form of the failure of educators to escape the school culture and begin to rely on the conditions at play in professional cultures,[52] as noted in my earlier discussion of "situated cognition.")

Consider the following scoring criteria for essay writing and the descriptor for the top point on the scale. Although this particular list of criteria is from New Jersey's writing assessment, it is typical of many state and district rubrics now in use:

Criteria:
  Organization/Content
  Usage
  Sentence Construction
  Mechanics
Descriptor for top score:

Organization/Content: Samples have an opening and closing. The responses relate to the topic and have a single focus. They are well-developed, complete compositions that are organized and progress logically from beginning to end. A variety of cohesive devices are present, resulting in a fluent response. Many of these writers take compositional risks resulting in highly effective, vivid responses.

Sentence Construction: Samples demonstrate syntactic and verbal sophistication through an effective variety of sentences and/or rhetorical modes. There will be very few, if any, errors in sentence construction.

Mechanics and Usage: Few, if any, errors.

What a bore. There is nothing in this scoring system that rewards style, imagination, or ability to keep the reader interested. Yet we see this limitation in almost every writing assessment, including those of the NAEP. In reviewing student stories contained in portfolios as part of a pilot project to score locally completed work, the NAEP rubrics emphasized only formal criteria. Here is a descriptor for a top-level story: "Paper describes a sequence of episodes in which almost all story elements are well developed (i.e. setting, episodes, characters' goals, or problems to be solved). The resolution of the goals or problems at the end are elaborated. The events are presented and elaborated in a cohesive way."[53] Surely this is not the best description possible of a good story! But habits of testing for merely formal problems run deep. In working with a department of English teachers on some schoolwide scoring rubrics, it took me two long sessions to get them to admit that whether or not a paper was "interesting" was of primary importance. But they had never been willing to grade for that criterion, nor were they confident that such a criterion should be in a formal rubric.

The reader should not infer that I believe that criteria of the sort listed above do not matter. They are important, of course; but they are merely necessary, not sufficient. To see how we might employ better criteria that are more closely linked to the reason writers write and the effects writers hope to have on an audience, while still being mindful of other, more formal criteria, consider *clarity, persuasiveness, memorability,* and *enticingness,* offered by

Allan C. Collins and Dieter G. Gentner.[54] Note that these criteria, which flow from a careful analysis of the purpose of the task, cannot likely be met if there are distracting errors of the organizational or mechanical kind. But we correctly alert the writer to the fact that writing ought to be worth reading, not merely formally "correct."

As an aside, it is worth noting that many practitioners do not understand this logic of assessment design. They rarely see, without a good deal of training, that the criteria of a competence must be explicit and logically prior to the design of any test task, based on an analysis of the characteristics of genuine success. One might well say that the tragic flaw that renders many teacher tests invalid is the teacher's habit of designing the task first and thinking through the validity concerns later. This is an inevitable problem, given the teacher's tendency to try to design effective instructional activities as opposed to tasks designed backward from the results one hopes to obtain; it is a problem that we must do a better job of addressing in professional development.

For scoring rubrics to be valid, the criteria have to be more than "face authentic," in other words. A test should enable us to effectively and validly *discriminate* between performances of different degrees of quality. As a result, scoring rubrics must be based on a careful analysis of existing performances of varying quality. We must possess models of exemplary and not-so-exemplary performance and tell the two apart on the basis of apt reasons. The discriminations we make must be valid, therefore, not arbitrary; here too, reliability is not enough. We should be basing our judgments on the most *salient* and *educative* distinctions, not on those most easy and uncontroversial to score. Rubrics that rely heavily on value-laden or comparative words are also guilty of sacrificing validity for reliability. For example, to say that a 6 is a "good" paper while a 5 is only "average," or that the better essays have "more" reasons than the not-so-good essays, is to make the judgment arbitrary—more like a norm-referenced test than a criterion-referenced test. The explanation is simple enough: we can easily imagine the arbitrary criteria *not* being met by excellent papers: many fine essays offer few reasons for a position; many dissertations with 400 footnotes have nothing to say.

The foreign-language proficiency guidelines of the American Council on the Teaching of Foreign Languages (ACTFL) show what all scoring systems should strive to emulate. In their scoring descriptors, the scores reflect *empirically grounded traits* about the speaker's performance, irrespective of the performer's age or experience, based on years of categorizing particular performances into levels of competence. Thus the guidelines identify typical errors for each stage of language performance. For example, the mistake of responding to the question, *"Quel sport préférez-vous?"* with the answer, *"Vous préférez le sport tennis"* is noted as "an error characteristic of speakers" at the midnovice level, where "Utterances are marked and often flawed by repetition of an interlocutor's words. . . ."[55] These are the kinds of standards that need to be developed in all subjects.[56]

Here again we see that the most valid design procedure involves working backward from the criterion performance and concrete models of diverse levels of performance. What too few practitioners seem to understand is that scoring rubrics are derived *after* we have a range of performances in hand, so as to ensure that our descriptors and discrimination procedures are not arbitrary. Put simply, no one should design any performance task "for keeps" without having first obtained a sample of diverse exemplary performances and a sample of the range of possible performance.

The Context of Testing

Contextual issues relate to test administration itself. There is no such thing as an invariant and generic test situation—one in which students can be assumed to always reveal what they "know." Contextual factors in the test situation itself can affect what is *really* being measured—irrespective of the test designer's intent, and especially if the test does not permit the student to explain answers. As Messick argues, there is a problem of "context of measurement," which includes "factors in the environmental background as well as the assessment setting."[57] He and others (notably, Harold Berlak, and John Fredriksen and Allan Collins[58]) have argued the issue more broadly by making the point that validity must be analyzed in terms of the context in which testing occurs—that is, whether the test is used for the purposes for which it was intended—and the consequences that accrue from it. Not only the meaning of test scores is important, but also their "relevance, utility, import . . . and the functional worth of scores in terms of the social consequences of their use."[59]

The implications are considerable, once we grasp the fact that student responses are colored by the particular task and setting: "We are thus confronted with the fundamental question of whether the meaning of a measure is context-specific or whether it generalizes across contexts [since the] very nature of the task might be altered by the operation of constraining or facilitating factors in the specific situation." That is why validity inheres in the *interpretation* of a score, not as a property of the test itself. Messick soberly concludes by urging "that the role of context in test interpretation and test use be repeatedly investigated or monitored as a recurrent issue."[60] Can test makers honestly admit that they do such monitoring regularly?

Consider the following example of what happens when context is not considered in testing. The kindergarten teachers in Ellenville, New York, were puzzled by the results on a commercial standardized test used in the district. Almost every student had gotten a simple question wrong. The question that caused the students trouble seemed simple enough: "Which one of the animals is a farm animal?" (In standardized testing for young children, the multiple choices are in the form of pictures, the "right" one to be selected after the test administrator reads each question.[61]) The choices: a picture of a whale (or porpoise?) diving in the water, a giraffe, and a chicken. Why was the chicken not selected by the students? Because not more than twenty miles from Ellenville is the Catskill Game Farm, where the star attraction (also represented on its large billboards in the area) is—you guessed it—a giraffe.

What seemed the only reasonable answer to the students was correct in context; what seemed the only apt answer to the test maker turned out to be wrong in a specific context. Therein lies an inherent problem with tests that are both generic and nonresponsive. In a country with no agreed-upon universal syllabi or texts, test questions must be stripped from their natural setting; yet by depriving students of situational feedback and detail, we violate one of the most basic norms of social interaction and the "tests" that it provides. All questions are normally asked in context, often assuming a purpose, culture, audience, and situational constraints—sometimes to the point that the "test" is about our ability to read the cues properly. If as we drive somewhere, you yell from the back seat, "When will we get to Chicago?" and I answer, "We've got 200 miles to go," my answer is not "wrong." You understand my answer as apt with a moment's thought (since we both know that the speedometer is visible and that you can see we are moving along at sixty miles an hour). Similarly, if your math teacher says, "Do the odd problems for tonight's homework," we can assume that she means the odd-numbered ones, not the most bizarre ones. (Though students can be masterful in exploiting such inherent ambiguity to their benefit.)

We fail to grasp the danger of traditional generic testing of students if we view the giraffe story as evidence of a mistake by the test company. On the contrary, as the Messick argument suggests, we may be assuming far too much about the stability and transferability of student knowledge and too little about the influence of testing conditions. The particular "mistake" concerning the giraffe may be a sign that important arguments about "the fundamental question of whether the meaning of a measure is context-specific or whether it generalizes across contexts" have not gotten an adequate hearing. Tests that are designed to yield stable scores, oblivious to the local syllabus, culture, and milieu—that is, the context—may end up testing only a trivial residue of a context-bound education; and ironically, tests of this sort make test items harder for students than they normally would be, because all typical contextual cues and responses are removed. And those researchers who caution us in the use of performance tests, advising that there is inadequate generalizability when tasks vary slightly, may be looking through the wrong end of the telescope: intellectual performance may be more contextually sensitive than we have heretofore been able to see or willing to admit, given a psychometric paradigm that (naively) assumes the student performer to be capable of consistent performance.

It is therefore not proper to say that a student either does or does not "possess" knowledge. Rather, the test taker acts knowledgeably or ignorantly—*in context*.[62] Context not only enables the student to know whether *chicken* or *giraffe* is the right answer *in this case;* it also lets the test scorer know whether an answer is right or wrong *in this case.* What, then, is being assessed when the student answers a question but the judge is mute or the environment fails to respond? Certainly not competence.

The use of the word *understand* as opposed to *know* makes the point more clearly: we do not understand things in general; we understand (or misunderstand) a person or an answer *in context*— "I understand what you mean," "I see what is required here," and so on. Perfectly bright and able people who are effective in one setting or job can screw up in another: competency is context-bound. There is an obligation on testers, therefore, to seek each test taker's rationale for answers. If they do so, there is no good episte-mological or cognitive reason to assume that test scores *should* be stable (as most test programs tacitly assume) if we vary the task or context slightly.

The same concern with the contextual nature of questions and answers applies to test formats. Though there is disagreement on the subject, Messick, Cronbach, Fredriksen, and others have all suggested that significantly varying the format of a test changes student scores and their meaning. Cronbach goes so far as to say that "the form of the task can be as important as the substance."[63] This seems particularly true if we begin with complex criterion situations instead of devising mere open-ended forms of indirect items.[64]

The argument for authenticity that I and others have made should thus be understood as something more substantial and less naive than some measurement folks would have us believe.[65] If validity refers to the implications or consequences of the inferences made, as Messick and others have argued, these issues cannot be ignored. As Messick puts it, in quoting Cronbach, " 'The bottom line is that validators have an obligation to review whether a practice has appropriate consequences for individuals and institutions, and especially to guard against adverse consequences. You . . . may prefer to exclude reflection on consequences from meanings of the word *validation* but you cannot deny the obligation.' But we would prefer a somewhat stronger phrasing, because the meaning of validation should not be considered a preference."[66]

Task Worthiness and Incentives:
Another Look at Face Validity

In a student-centered view of assessment, we perhaps ought to res-
urrect an old concept that is now often pooh-poohed by psychometricians: face validity. Is the test, "on the face of it," a proper test
of the ability or knowledge in question? Though this concept was
once dignified enough to warrant discussion in measurement texts,
few modern experts give any formal consideration to the matter
these days.[67]

In one standard educational measurement textbook that addresses the issue, the authors state that, in determining criterion-
related validity, "we care very little what a test looks like." Yet a
footnote to this sentence adds that the claim is not "entirely true,"
since what the test looks like "may be of importance in determining
its acceptability and reasonableness to those who will be tested."
Ironically—and tellingly, as I noted in Chapter One, in discussing
the legal issues surrounding validity—the example chosen concerns
adult pilots, not young students: "Thus, a group of would-be pilots
may be more ready to accept an arithmetic test dealing with wind
drift and fuel consumption than they would the same problems
phrased in terms of cost of crops or of recipes for baking cookies.
This appearance of reasonableness is sometimes spoken of as face
validity."[68]

Messick, in his analysis of the concept of validity and its
history, notes that, although "in the technical sense" face validity
is not a form of validity, "whether the test is judged relevant to its
objectives . . . can affect examinee cooperation and motivation. . . .
Therefore, it is argued that face *in*validity should be avoided whenever possible."[69] (Surprisingly, in an otherwise exhaustive account
of how consequential validity might be better established, Messick
offers no specific consideration of the consequences of a test to the
individual test taker.)

Anna Anastasi has probably written the most about face validity and its role in validation. In the most recent edition of her
textbook on psychological testing, she argues that while face validity "is not validity in the technical sense" (since it refers "not to

what the test actually measures but to what it appears to measure"),
it is vital for "rapport and public relations." In fact, she argues that
"face validity itself is a desirable feature of tests." She too cites
examples of adult negative reactions to items that were too much
like school items; they were "frequently met with resistance and
criticism." Having argued that the issue is one of rapport merely,
she goes on to say more forcefully that "if test content appears
irrelevant, inappropriate, silly, or childish, the result will be poor
cooperation, *regardless of the actual validity of the test.*"[70]

It is this last phrase that needs to be pondered. To take an
extreme case, why would we *assume* that a test is "technically" valid
if it is universally ridiculed and resisted by takers or users? How can
an inference about a score not be conditioned by the user's response
to the test? (Of note in this regard is that Anastasi speaks only of
the content of the test, not its form). If, for example, performance
tasks are in fact "far more likely to elicit a student's full repertoire
of skills," as Howard Gardner's research shows, then why is the
validity of tests that do not evoke these responses not open to question?[71] What if there is *always* a more engaging immediacy (and
hence better evocation of know-how) provided by direct assessment?
What if indirect forms of assessment so distance some students from
contextual "tests" of understanding that they lose interest in the
ultimate criterion? While the relative merits of directness and indi-
rectness in test construction have been argued on technical grounds
in the testing literature, there is no mention of the possible effect
of this technical decision on the test takers.[72]

Thus, although face validity should be considered, to focus
only on it is to miss a more important point about the incentives
to perform well that might be found to inhere in more authentic
forms of assessment and that might change the implications of
scores. Gardner, for example, suggests that assessment in the "context of students working on problems, projects, or products which
genuinely engage them" can "hold their interest and motivate them
to do well," suggesting that a more substantive question about validity is at stake.[73] And John Raven is prepared to question the
validity of any test that ignores motivational issues: "Important
abilities demand time, energy, and effort. As a result, people only
display them when they are undertaking activities which are impor-

tant to them. It is meaningless to attempt to assess a person's abilities except in relation to their valued goals."[74] Raven acknowledges that such views are in "sharp conflict" with traditional views, but there is a commonsense appeal here that deserves better exploration at least.

Anastasi approvingly cites a "provocative" article calling attention to the "paucity of available research on face validity, despite its probable contribution to prevalent attitudes toward tests."[75] In that 1985 report by B. Nevo, the results were so promising that the author recommended that both qualitative and quantitative data about face validity be regularly reported in test manuals.

It therefore seems not only reasonable and fair but apt for more comprehensive validation to give the (older) student (and/or teacher, when the test is externally devised) a chance to judge a test's appropriateness, especially considering how easy it is for all adult parties to confuse their intent with their actual effect. (New York does give teachers this opportunity in the Regents exam program.) Consider, for example, the student questionnaire shown in Exhibit 7.3, which I devised as a simple way for teachers to assess the students' sense of a test's aptness and fairness. It can be given out after every major middle or high school test.

I am not proposing that students have the final say, nor would I claim that their judgment is necessarily accurate or in any way technically informed. What I am asking is this: What if we find that particular tests or sets of test questions are found to be of significantly less value or justification from the test taker's and test user's point of view than other tests they encounter? Surely it is in the tester's interest to give the student a voice, as one factor in considering the matter of validity. Many respected testing specialists have advocated such techniques as part of all test piloting.[76]

How one's work and talents are judged is of paramount concern to everyone. Thus fairness demands that the test taker's response be solicited and pondered. We routinely assume that adults have the right to a say in performance appraisal systems, through either tacit or explicit discussion (and often through formal negotiations). So why should students be perpetually shut out of the discussion?[77]

Exhibit 7.3. Student Questionnaire on the Test.

Please circle the number that best represents your response to each statement (from "strongly agree," 1, to "strongly disagree," 5).

1. This was a fair test of what we learned.	1 2 3 4 5	
2. This test was easy, if you studied for it.	1 2 3 4 5	
3. This kind of test really makes you think.	1 2 3 4 5	
4. This kind of test is new for me.	1 2 3 4 5	
5. I did a good job of preparing for this test.	1 2 3 4 5	
6. You did a good job of preparing us for the test.	1 2 3 4 5	
7. I was unfortunately surprised by the questions you chose.	1 2 3 4 5	
8. The directions were clear.	1 2 3 4 5	
9. You provided lots of different ways for us to show that we understand what was taught.	1 2 3 4 5	
10. There was enough choice in the questions we could select to answer.	1 2 3 4 5	
11. Some questions should have been worth more points and/or others worth less.	1 2 3 4 5	
12. We were allowed appropriate access to resources (books, notes, and so on) during the test.	1 2 3 4 5	
13. I expected the grade I got, once I saw the test questions and then later found out the right answers.	1 2 3 4 5	
14. There wasn't enough time to do a good job; I know more than I was able to show.	1 2 3 4 5	

The "Value" in Validity Concerns

One reason that validity concerns are so easily finessed is that they demand more than technical measurement expertise. Any inference about test results is a complex act of judgment involving the consideration of different kinds of data and our intellectual values.[78] As Messick has cast it, "To validate an interpretive inference is to ascertain the degree to which multiple lines of evidence are consonant with the inference, while establishing that alternative inferences are less well supported."[79] As he notes, establishing the validity of scores is thus akin to establishing the worth of a theory in science: we look for patterns and consistency; we examine multiple points of view and try out other possible inferences (which are always available) to see which one is least susceptible to criticism. This process is more complex and demanding than calculating reliability coefficients.

I am not arguing that indirect tests are inherently defective or prone to invalid inferences about performance. I am fully aware that certain constructs, such as critical thinking or reading comprehension, do not easily admit of direct testing. I am also aware that an indirect test can yield positive correlations with some criterion situations (for example, vocabulary tests as predictors of verbal-role success.) My fear is that validity has deteriorated in mass educational testing to excessive concern with *content* validity, the use of highly questionable methods for instantiating certain constructs, and mere correlations with other indirect tests (in an endless circle of results on questionable tests being used to validate questionable tests, in other words).

At bottom is a philosophical problem of major proportions about the purpose of schooling: Is schooling meant to yield common knowledge? If so, then it makes perfect sense to think of tests as properly focusing on what students hold in common. But what if education is a personal, idiosyncratic affair, where the meaning and personal effectiveness that I derive from coursework is more important than what knowledge we all end up holding in common? In that case, a standardized, indirect test—of any kind—would make no sense: What could we possibly mean by a standardized test of the meaning of educative experience? What, then, of the validity of aptitude tests if I cannot state with precision: aptitude *for what future role or aspiration?*

Consider Albert Shanker's long-held view that the determination of achievement should be thought of as Scouts think of merit badges: the determination of achievement should be based on a person's demonstrated ability to use knowledge "in the field" (literally, in his case; he is a bird-watcher and received one of his Scout badges in that activity), resulting in an *inherently* personalized collection of badges. ("That's the kind of knowledge that doesn't leave you."[80]) Nor are the collections of badges uniform across students even if each badge requirement is standard (and to a high standard).

As I mentioned in Chapter One, this is the deeper issue raised by the SCANS report with regard to the meaning of a transcript. If a transcript is really better thought of as a résumé, as SCANS claims, then what does that suggest about testing, about teaching, about curriculum design, and about the current myopic search for a "national standard"? It suggests, at the very least, that a penchant for testing everyone on the same things is misguided. While the issue is debated further, let us at least demand that test makers become more obligated to link their tests to the tasks, contexts, and "feel" of real-world challenges.

Notes

1. Readers who want to review the most up-to-date thinking on this score are encouraged to review J. Millman and J. Greene, "The Specification and Development of Tests of Achievement and Ability," in R. L. Linn, ed., *Educational Measurement*, 3rd ed. (New York: American Council on Education/Macmillan, 1989), J. L. Cronbach, *Essentials of Psychological Testing*, 5th ed. (New York: HarperCollins, 1989), R. Linn, E. Baker, and S. Dunbar, "Complex, Performance-Based Assessment: Expectations and Validation Criteria," *Educational Researcher* 20 (1991): 15–21.

2. L. B. Resnick, "Tests as Standards of Achievement in School," in Educational Testing Service, ed., *The Uses of Standardized Tests in American Education*, Proceedings of the 1989 ETS Invitational Conference (Princeton N.J.: Educational Testing Service, 1990).

3. See E. Baker, M. Freeman, and S. Clayton, "Cognitive Assessment of History for Large-Scale Testing," in M. C. Wittrock and E. L. Baker, eds., *Testing and Cognition* (Englewood Cliffs, N.J.: Prentice-Hall, 1991).

4. R. Glaser, "Expertise and Assessment," in M. C. Wittrock and E. L. Baker, eds., *Testing and Cognition* (Englewood Cliffs, N.J.: Prentice-Hall, 1991), p. 28.

5. W. G. Perry, Jr., *Forms of Intellectual and Ethical Develop-*

ment in the College Years, rev. ed. (Troy, Mo.: Holt, Rinehart & Winston, 1970).

6. R. Glaser, "Cognitive and Environmental Perspectives on Assessing Achievement," in Educational Testing Service, ed., *Assessment in the Service of Learning,* Proceedings of the 1987 ETS Invitational Conference (Princeton, N.J.: Educational Testing Service, 1988), p. 47.

7. The passage purported to be from a textbook considered for adoption is from Department of Health, Education, and Welfare, ed., *The American Revolution: Selections from Secondary School History Books of Other Nations,* HEW Publication OE 76-19124 (Washington, D.C.: U.S. Government Printing Office, 1976), pp. 59–74.

8. Glaser, "Expertise and Assessment," pp. 28–29.

9. From L. B. Resnick, *Education and Learning to Think* (Washington, D.C.: National Academy Press, 1987), p. 3.

10. B. S. Bloom, ed., *Taxonomy of Educational Objectives,* Vol. 1: *Cognitive Domain* (White Plains, N.Y.: Longman, 1956), pp. 162, 173.

11. It is worth noting that "application" in this sense was *not* a higher-order skill for Bloom and his colleagues; and rightly so.

12. See W. C. Ward "Measurement Research That Will Change Test Design for the Future," in Educational Testing Service, ed., *Assessment in the Service of Learning,* Proceedings of the 1987 ETS Invitational Conference (Princeton, N.J.: Educational Testing Service, 1988), and C. V. Bunderson, D. Inouye and J. Olsen, "The Four Generations of Computerized Educational Measurement," in Linn, ed., *Educational Measurement.*

13. William James made this same point 100 years ago in *Talks to Teachers* (New York: W. W. Norton, [1899] 1958).

14. Some readers might think I am forgetting about test reliability with such a claim. On the contrary. The standard psychometric conception of reliability assumes that the *performer* is always reliable—that only *scores* can be unreliable. As we shall see below, this is a fundamental epistemological error as well as a violation of common sense.

15. M. McCloskey, A. Carramazza, and B. Green, "Curvilinear

Motion in the Absence of External Forces," *Science* 210 (1980):
1139–1141, and H. Gardner, *The Unschooled Mind: How
Children Think and How Schools Should Teach* (New York:
Basic Books, 1991). As the history of such "fantastic" ideas as
calculus shows, a new conceptual insight is often resisted by
sophisticated adult professionals. All new ideas face powerful
resistance, suggesting Piaget's prescience when he proposed a
"cognitive unconscious" parallel to the affective unconscious
and the resistance it exerts as postulated by depth psychology.
(See J. Piaget, "Affective Unconscious and the Cognitive Unconscious," in *The Child and Reality: Problems of Genetic
Psychology* (New York: Grossman, 1973).

16. J. Dewey, "Moral Principles in Education," in J. A. Boydston,
ed., *The Middle Works of John Dewey: 1899–1924* (Carbondale: Southern Illinois University Press, [1909] 1977). See T.
S. Kuhn, *The Structure of Scientific Revolutions*, 2nd ed.
(Chicago: University of Chicago Press, 1970), for a more modern and detailed account of this view of the history of science.

17. Let me offer a caution to the language-sensitive reader: I am
speaking about higher-order habits—what are often referred to
as "dispositions." For a good account of the technical differences between "habits" and "dispositions," see G. Ryle, *The
Concept of Mind* (London: Hutchinson House, 1949), and J.
Passmore, *The Philosophy of Teaching* (Cambridge, Mass.:
Harvard University Press, 1980).

18. The literature on critical thinking is ironically muddled on
this issue. The "dispositions" are treated with obvious unease.
Everyone acknowledges the importance of certain habits of
mind in the development of thinking skills, but no one knows
how to assign them a logical status or draw out the proper and
far-reaching curricular and assessment implications. See, for
example, the work of R. H. Ennis, one of the pioneers in the
field. He now lists "thirteen essential dispositions" (Ennis, in
Baron and Sternberg [1987], also Ennis [1985]). He describes
a course that would develop critical "abilities" (meaning skill)
and then adds, confusingly, "The dispositions would be introduced when students are ready and would be continuously
emphasized thereafter." After an extensive analysis of the req-

uisite skills, he devotes a short paragraph at the end to the topic of dispositions: "Critical thinking is not enough. One must have these critical thinking dispositions as well," (p. 24). Yet, after lamenting that the appropriate dispositions are often absent, Ennis offers no curricular insights on how to develop them. Baron, in the same anthology, notes that "program goals for teaching thinking too rarely include references to changes in students' attitudes and dispositions. . . . This area is ripe for creativity and invention" (p. 242).

19. Dewey, "Moral Principles in Education," p. 290.

20. J. Dewey, *How We Think: A Restatement of the Relation of Reflective Thinking to the Educative Process* (Lexington, Mass.: Heath, 1933), pp. 119–120.

21. See A. Chickering and C. Claxton, "What Is Competence?" in R. Nickse and others, *Competency-Based Education* (New York: Teachers College Press, 1981), pp. 9 –11.

22. A. Binet, and T. Simon, "The Development of Intelligence in the Child," in *The Development of Intelligence in Children* (Salem, N.H.: Ayer, 1983), p. 42.

23. Ryle, *The Concept of Mind*, p. 47.

24. Office of Strategic Services, *Assessment of Men: Selection of Personnel for the Office of Strategic Services* (Troy, Mo.: Holt, Rinehart & Winston, 1948), pp. 39, 49.

25. N. Frederiksen, "The Real Test Bias," *American Psychologist* 39 (1984): 193–202, p. 199.

26. See R. Gagné, "Learning Outcomes and Their Effects: Useful Categories of Human Performance," *American Psychologist* 39 (1984): 377–385.

27. This definition, used by the Fund for the Improvement of Post-Secondary Education, was formulated by T. Corcoran and is quoted in Nickse and others, *Competency-Based Education*, p. 10.

28. G. Grant and Associates, *On Competence: A Critical Analysis of Competence-Based Reforms in Higher Education* (San Francisco: Jossey-Bass, 1979), p. 6.

29. S. Messick, "Meaning and Values in Test Validation: The Science and Ethics of Assessment," *Educational Researcher* 18 (1989): 5–11, p. 10.

30. R. Bond, "Making Innovative Assessment Fair and Valid," in Educational Testing Service, ed., *What We Can Learn from Performance Assessment for the Professions*, Proceedings of the 1992 ETS Invitational Conference (Princeton, N.J.: Educational Testing Service, 1993), pp. 64–65.

31. E. F. Lindquist, as quoted in Millman and Greene, p. 348.

32. D. McClelland, "Testing for Competence Rather Than for 'Intelligence,'" *American Psychologist* 28 (1973): 1–14, pp. 7–8.

33. Frederiksen, "The Real Test Bias," pp. 199–200.

34. Office of Strategic Services, *Assessment of Men*, p. 42.

35. From "Educational Lessons from Wartime Training," as quoted by W. Neumann, "Educational Responses to the Concern for Proficiency," in Grant and Associates, *On Competence*, p. 85.

36. Office of Strategic Services, *Assessment of Men*, p. 42. Frederiksen ("The Real Test Bias") notes that most validation research is done "backwards," in that studies of the appropriateness of indirect tests usually involve other indirect but open-ended tests. Similarly, McClelland ("Testing for Competence Rather Than for 'Intelligence'") observes that almost all validity coefficients derive from either other indirect tests or college grade-point averages.

37. Office of Strategic Services, *Assessment of Men*, p. 42.

38. L. J. Cronbach, *Essentials of Psychological Testing*, 5th ed. (New York: HarperCollins, 1990), pp. 414–415.

39. See G. Wiggins, "A True Test: Toward More Authentic and Equitable Assessment," *Phi Delta Kappan* 70 (1989): 703–713.

40. R. Fitzpatrick and E. J. Morrison, "Performance and Product Evaluation," in F. L. Finch, ed., *Educational Performance Assessment* (Chicago: Riverside/Houghton Mifflin, [1971] 1991), pp. 92–93.

41. Chickering and Claxton, "What Is Competence?" p. 11.

42. Office of Strategic Services, *Assessment of Men* (emphasis added).

43. Bloom, ed., *Taxonomy of Educational Objectives*, p. 168.

44. See G. Rogers, *Validating College Outcomes with Institutionally Developed Instruments: Issues in Maximizing Contextual*

Validity (Milwaukee, Wis.: Office of Research and Evaluation, Alverno College, 1988).

45. J. S. Brown, A. Collins, and P. Duguid, "Situated Cognition and the Culture of Learning," *Educational Researcher* 18 (Jan./Feb. 1989): 32-42, p. 34.

46. See Nickse and others, *Competency-Based Education.*

47. C. Gragg, "Because Wisdom Can't Be Told," in M. P. McNair and A. Hersum, eds., *The Case Method at the Harvard Business School* (New York: McGraw-Hill, 1954). Available as a reprint from the Harvard Business School Publishing Division, Boston, Mass.: HBS Case 9-451-005, p. 6.

48. See Linn, Baker, and Dunbar, "Complex, Performance-Based Assessment," for further discussion of validity issues.

49. However, many New York State tests do allow the student what amounts to unlimited time (all day), given the shortness of the test. And in most cases, certifiably learning-disabled students are allowed unlimited time on the SATs and many state achievement tests.

50. B. S. Bloom, G. F. Madaus, and J. T. Hastings, *Evaluation to Improve Learning* (New York: McGraw-Hill, 1981), p. 268 (emphasis added).

51. Yes, yes, I know the issue is *really* one of cheating: let the teacher "sign off" on the papers, then, certifying authorship, as schools have long done in Australia (and now in Vermont) when the state assessment is built, in part, out of local work submitted to external examiners.

52. See Brown, Collins, and Duguid, "Situated Cognition and the Culture of Learning."

53. C. Gentile, *Exploring New Methods for Collecting Students' School-Based Writing* (Washington, D.C.: U.S. Department of Education, 1991), p. 20.

54. A. Collins and D. Gentner, cited in J. R. Fredriksen and A. Collins, "A Systems Approach to Educational Testing," *Educational Researcher* 18 (Dec. 1989): 27–32, p. 30.

55. American Council on the Teaching of Foreign Languages, *ACTFL Provisional Proficiency Guidelines* (Hastings-on-Hudson, N.Y.: ACTFL Materials Center, 1982), p. 7.

56. Note that most of the British scales mentioned earlier and the

proposed scales in New York and other states do not solve this problem. The rubrics use vague, general language that invariably leans too heavily on relative comparisons—a 5 paper is "less thorough" than a 6 paper, for example. There is thus no criterion-referenced standard at work. Look at state writing assessment rubrics used for different grade-levels: they are almost indistinguishable, showing that the "standard" is relative to the anchor papers assessors choose, not embedded in the language of the rubric.

57.   S. Messick, "Validity," in Linn, ed., *Educational Measurement,* p. 14.

58.   H. Berlak and others, Toward a New Science of Educational Testing and Assessment (New York: State University of New York Press, 1992); Fredriksen and Collins, "A Systems Approach to Educational Testing."

59.   Messick, "Meaning and Values in Test Validation," p. 5.

60.   Messick, "Validity," pp. 14–15.

61.   Reliability problems abound in testing our youngest children this way (one must constantly make sure that the students are looking at the right line of pictures), which is why many districts and states have banned such testing. The test companies use little icons or tokens for each line of choices in the test booklet; the five- and six-year-olds pick up a token and move it to the appropriate line of answer options on verbal command.

62.   See Ryle, *The Concept of Mind,* for the definitive account of "knowledge" as intelligent performance, not the "mental" application of declarative propositions to situations.

63.   Cronbach, *Essentials of Psychological Testing,* 4th ed., p. 146.

64.   As reported by Frederiksen ("The Real Test Bias") in reviewing the literature on the subject.

65.   See Wiggins, "A True Test," and D. Archbald and F. Newmann, *Beyond Standardized Testing: Authentic Academic Achievement in the Secondary School* (Reston, Va.: NASSP Publications, 1988). Compare F. L. Finch, "Issues in Educational Performance Evaluation," in Finch, ed., *Educational Performance Assessment,* for the view that the idea of authenticity is a big fuss about a naive idea.

66. Messick, "Meaning and Values in Test Validation," p. 11.
67. See A. Anastasi, *Psychological Testing,* (New York: Macmillan, 1954.)
68. R. L. Thorndike and E. P. Hagan, *Measurement and Evaluation in Psychology and Education,* 4th ed. (New York: Wiley, 1955), p. 60.
69. Messick, "Validity," p. 19.
70. Anastasi, *Psychological Testing,* 6th ed., p. 144 (emphasis added).
71. Gardner, *The Unschooled Mind,* p. 93.
72. Millman and Greene, "The Specification and Development of Tests of Achievement and Ability," p. 348.
73. Gardner, *The Unschooled Mind,* p. 93.
74. J. Raven, "A Model of Competence, Motivation, and Behavior, and a Paradigm for Assessment," in Berlak and others, *Toward a New Science of Educational Testing and Assessment,* pp. 89–90.
75. Anastasi, *Psychological Testing,* 6th ed., p. xxx.
76. Anastasi, *Psychological Testing,* 4th ed. See also W. Haney and L. Scott, "Talking with Children About Tests: An Exploratory Study of Test Item Ambiguity," in K. O. Freedle and R. P. Duran, eds., *Cognitive and Linguistic Analyses of Test Performance* (Norwood, N.J.: Ablex, 1987).
77. As I noted earlier, the New York truth-in-testing law that led to test companies having to publish test questions after the fact was possible (according to measurement expert Walt Haney) only because the suit was brought by politically powerful college and graduate students. Minors have no lobbying group or advocacy group other than groups such as FairTest.
78. See Cronbach, *Essentials of Psychological Testing,* and Messick, "Meaning and Values in Test Validation," for example.
79. Messick, "Meaning and Values in Test Validation," p. 13.
80. A. Shanker, "The Social and Educational Dilemmas of Test Use," in Educational Testing Service, ed., *The Uses of Standardized Tests in American Education,* Proceedings of the 1989 ETS Invitational Conference (Princeton, N.J.: Educational Testing Service, 1990), p. 10.

8 | Accountability: Standards, Not Standardization

Various people who reviewed the initial draft of my manuscript suggested that the book required a discussion of accountability, even though accountability is a concept tangential to my purpose. I have somewhat begrudgingly complied—reluctant not because the topic is not important (it is) but because even calm, rational folks get carried away on this subject. We simply assume, without much thought, that accountability is possible only through standardized testing. That just is not true, however, as a look at other institutions—especially private sector ones—reveals, and as the following remark from a Dow Chemical vice president suggests: "Quality is the customer's perception of excellence. Quality is what the customer says he needs, not what *our* tests indicate is satisfactory."[1] This final chapter is devoted to a discussion of why this is so.

Accountability as Structured Responsiveness

The opinions that we, as a country, hold on the subject of accountability are woefully habit-bound. One indication of this is the fact that the most heat I have ever taken for a position came in response to this question, posed in a discussion paper for a working group looking at kindergarten-through-graduate school assessment policy: Who really wants and needs easy comparability of schools anyway? A dozen intelligent folks, from within education and from the policy and legislative world, reacted as if I had said something

256

preposterous. It is *obviously* necessary to think of accountability as comparability, they said. But who is it who so obviously wants such comparability—especially as a function of test scores? When have test scores led to school improvement of an essential kind? More to the point, to whom are schools truly accountable (in the sense of morally responsible)? If the answer is "the school's clients and customers" (not oversight agencies), as I believe it must be, then standardized testing has little to do with accountability, since the client's satisfaction or dissatisfaction will be due to more routine and direct indicators.[2]

Accountability exists when the service provider is obligated to respond to criticism from those whom the provider serves. The ability to hold the service provider responsible depends upon a moral-legal-economic framework in which the client has formal power to demand a response from the provider, to influence the providing, and to change service providers if the responses are deemed unacceptable. Any tests required should merely make it easier for clients to exercise their rights; they should merely help them better understand the quality of the service provided.

The dictionary definition of *accountability*, which includes a formal, legal element, makes this clearer. *The Oxford English Dictionary* defines the adjective *accountable* as "liable to be called to account, or to answer for responsibilities and conduct: answerable, responsible, amenable." Accountability is a moral (and sometimes, by extension, legal) obligation to be responsive to those with whom I have a formal relationship. And as the word's roots in legal history suggest, accountability presumes moral equality: no one is above the "law." Teachers and administrators are obliged to answer questions about how their students are doing, irrespective of what they choose to report.

Tests may provide more information to those in such a relationship, but they do not improve the "accountability" (that is, the responsive quality) of the relationship. For example, requiring yearly physical exams of all fathers will not increase fathers' accountability to their families. As a father, I have that family obligation before I go to the doctor. The test results will affect my conduct only if they tell me things I could not have known beforehand—for example, that my blood pressure or cholesterol level is too high. I am "accountable" for these new test results only if (1) I am capable of changing the results and (2) those to whom I am obligated—my family—know, understand, and can use the results (and can use moral suasion to induce me to change my unhealthy habits).

Let us look at a simple example of a client-institutional relationship—car owner and car manufacturer—to see how accountability depends upon a relationship of responsibility, a relationship of moral equals. In what way is the powerful Ford Motor Company "accountable" to me, based on the performance of my Taurus? There are different answers: I have an explicit contract (my warranty). (Schools, of course, do not ever provide warranties; see below.) A failure to honor the contract can lead to my seeking redress. But in the long run, there is a more powerful (though less formal) form of accountability: I can buy a car from a different manufacturer next time. We certainly make a great mistake if we believe that accountability derives from the oversight provided by the Federal Trade Commission or the Department of Transportation and Highway Safety.

Now consider the role of comparative testing. Do I *need Consumer Reports* to hold Ford accountable for my Taurus? Think carefully, now: I am not asking whether the tests are useful and informative; they surely are. The question is whether *accountability* depends upon those tests and rankings. The answer, I think, is mostly no. In one sense, though, yes: the average car buyer cannot conduct all those tests, and the tests get at hidden but vital aspects of buyer satisfaction; the more people read the comparisons, and the more the comparisons are judged to be credible, and the more the cars with hard-to-see defects receive bad ratings, the more the manufacturer will pay the price in lower sales. But the bottom line is that I can and do vote with my pocketbook: if I am unhappy with my Ford Taurus, I will return it, sell it, or junk it. We do not need any test other than our own satisfaction or dissatisfaction to keep Ford accountable, because the car company is dependent upon my continued satisfaction.

This organizational dependence on my satisfaction has not characterized public schools until quite recently. With the monopoly that public schools have had, they have not needed to worry about the dissatisfaction of the student, the parents, or the receiving institution (the "institutional customer" of the school). This becomes much clearer if we reverse the Ford vignette and ask, What accountability was there in the automobile industry of the former Soviet Union when there was only one car to buy, the Trebia?

For a second example of the accountability relationship, let us look at the game of baseball. In this more complex system of performers, the clients are in a removed position, just as they are in schooling. The fans are the clients; they pay the bills. Yet they do not manage the team, and they *should* not (just as students and parents should not manage the teaching). How are teams "accountable" to them? More indirectly, through the pattern of actions of management and players—just as in schools. To whom is the team responsible? Its fans, if anyone.

By what mechanism is the team accountable to its fans, then? Through its game performance, that most basic of tests, as evidenced in its won-lost record? Yes, the record is unequivocal—in this case, the "test" *defines* the domain (making all inferences valid), and having 162 games solves all our reliability problems— but it is not the mechanism of accountability. The won-lost record is not always the best indicator of optimal performance (teams, like schools, can do modestly well with limited talent); nor does it always correlate with satisfaction (look at the perpetually dismal record of the Chicago Cubs, with their high attendance).

Where, then, *is* the accountability in baseball? It derives in large part from the real possibility that fans, advertisers, and players can and do desert bad teams. The "test" (season record) does not provide the accountability; the possibility of a direct and forceful response to the results of the test by the many "clients" provides the accountability—the "exit option," as Albert H. Hirschman calls it.[3] Even while immune to antitrust legislation, every baseball team that seeks to stay in business has a direct interest in improving itself. Alas, most schools do not have such an interest at present; parents, students, and teachers rarely desert their schools.

The biggest problem with envisioning a school accountability system based on the baseball analogy is that school testing does not work like the season of games. Each test is one-shot, not a season; it is an indirect and generic measure, not the criterion performance; and the test is imposed, not a natural part of the environment and mission of the schools. The parallel in baseball would be determining the health of a team on the basis of one arbitrarily chosen game per year. Each team would be "tested" by an impatient group of baseball overseers and compared against other teams, arbitrarily chosen, using a complex, little-known set of statistics and equating formulas so arcane that only the psychometricians would understand it. How would that improve accountability? If a given measurement is not of self-evident meaning and value, how can it hold anyone responsible for anything? To find out how our schools are doing, we would be better off assessing student performance over 162 days in school, just as players are "tested" all season.

Even if we have credible and multifaceted statistics for each baseball player, we have no single, aggregate statistic representing each player's achievement; there is no *single* "test score," in other words. Batting average, runs batted in, runs scored, home runs, stolen bases—these and many other statistics are part of a complex assessment of a player's worth, based on *incommensurable* variables. Even with reams of objective data, summary conclusions— summary *judgments* based on the act of placing value on certain traits as opposed to others—are hard to come by: consider recent salary-arbitration cases in which players' agents have hired statisticians to provide new (and often arcane) measures of their clients' true value. Yes, I hit few home runs, but my total run production is high; yes, I strike out a lot, but I have more hits in clutch situations (two outs, late innings, when we are behind) than other players, and so on. In fact, in baseball as in school, many players' statistics relate to and are dependent upon other people's statistics: I cannot have many RBIs if my teammates do not get on base; I am likely to hit for a low average and draw more walks if I am the only good hitter on the team (since pitchers will pitch around me and I will get fewer good pitches to hit). Students and teachers are ill served by having complex performance reduced to an arbitrarily single number.

Nor should we be looking at only one baseball season, if the analogy is to be apt. In any given year, some teams are weak and some are strong. If those strengths and weaknesses simply played themselves out over time, the rich would get richer and the poor poorer. How can there be accountability if there is little possibility of fundamental reform and injection of better talent? Well, the game is designed so that reasonable balance—equity—is built into it over time. The new-player draft enables poor teams to get first crack at the best young talent, for example, and the free-agent system and a system for making trades enable any team to quickly improve itself if it acts wisely. Even in something as "Darwinian" as professional sports, we can have accountability, because there is both a built-in possibility of dramatic change and possible improvement, and the freedom to exit.

The absence of *credible* tests makes summary judgments about school (never mind teacher) performance almost impossible. And whatever tests we use, if union contracts and custom prevent teachers from being "traded" or acting as "free agents," it is far less likely that schools can be changed. And if they cannot be changed, they are not accountable.

It thus makes no sense to think of accountability as a system devised by the state (or other agencies) to exert *its* influence, based on test scores. Accountability is dependent upon the client's freedom and power to exert influence—irrespective of the source of the information on which client decisions are based—and dependent, therefore, on a system that confronts teachers more directly with their successes and failures. What the Ford and baseball analogies suggest is that we should be more cautious about assuming that accountability *depends upon* state or national testing. Because if accountability is a form of responsibility—hence responsiveness— then accountability may actually work better if we "think local" and help clients to exert influence, in a context where an institution must face direct consequences as a result of its responsiveness to clients (or its lack of it).

Readers of John Chubb and Terry Moe's lively account of schools and choice will no doubt be saying that this all sounds familiar.[4] I applaud these writers for their analysis of the problem; and I agree that school reform will not likely work, even with moves toward site-based management, unless this structural unresponsiveness to clients and institutional customers is changed. But for reasons that I can only sketch here, I think that their prescription— school choice by parents—is off the mark. As I will argue, the mechanism of choosing a school is too unresponsive a mechanism to improve schools. What is wanted is a better system of responsiveness to the everyday frustrations of students and parents—a system that gives a voice to former students and future "institutional customers" of the school. School testing has as little to do with that problem as the leading economic indicators have to do with reform of my neighborhood hardware store.

Chubb and Moe argue that there are basic reasons that private schools are more responsive than public schools (tied as the latter are to all manner of constituency interests other than those of the clients). Though public schools operate "under a system of democratic control, [they] are governed by an enormous, far-flung constituency in which the interests of parents and students carry no special status or weight. When markets prevail, parents and students are thrust onto center stage, along with the owner and staff." Markets work to ensure that parents and students play a more central and influential role by three means, according to the authors, "1. Those who own and run the schools have a strong incentive to please a clientele of parents and students by the decisions they make. This sort of responsiveness is perhaps the most obvious path by which markets promote a match [between clients and school]. 2. People have the freedom to switch from one alternative to another. 3. Natural selection."[5] An irony here is that despite the almost complete control granted to operators of private schools, they must be responsive to parents and students or go out of business.

As any parent, teacher, or building administrator knows, the unresponsiveness of schools has a great deal to do with the fact that union rules, bureaucratic traditions, and custom make it virtually impossible to shape public schooling around the learner-client's perceived needs. Students are assigned to teachers with little or no say. Classes are designed and organized to suit the temperament, style, and (especially) pace of the teacher and the aggregate class. If a student gets a poor teacher or has a relational problem with a teacher, too bad: few schools allow students to change classrooms or teachers based on the client's unhappiness with the service. (Principals and board members hate parents who persist in such matters.) As Albert Shanker often remarks in his speeches, if a doctor's prescription and advice fail to work for a particular patient, the doctor is obligated to try an alternative approach; in school, they yell at you if you do not respond to their medicine.

This would seem to argue in favor of school choice—the

"exit option" from the public school that fails to serve. But what do you do if, after choosing a new school, you end up with the same old ineffective methods and still have little opportunity or apparent right to demand change of teacher, classroom, or program? Put differently, what if the school you have chosen does not feel particularly obligated either to accommodate differences in learning style or to respond to parental and student complaints about existing methods and approaches? Indeed, this is the situation in almost all schools, public and private. We are still light-years away from treating students as clients seeking a service—clients who are able to seek and receive changes in the (daily) service when the methods used and prescriptions made by teachers fail to help them.

As odd as it may sound, I believe that the individual teacher is and has historically been mostly *immune* from accountability. It is almost unheard of for teachers to have their ineffective methods challenged, their questionable grades overturned, or their classroom duties altered because of a failure to serve the clients well (as judged by the clients or the clients' guardians). Only dramatic and extreme malfeasance leads to such actions.

What is wanted is the ability to be heard on a regular basis about practices to which one is opposed within the organization. Chubb and Moe borrowed the "exit option" idea from Hirschman, but they failed to borrow a companion concept from their reading— namely, the importance of the concept of "voice": the ability of insiders to have opportunity to give voice to their complaints. The exit option alone is insufficient to reform schools, especially in exurban and rural regions. (The folks in Warsaw, New York, with one elementary school, are not likely to drive their kids thirty-five minutes away to Geneseo and its one elementary school, despite my hometown district's good reputation.) As Hirschman put it, "The voice option is the only way in which dissatisfied customers or members can react whenever the exit option is unavailable. This is very nearly the situation in such basic social organizations as the family, the state, or the church." (Is the lack of reference to school here a telling omission about what we have tended to assume about this right in schools?) Indeed, Hirschman argues something that Chubb and Moe seem to ignore: "The presence of the exit alternative can therefore tend to *atrophy the development of the art of voice.*"[6]

The primary "unit" of accountability is thus not the district officials or even the individual school as an impersonal entity (both of which are too distant from the client's interests), but the *particular* set of teachers and administrators that are *directly* responsible for each child's experience and achievement. This is a crucial distinction in terms of an effective (that is, responsive) system of accountability. I want to be able to be heard by my teacher if I am a student. My most important "choice" should be about the quality of my relationship with that teacher, and if I cannot influence it for the better, then I should be able to change teachers. Consider the medical equivalent. I want to be able to influence the care provided by my doctor: I want to be heard when I am poorly served, and I want to change doctors if I am not heard and am therefore dissatisfied by the service. I certainly do not want merely to be able to change hospitals, in a system whose hospitals are bound to be virtually indistinguishable and not really interested in my particular case when I get there.

Schools would thus be instantly more accountable if we worried less about arcane psychometric proxy tests and worried more about making the teacher's daily work public and giving the student performer a more powerful voice. "If customers are sufficiently convinced that voice will be effective, then they may well postpone exit."[7] What if teachers were obligated to consider individual learning styles, not because of some mandate but because the student could transfer into another class on demand? What if each teacher had to display monthly the best work from *each* student in a public place of the school? What if academic teachers (as many vocational teachers now do) had to meet yearly with a "consultant committee" of professionals from their field to review their work? What if performance appraisals were centered on teacher self-assessment in reference to a range of student work from a major assignment? These are the kinds of mechanisms that would improve accountability immediately and forcefully.

If we argue that the student performer is the primary "customer" for assessment information (as I have tried to argue, in different ways, throughout the book), then it follows that students ought to give *teachers* regular feedback, not about the abstraction of an entire course or program but about the quality and usefulness of the instructional help and assessment information they receive. As a simple example, one of my former school colleagues used to hand out index cards each Friday and ask students to describe, on one side, what "worked" for them that week and, on the other side, what did not work. These cards were far more effective and responsive than formal course evaluations, which ultimately shield teachers from reacting to dissatisfaction (though they are surely better than nothing). (Notice that my colleague's informal questionnaire, like a questionnaire to the student about test feedback, does not ask the students questions about which they are not experts. Students are not only the *best* judges but the *only* judges of the quality of the assessment feedback they receive and whether the lessons work for them.)

These index-card questionnaires are really no different than the questionnaires given out at the hotels I visit each month as part of my consulting work. In client-centered service businesses, a critical piece of the formal accountability is always provided by the client's formal evaluation. Equally valuable are the surveys used in many high schools of graduating students or alumni to assess the programs and services that they found of most and least value. What matters is not the "truth" of the students' claims but the importance of taking their perceptions seriously.

I am *not* saying that the only (or most important) way to improve school accountability is to use survey data from students. That information is only a small piece of a much larger assessment puzzle, in which we "triangulate" similar kinds of information gained from our many clients and institutional customers—from parents, teachers at the next level, former students—with the test and admissions data we find most credible. I *am* saying that we will never understand or achieve real accountability until we see that tests per se do not provide it, but mechanisms that increase responsiveness to clients do.

Another reason that the exit option alone does not ensure accountability is that it has little value to the receiving institution— the institution to which the student graduates. One of the most important features of private schools, never adequately discussed by

Chubb and Moe, is the ability to set *entry*-level standards, (as well as or instead of exit-level standards). It is not inconceivable to organize such a voice in the public sector. Some schools already have done so: Littleton (Colorado) High School, as part of its move to a performance-based diploma, has a K-8 articulation committee to both better understand incoming students and influence middle schools. Edmonton, Alberta, schools have achievement tests on the "cusp" years of schooling, designed and scored by teachers from both schools. While one may not be able to "reject" incoming students in the public sector, one can certainly exert greater influence on the institutional "suppliers" through such moves.

Nor need we think about the "voice" of the receiving institution so formally. How many schools routinely survey their former students as to the value of their former education? How many high schools organize focus groups of college professors to find out how their syllabi, assignments, and tests are viewed? How many middle schools require that their faculty spend a day with high school faculty to learn how well or poorly their former students have been prepared? (Management consultants in business routinely advise managers to spend far more time with the external customer than they are inclined to do.) These questions suggest not only that the voice option has not been adequately considered as a part of school policy but that Chubb and Moe's distinction between "consumers" and "constituencies" is too narrowly drawn: the next level of the educational system has a more direct and practical concern with the quality of each student's exit-level performance from the current level than other constituencies in the public sector.[8] And the next level's voice, if it had to be heard as part of a formal accountability mechanism, would provide far more useful and compelling feedback than that from any test.

School Accountability and Value Added

Results from credible teacher- and learner-useful tests are nonetheless an important part of any accountability system. But the key words are *credible* and *useful*—to the teacher, learner, and parents. Obtaining credibility and usefulness depends upon more than just a move from indirect to direct tests. If the testing we do in the name of accountability is still one-event, year-end testing, we will never obtain valid and fair information. We need to ensure that any accountability-related testing reveals the "value added" by the school if we want to know whether or not a school is "effective." (That is why Chubb and Moe properly analyzed performance *gains,* using a comparison of test scores of the sophomores and seniors studied, to argue their case.[9])

The analogy of automobile purchasing that we used to explore this issue initially was limited by an important fact: the automobile industry can be properly viewed as an almost perfect "outcomes-based" system. We think that we can fairly and properly assume that the vagaries of the "inputs" (quality of the steel and the production process, quality of the workers) can be almost completely minimized through what we rightly call "quality control." But schooling is not like that. The quality of the "inputs" has a great deal to do with the quality of the result. Who our students are when they enter makes a profound difference when we compare schools or districts. Then add student mobility to the mix: in some urban districts, students start at, leave, and then return to the same school during the year—sometimes repeatedly. Some urban schools have mobility rates of as high as 210 percent per year. What in the world are we measuring, then, if we use one-event testing to provide accountability? More to the point, how can one-event testing ever provide leverage for accountability?

Any sensible plan for school and district accountability needs to look at both "inputs" and "outputs"—in other words, it needs to look at the "value added" by the faculty and the school. Whether we consider a simple pretest/posttest system or a more sophisticated approach to longitudinal assessment, we should look not just at isolated results but at changes effected by the school. As Alexander Astin, a long-time researcher in this area of so-called value-added measurement, remarks, "The output of an institution . . . does not really tell us much about its educational impact or educational effectiveness in developing talent. Rather, outputs must always be evaluated in terms of inputs."[10]

Value-added assessment of institutions has a complex history over the last twenty years, as Peter Ewell points out in his review of assessment in higher education.[11] In fact, the concept of value added has been altered by many of its proponents to focus on overall "talent development" of students (as opposed to specific "value" added by the institution.) The shift is more than semantic, and the revised model requires far more statistical sophistication than a pretest/posttest model. We end up with a clear picture of the extent to which intellectual talent can be developed only as we do complex multivariate studies on the various student-ability and school-context factors at work. Astin, for example, now refers to his model as an "input-environment-output" (IEO) model. The "input" represents the talents that students bring, the "environment" represents the contextual factors that amplify or impede talent development, and the "output" represents the best work achieved by the students while in residence. Any accountability system should study all three factors to get a clearer sense of what precisely was the value added by the school. As Ewell points out, such a model is more than complex: it represents a fundamental shift away from a simple physical-science-experiment model of measurement (pretest/posttest, with the variable being school) and toward a "multivariate statistical control" model that is "more akin to the disciplines of sociology and econometrics."[12] At the very least, we see that whatever testing we do as part of such a system will look more like a pretest/posttest model in reference to cross-disciplinary outcomes. (Merely getting out of the habit of testing a cohort once, in June, on isolated achievements, would be a major step forward.)

We can perhaps best appreciate the idea of value added (which is, after all, a term from economics) by once again casting things in moral language. Fairness and equity must be a part of any accountability system. It is more *fair* to use a value-added model than an outcomes-based model because good schools may be good only because of what already-bright, already-capable students bring to the school. (Remember, for example, that the socioeconomic status of student bodies is often a highly reliable indicator of achievement.) If comparing is what we feel we need to do, we should at least compare apples to apples, not apples to oranges. What kind of accountability is it that compares economically depressed New York City schools (with their 70 percent bilingual population and 90 percent mobility rate) to the best suburban schools in Scarsdale or Bronxville? Good Lord, we don't do that even in athletics: we have different divisions and conferences in high school and college sports. On the same rationale, South Carolina has experimented with placing schools in different "bands," based on the socioeconomic status of each school's population.

The new Kentucky system takes the value-added concept to its logical extreme, where testing is concerned. Traditional comparability has been dropped altogether: instead of comparing schools to each other, schools are compared to themselves, over time, against standards (as I noted in Chapter Five). This does two things that improve accountability: it makes it possible for local communities to better understand how their schools are doing, and it makes it far more likely that local faculties will see it as in their self-interest to improve both their ongoing assessment of performance and their level of performance, no matter how "bad" or "good" the current results. Such a plan can easily be carried out at the district level as well. Edmonton, Alberta, has a site-based decision-making system that requires each site team to set yearly performance goals, based on identified local priority weaknesses. And the Fairport schools in western New York have just begun an interesting experiment: teams of teachers across grade levels will be competing against other teams of teachers for modest bonuses in terms of aggregate student performance, using an array of assessments that they are designing.

Fairport's efforts are in keeping with the plan for the entire state of New York. The "Compact for Learning," a report formulated by Commissioner Tom Sobol and the board of regents four years ago, calls for a fundamental recasting of the relationship between local schools and the state, and it places great emphasis on local assessment as the cornerstone of accountability. And a recent task force on curriculum and assessment, put together by the commissioner as part of the work called for by the "Compact for Learning," has called for the state to get out of the business of pupil testing entirely—to become an *auditor* of local performance and assessment (as opposed to an enforcer of its own standards through its own tests). (The task-force's proposal recommends that the state continue to do program-evaluation testing, but only on a sampling basis, similar to what is done by NAEP.)

Such a plan is increasingly necessary as public education becomes more diverse and privatized in fact or in spirit. As we see clearly when we look at private education and higher education, traditional cross-school comparisons make less and less sense if (and since) there are few shared outcomes or values across institutions. That is why the process of school accreditation is built out of a self-assessment: given your mission and philosophy, what is the gap, if any, between our intent and your effect? Though many of the accreditation procedures (and histories) leave a great deal to be desired in practice, the idea is sound: it recognizes the appropriate diversity of institutions and missions, and it asks faculties to investigate their actual effects, not just their imagined or hoped-for results. New York State is looking seriously, through a pilot project, at the British Inspectorate model of school assessment, which formalizes this idea. The challenge is to make the feedback loop more timely and less pro forma.

The main reason for thinking of accountability as a characteristic of the local school is that oversight agencies have no real pressure to exert on classroom-level conduct. The state neither can nor should demand improvements from each classroom; that is properly a local matter. And single test scores provide no useful leverage, because they cannot be used in a timely, appropriate fashion. Most important, however, conventional standardized test results cannot be used *by the clients* to influence schools, since so many psychometric tricks are at work in the design and scoring of the tests that their meaning is never self-evident to anyone but the (external) designers.

Toward a Natural Meritocracy

Most intelligent observers now see that free economic trade is superior to "command" economies, with their complex quotas, tariffs, and price supports. But school reform is still being viewed as a kind of Eastern European communism: we are mandating outputs (national goals, national tests, national standards) in rooms and buildings that remain isolated from one another and in which there is little or no incentive to break ineffectual educational habits. What we need instead are incentives that unleash and reward entrepreneurial behavior in every school.

No doubt school and teacher choice by parents are important. But perhaps the people who need school choice most to effect

change are *teachers*. If accountability requires responsiveness, then
it is imperative that teachers be allowed to band together to form
programs and schools that adhere to their pedagogical aims and
values—irrespective of what the union or the faculty as a whole
would choose to do. That is why the idea of the "charter school"
is such an important one: any group that wanted to could be "chartered" by the school board to open a "school" within the school
system. We must allow our best teachers to have greater freedom of
alliance, program development, and authority, in this way and others. There can be no accountability in a school world that views all
teachers as equally accountable and successful by *fiat*—that is, in a
world where unions and management allow the perpetration of the
myth that all teachers are equally competent and that "we are all
responsible" for children's welfare. If we are *all* responsible, then
no one is.

For there to be accountability in schools, then, there must be
freedom and opportunity for entrepreneurial teachers to take reform
ideas beyond their own classrooms. Even the charter school approach is not enough, however, if teachers cannot gain increasing
access to the system's resources for a good idea that works. In addition, there have to be both opportunities and incentives in the
system for non-risk-taking teachers to adopt reform tactics and solve
client problems *because the job demands it,* not because it is a good
idea or because "thoughtful professionals" do such things.

We need to build a performance-based meritocracy, in short.
There are few opportunities for outstanding educators to be noticed
and sought out, never mind properly rewarded with power and
authority. In other words, we need an accountability system in
which teachers feel *obliged* to know what the *best* teachers, programs, and schools do, in which"benchmarking" (to use an industry term) is both a job requirement *and* in one's enlightened self-
interest. We need to create a new kind of capital whereby successful
educators receive "investable" educational resources or power to
expand their efforts. The recently established National Board for
Professional Teaching Standards established within recent years
will help; now we need to consider what might be similar market
forces that increase leverage on individual schools to do what works
rather than what suits faculty habit, union contracts, and school

boards. Consider the current paucity of promotion possibilities in public schools as a sign of the problem. Unlike independent schools and private colleges, where the jobs of academic dean and department head are significant and are used to reward good teachers, public schools either have no such jobs or they make them excessively bureaucratic.

A simple case in point to illustrate how our K-12 world is antimerit: the School Without Walls in Rochester (New York) has been lauded by the state as exemplary, is a long-time member of the Coalition of Essential Schools, and was publicly and frequently praised by former Superintendent McWalters and Adam Urbanski, head of the teachers' union—*but the school has no credibility with rank-and-file teachers in other Rochester high schools.* Nor, for that matter, have any local public school leaders felt obliged or been obliged to inquire into its success. It is dismissed—as an "alternative" school, and it struggles to get funding for its increased student load. It is this systemically tolerated cynicism that makes accountability impossible.

Being "interested" in successful ideas is not the same as perceiving that they are in my interest. Why *should* a teacher or faculty persist with a process as cumbersome, complex, and prone to discord as school change without sustained incentives? In the current system, one's "success" as an experimenter often earns the enmity of one's peers, lots more work, and more students (but no concurrent increase in resources).

Thus an accountability system requires incentives, not just mandates and threats. We must finally learn to escape the puritanism that still haunts American schooling in the assumption that people should *want* to do the right thing. We need incentives that cause the cynical, the lazy, the diffident to feel that experimentation is more rewarding than sitting still. (An incentive, as we noted in Chapter Five, is what causes you to do and persist with something that you probably would not do without the incentive, but without making you feel coerced. Money can thus be used as both a disincentive and an incentive, depending upon how it is used to foster a climate of client-centered experimentation.)

Here are some examples of school systems that are getting

some of the incentives right (for kids as well as adults), leading to better accountability:

- In Cherry Creek, Colorado, schools have sharply reduced the number of district-level subject heads. They have used the monies saved to develop a request-for-proposals process whereby the district supports the most promising ideas in each subject with funds, a mini-sabbatical, and a secretary for the teachers whose proposals are accepted.

- In Edmonton, Alberta, central-office people are called "consultants" and control little budget. The consultants are "hired" by each school, and they are only *re*hired on the basis of helpful performance. In addition, the evaluation process is the reverse of the chain of command: the superintendent is evaluated by the cabinet, administrators are evaluated by teaching staff, teachers are evaluated by students, and so on.

- In one Louisville, Kentucky, middle school, the principal required faculty members, in pairs, to engage in experimentation for a year on a cutting-edge issue of their choice. Each teacher was evaluated that year on the quality of that pair's experiment.

- In schools in Upper Arlington, Ohio, students in language arts are required to produce quality work to be promoted. They place their best work in the district portfolio, and that work must be deemed good or excellent for promotion to occur. Thus quality is not an option, but a requirement for all.

- In all New York vocational high schools, each teacher works with a "consultant committee" made up of people from the teacher's field (welding, cosmetology, and so on). The committee assists the teacher in evaluating the quality of the program, participates in the teaching and assessing process, and becomes involved in standard-setting.

- In Kentucky's new accountability system, each school is compared to itself, over time, on new performance, portfolio, and short-answer tests. Over time, each faculty must get an increasing percentage of students up to standard, not just increase school averages.

We must help policy makers and state departments of education to see this as part of their role: the establishment of an incentive-driven, as opposed to a mandate-driven, system of educational reform.

Virtues are upheld or undermined daily in our schools. Increased excellence will not come through state fiat and once-a-year tests but through a strong commitment to local "structures, interactions, ideology, habits, rituals and symbols."[13] Nor can national multiple-choice tests ever *raise* standards, if "standards" are derived as statistical artifacts from test items (as they are in some NAEP scales and as is proposed for future NAEP results). Why do the impatient policy makers not see that they are recapitulating the terrible history of the school-efficiency movement of 1910–1920, when simplistic "scales" were devised to judge teacher performance?[14] Why not instead establish *standards for local standards*, and *better incentives* for meeting them?[15]

As an intermediate solution, we ought to endorse policies that lead to shared values, as in large-scale judgment-based testing. We need, in other words, standards for the *tolerable variance in grading student work across teachers, departments, schools, and districts*. The state should ask all districts to set grading standards and parameters of tolerable variability for across-teacher grading of similar work, saying, in effect, "We do not feel that it is our place to tell you how to assess student work in mathematics, but we expect different teachers to agree on grading policies and to score similar work within 10 points on a 100-point scale—whatever the criteria being used." The state would then periodically seek from (or oversee in) each district an audit of its grading practices.

Toward a Real System

To speak of schools and districts as "systems" is to speak contradictorily, after all. Districts and schools alike are really webs of profound isolation. And it is a long-standing alienation: of teachers from teachers, teachers from their subjects, grade levels from other grade levels, schools from other schools, and districts from their institutional clients (colleges and businesses). I have heard high school teachers described as self-employed entrepreneurs—a characterization that bolsters their immunity from formal criticism, especially in regard to the incoherence of high school programs.

(Indeed, in many large high schools, full faculty meetings are rarely held.) How can policy makers hope to "leverage" change by tests or any other means if the "mass" being moved crumbles into many isolated bits on contact? It is these webs of habit-bound isolation that policy makers should rethink, because with no real school *system*, we have no *possibility* of real accountability.

In a recent editorial in the *Rochester Democrat and Chronicle,* a local New York newspaper, the editors cited a state report on a school currently being reviewed for its poor performance (February 24, 1993, p. 12). In that state report, the harshest words were reserved for the "educational anarchy" that resulted from teachers designing courses and programs in isolation from one another. This "anarchy" is the norm in every American school district. There is no formal obligation or set of practices to ensure that the right hand knows what the left hand is doing. Yet it is what one might call "structural obligations" to be responsive to other elements of the system that determine whether there is or is not accountability; tests do not make that determination.

All the testing in the world will not change the fact that teachers are presently immune from formal responsibility for their *later, long-lasting* effects on children, as unthinkable as that seems. Schools that fail to include in all teachers' job requirements the seeking and use of feedback about the consequences of their teaching allow teachers—even encourage them—to rationalize, rather than empirically justify or soul-searchingly examine, their habits. When students are bored, Mr. Vasco will see a discipline problem, and no one will be able to challenge him on it; when Johnny flunks out of science class in the eighth grade, Miss Julliard (in the third grade) will not know, much less *see,* her part in it. This alienation from one's effects means that school is whatever the adults who inhabit it say it is, and success is wherever they find it. This is the exact opposite of any robust meaning of accountability. And imposing one-shot indirect tests will have absolutely no impact on this blind spot, because such tests lack credibility and diagnostic insight into the problem, are given when it is too late to do anything about the problem, and take us no further in the much harder work of establishing more intelligent lines of command and job descriptions.

What John Dewey said seventy years ago on this subject remains true today: "We make a religion out of education, we profess unbounded faith in its possibilities. . . . But on the other hand, we assume in practice that no one is specifically responsible when bad outcomes show themselves. . . . [W]hen results are undesirable we shrug our shoulders and place the responsibility upon some intrinsic defect or outer chance."[16] Too many teachers and administrators are in the habit of accepting praise for student success while explaining why student failure is not their fault (blaming family or psychological problems, outside jobs, television, and so on). We cannot have it both ways: either school is having an effect, or it isn't. We must therefore do a better job of measuring that *effect* and assigning responsibility.

In our wish to respect the dignity of school personnel and the nobility of their intentions, we resist acknowledging a politically incorrect but important truth. In the absence of an accountability system that would make teachers worry more about the effects of their teaching than their intent, many educators still do not understand their jobs: many wrongly come to think that their purpose is to teach what they know and like, on a relatively fixed schedule— *irrespective of the learning that does or does not ensue.* Far too many persist in resolutely moving through their syllabi even when things are clearly not working, when important ideas are not yet understood. They will tell you that they cannot slow down because they must cover the content, yet it is not quite clear why: rarely can they cite a specific mandate, job description, or penalty that makes this more than myth, and variance options go begging in every state. Besides this argument makes no sense if the aggregate final achievement of all students is what we measure. In short, teachers are not now obligated, either by job description or direct pressures on the institution from other institutions, to *really* know how they are doing and to do something about it when things go badly.

By contrast, professionals and coherent institutions are always adaptive and responsive, so clear in their purpose and necessarily focused on their clients that they can be *systematically and quickly attentive to the gaps between intent and effect;* the members and the "structures" all bend to a common goal. Stanford football is the quality of the execution and *adjustment* of Bill Walsh and his players—not Bill Walsh's values or strategic philosophy. The Metropolitan Museum of Art is its displays and the revenue generated by those displays, not its vast collection and the tastes of its directors. Apple Computer is its computers, the niche it chooses, and the market share it earns, not the technical and design values of its executives. Like any other organization, a school should be defined by the quality of the products and performances produced by its "workers"—namely, the work of *students*—and by the ability of teacher-managers to fundamentally adjust their approach, schedule, or use of resources if performance is not up to standard.

Let me offer a simple example from my own experience. In my third year of teaching, I also coached junior-varsity boy's soccer. With wonderful intentions (and after lots of summer lesson planning), we began the season in September. By mid October we were 0 and 6. As any coach would do, I had to fundamentally alter those initial plans (no matter that the lessons were "essential" and had been planned as part of a logical and thorough soccer "syllabus"); I had to carefully analyze performance weakness, make basic adjustments, and work on the major causes of the current failure. But when did a faculty ever think or act this way? (When did *I* ever think this way as an English teacher?) When did a group of reading or science teachers ever say, in "midseason," "We're 0 and 6 and we'd better make fundamental changes in our program, our use of time, and our use of personnel"?

"Ah, but there were twelve 'standardized tests,' not just one, in your soccer season," the critic will say. "This only supports the idea that accountability depends upon testing that provides comparability. Let's use test scores and teacher tests to compare teachers." Bad analogy. For one thing, soccer is tested by *playing soccer*. We do not use an indirect generic test, given once a year to all athletes in all sports everywhere. Imagine what little value would accrue from the imposition of a generic proxy test of "athleticism" in an attempt to make each specific varsity sport program "more accountable." Further, it is not the *number* of tests that matters: although it is not uncommon for systems to give a dozen tests over the student's career, what have poor results led to in terms of school improvement?

No, what makes soccer coaches accountable and English teachers not accountable is the public nature of the games, the im-

mediacy and credibility of the game results, and the inherent col-
legiality and mutual interest of the coach-player relationship. When
something works for my "clients," we do it; if it fails to work, we
stop doing it. I am more accountable not because I receive more
feedback but because my failure to act on the feedback is public and
tangibly consequential. Nor does all the vital feedback come from
game scores: as every coach knows, my ongoing responses to the
players' demands and their perceptions (of themselves, of each
other, of me, of other teams) are as important as what happens on
the field, if we are to have a successful season.

For all our talk about oppressive standardized tests, head-
strong administrators, impetuous school boards, and meddlesome
state departments of education, the simple fact is that few teachers
receive formal, *obligating* feedback from colleagues and recipient
schools that challenges their current habits; it is almost unheard of
for teachers to be formally saluted or disciplined for the academic
performance of their students, based on hard evidence. It is a rare
school that organizes site-based management around student performance reviews and a self-obligation to student performance targets.
Site-based management will fail unless we stop allowing the site
teams to talk about whatever they want and to bog down in process
and turf details. They should be chartered not as a process but in
terms of a product: their obligation is to improve student performance, and they should submit yearly plans that outline how they
will set student performance goals, monitor student performance,
and adjust their own performance.

The evidence of this lack of obligating feedback is abundant:

- Fourth-grade teachers rarely meet with fifth-grade teachers to
  ensure that where the former end up is where the latter need to
  start.
- It is usually no one's formal job responsibility to know how
  former students fare in later academic or work settings and to
  disseminate that information to all faculty for action.
- Local tests are neither formally validated nor benchmarked
  against wider-world tasks, criteria, and standards; teachers can
  give grades inconsistently and unreliably; there are no precedents or standards for grading audits.

- Teachers are typically evaluated either on their own behavior or through arbitrary tests of their students, not on their success in getting students to perform the most important tasks of their institutional clients. (Coaches, band directors, and vocational teachers are the exception.)
- Most school faculties are not officially obligated to study the success of other schools.
- It is rare for schools to collect and analyze exemplary student work and teacher-graded work to ensure that standards are clear and held in common. It is equally rare to see the analysis of student performance errors as a regular item for faculty-meeting discussion.
- Few schools *redeploy* teachers and other resources midyear when performance for a predictable group of students is not up to par.

Though hard pressed on all sides by children and chores, faculty are isolated from obligating, systemic feedback. The complaints of students, parents, the next grade level, the next level of schooling—all these can easily go unheard (and unsolicited) with impunity; responsiveness is an *option*. Where, for example, are teachers formally obligated to alter their lesson plans on the basis of early-year failures by some of their students? How many faculties can state (or are required to find out) what the alumni believe the strengths and weaknesses of their former education to be? When alumni complaints *are* heard, how many faculties do something about them? How many schools regularly meet with schools at the next level (or with professions) to determine whether their objectives and programs articulate with those at the next level? Being formally bound by contract and job description to seek and respond to such feedback would compel teachers to push performance so that it transcends our powerful self-fulfilling prophecies based on habitual and shut-in expectations.

Though some accrediting organizations have moved to an outcomes-based focus (most notably, the North Central Association), the accreditation process is still too infrequent, lengthy, and pro forma to compel schools to worry about their record. What we need is a more timely and frequent self-assessment by teachers and schools, in reference to appropriate indicators of outcomes, gains, and environmental health. The absence of such feedback is due, in part, to our penchant for inauthentic generic testing, whether imposed or locally designed. By using indirect proxy tests of achievement, we reward schools for the socioeconomic status of their students instead of the value-added achievement produced by the faculty. In the absence of value-added indicators, each school can easily claim to be unique, fancying itself to be doing as well as it can be doing—*given* its students, faculty, and budget.

The absence of effective feedback is due also to a myopic habit of school evaluators: the habit of assuming that "input" indicators are more important than indicators of gains in student performance. For example, in an otherwise helpful and well-written book on school self-improvement, Brian C. Caldwell and Jim S. Spinks list twenty-three indicators of effective schools, of which only three relate to outcomes. The indicator linking testing to outcomes states, "Scores on tests reflect high levels of achievement."[17]

In the absence of credible measures of gain, we become impatient and settle for glib comparability. We thus witness the ironic return of policy solutions as obtrusive as those detailed by Callahan in his seminal treatise on the politics of school reform written thirty years ago.[18] Standardized tests and "scales" were first imposed on teachers in the early twentieth century for reasons identical to those being offered today. Policy makers then, like policy makers now, mistrusted the local report card and transcript—often, of course, for sound reasons. (Since teachers are inclined, for both noble and self-interested reasons, to see the child's performance in the best possible light, and since teachers grade in isolation from one another and the wider world's standards, it becomes necessary to demand an "accounting" of the teachers' accounting.) But if we knew that we had (1) adequate collaborative, disinterested scoring of student work at the local level, (2) an oversight system to ensure that the standards and criteria being used were both apt and rigorously employed, and (3) an appeal system that could be used by students, parents, *and teachers at other levels* to contest a grade, then it is very unlikely that more testing would contribute to accountability.

In the absence of these ideals, testing thrives. And it thrives because schools have always been under various political pressures to promise unrealistic change. Administrators have been quick to adopt mass testing in self-defense, as Callahan points out, for reasons similar to those that prevail now. He quotes an NEA official of 1913: "The ultimate problem of this Committee . . . is that of creating a new kind of confidence on the part of the public in the work of the public schools."[19] As a solution, "efficiency scales" and other simple indicators and language were recommended, so that "businessmen" would be able to understand how schools were faring. Narrow and literal compliance with such procedures, not quality, is the inevitable legacy of accountability by the "standard" of standardized tests. As a modern CEO of a major service business commented to Phillip Schlecty, "You in education have made a terrible mistake by relying on standardized tests as the only measure of performance: you have handed over quality control to the accountants."

Sad but true. We judge the standards of an enterprise by the quality—the *qualities*—found in its daily work. We do not judge Xerox, the Boston Symphony, the Oakland Athletics, or Dom Perignon on the basis of indirect indicators or single scores fixed by others. Rather, we judge their quality on two essential but independent criteria. The first is this: Is the daily work that is produced standard-setting (or at least standard-upholding)? In other words, is the customer *always* satisfied, and does the organization have the customers it wants? The second criterion has to do with quality control, with consistency across individual performances: Is there *minimal* variance between the best and worst work? (As I noted in Chapter Five, our failure to judge schools by the *range* of performance as well as by the mean or best performance ensures that the worst effects of tracking and inequitable distribution of teachers and resources will continue in schools.)

Let us finally be honest about the ongoing cry for test-driven accountability: the schools are being treated hypocritically. Those who propose high-stakes, uniform audit-tests as the sole measure of school performance would never tolerate similar reductionism of or interference in their own affairs. (Instructively, our best colleges are not subject to a similar policy.) You did not hear state legislatures or Congress calling for standardized tests when the savings and loan scandal hit in the 1980's, for example. No, the critics of schools are not about to improve *their* workplace or define "quality" in *their* domain of policy making or politics by the use of standardized tests or other imposed, generic indicators. Why should schools be different?

Standards

If we subscribe to a vote-with-your-feet view of accountability, then it follows that we do *not* need common national tests and imposed national standards. If the private school sector gets by quite well without those tests and standards (and it *does* get by well: private schools are generally judged to serve their clients responsibly and responsively), why in the world would we want to impose them more on our public schools?

In fact, one of the great mysteries of the current debate in education is the frequent claim by policy makers that we lack national standards. What an odd and erroneous claim: we have the Advanced Placement program, achievement tests in every secondary subject linked to college demands, as well as to programs such as the International Baccalaureate and criterion-referenced tests such as the National Assessment of Educational Progress. What we lack is the will to apply such existing standards to *all* students instead of a handful, if academic reform is what we are after. We lack not standards but policies and incentives that would get not-so-good schools and teachers to take notice of what good schools and teachers accomplish.

Standards are never the result of imposed standardization, as I have elsewhere said.[20] Standards, like good assessment, are contextual. The standards at Harvard have little to do with the standards at St. John's College or the Juilliard School; the standards at all our best independent schools and colleges are determined by each faculty, not by policy-maker mandate. Standards relate to jobs done well by *individuals,* as judged within a context of particular purpose and effect. Yet, as Dewey lamented, Americans are "irretrievably accustomed to thinking in standardized averages. . . . In spite of all our talk about individuality and individualism we have no habit of thinking in terms of distinctive, much less uniquely individualized, qualities."[21] Little has changed for the better with respect to testing in this regard; we seem more prone to standardization than ever, even as business and government head in the opposite direction—namely, toward privatization and decentralization in management and toward worker-led benchmarking processes by which standards are set locally (but mindful of world-class performance standards).

Standards are not fixed or generic, in other words. They vary with a performer's aspirations and purpose. To quote Dewey again: "There are as many modes of superiority and inferiority as there are consequences to be attained and works to be accomplished."[22] (Sizer correctly asks not *"Which* standards?" but *"Whose* standards?" to better expose this point and the disingenuous tenor of the current official talk.) There is no such thing as *a* standard for secondary education; there are as many standards as there are colleges, professions, venues for performance, and aspirations. When schools give good guidance to students and are responsive to wider-world demands, there can be as many standards as there are students, programs, and career options—*with* accountability. There is a college for everyone; there are fine programs that do not care if the student lacks certain credits or has a high school diploma. To "raise" performance standards requires not standardization of expectation but heightened demands for quality work from each student in each course. The establishment of reasonable criteria for the exiting of school, from which more personalized judgments would be made about each student's work (the system used in graduate school), should not be compromised by some felt need for a consensus on what "our standards" ought to be.

We surely do *not* need a single set of mandated academic standards (and pressure to meet them). I watched sixteen students build a beautiful $250,000 house to contract and code at a Finger Lakes–area vocational high school. But all the students were academic "failures" in New York's Regents-syllabus-and-exam system and in terms of the national standards debate laid out by the governors and the president a few years ago. This makes little sense and causes much harm. We turn the proper relationship between accountability and education upside down if we assume that everyone must have the same education—if what we are really doing is designing a system that makes it merely easier for us to hold students and schools accountable on the basis of comparability.

It is true that we use the word *standard* as if there were a single excellence. But that hides the fact that different criteria and contexts lead to different single excellences. Yo-Yo Ma and Wynton Marsalis each set a distinct standard for other musicians; Tom Wolfe and Mark Twain each set a distinct standard for American writers. These (different) standards are educative and enticing. There is no *one* model of excellence; there are always a variety of exemplars to emulate. And someone excellent in one category, genre, or performance can be mediocre in another. There is thus no possible generic test of whether student work is "up to standard." The aptness of standards and criteria depends upon the context and purpose of the assessment: the artist who selects works to show at a job interview, selects works to hang in a juried exhibition, and selects works for his or her own living room walls uses different standards and criteria each time. The portfolio changes as the demands of each context change. Excellence is not a uniform correctness but the ability to unite personal style with mastery of a subject in a product or performance of one's design.

This is clearer when we use the word *standard* in the plural to describe character. A person with "standards" is a person with a passion for excellence and habitual attention to detail in all work done (even when a teacher's or the state's guidelines leave room for less). High standards, whether in people or institutions, are revealed through reliability, integrity, self-discipline, and craftsmanship—as *character,* in short. Raising test scores will *not* raise standards, therefore. Raising standards locally (through changes in the kinds of work and conduct tolerated) *will* raise test scores. But to raise standards locally, faculties will have "to agree to agree" and benchmark their work against appropriate wider-world standards linked to their (many) institutional customers. This can happen only when teaching is redefined to include assessing and when structures are created to compel teachers to talk to one another and agree about performance outcomes and how to assess them.

Let us take the idea of personally upheld standards back to the classroom. Accountability begins with teachers not accepting work that is shoddy: it isn't done until it's done right. Consider the English teacher, mentioned earlier, who instructs peer editors to mark the place in a student paper where they lost interest and to hand the paper back for revision; the paper is not done until all the peer editors get to the end. Consider the school system that requires of each student a language arts portfolio containing samples of work that earned B's or better. Consider the school system that uses an A, B, I (incomplete) grading system. Consider the new British curriculum and assessment system, in which students must earn at least a 6 (on a scale of 10) in every course to graduate—no matter how long it takes. Consider accountability reform that begins with such simple actions as requiring every faculty, team, or academic department to formulate policies that ensure that quality work is not merely an *option*.

Standards Versus Expectations

Many faculties with whom I have worked have a difficult time buying the idea that they should set standards that some students cannot reach. This shows how far we are from understanding standards and accountability. Standards are *always* out of reach; that is the point. The standards of performance and the standards of self-discipline in one's work are always "ideals" for all but the world's best performers in every field. Thus I do not "expect" most people to meet the standards set by the best. My "expectation" is that everyone will strive to improve his or her work by studying what is best and working continuously to narrow the gap between the current level of performance and the ideal level of performance.

In industry, the standard "zero defects per million" is commonly used. Although that standard can obviously never be met by mere mortals, it serves as the appropriate benchmark for all work. Similarly in writing, we should anchor our scoring systems not by the best work we happen to have in our possession but the best work that is *possible*—even showing professional samples for some of the assignments we give, as necessary. (We offer professional standards in the performing arts and athletics without hesitation.) Otherwise, we have unwittingly reinvented norm-referenced testing.

"But what about the student who can never get close to the standard?" There, in a nutshell, is the belief that continues to make education less than a profession. The only possible response is, "Having spent only six months with that student, how can you know that he or she cannot get close? And what chance will the student have of ever approaching the standard if you do not assess work in terms of it?" It is our pervasive and unsubstantiated fatalism about student performance that should be the focus of all accountability efforts.

Assessment in terms of standards is not to be confused with grading in terms of our expectations. Johnny's work may well be a 1 on a scale of 10, but that may be what we expect—for his age and experience. The standard-referenced score should not and need not be mechanically translated into a grade. Think of the difference between beginning divers and Amateur Athletic Union divers, both of whom get a 4.5 on a dive. Similarly, the ninth-grader's B and the twelfth-grader's B are quite different, based on our expectations— and properly so (as long as we communicate effectively to student and parent the difference between standard-referenced and norm-referenced scores and grades.)

We make a similar mistake in confusing growth with progress, especially at the elementary level. Growth is measured in terms of change in the individual: How far has the student come? Progress, however, is measured *backward* from the destination, the standard: How much closer is Johnny to the goal? It is possible, in other words, to experience a good deal of personal growth but little progress. Teachers do students and parents a great disservice when they report results as growth and not progress, because they invariably make it seem as if the student is closer to meeting a valid standard than the comment about growth really implies.

It makes no sense, therefore, to set standards for each grade level only. That is why the outcomes-based movement is so sensible. A standard offers an objective ideal, serving as a worthy and tangible goal for *everyone*—even if, at this point in time, for whatever reason, some cannot (yet!) reach it.

The following list summarizes what standards of performance are (and are not):

- *Concrete exemplars or specifications, not general goals.* A standard is a specific, valued, measurable result—"the four-minute mile"—not vague results such as "very fast running." In effect, a standard answers the question, "How *specifically* excellent does one have to be?"

- *Benchmarks, not norms.* Doing well relative to others is not necessarily doing well. In fact, as NAEP results show, *most* students are doing very poorly when measured not against other students but against specific performance standards in reading, writing, and mathematics.
- *The quality of acceptable performance demanded, not the scoring criteria by which we distinguish acceptable from unacceptable performance.* Criteria are the specified traits of any successful performance; they tend to be the same across age and experience, while expectations vary across age and experience. (In other words, the criteria for a successful high jump or a persuasive essay are the same, regardless of the experience of the performer.) "Thorough and well written" as a criterion, for example, implies no standard until a *specific,* exemplary paper is chosen to represent that language. *The choice of an exemplary paper sets the standard.* (The standard "anchors" the scoring scale; the descriptors alone cannot.)
- *The quality of the performance, not the degree of difficulty of the task.* By relying on testing to set standards, we perpetually conflate input standards with output standards. Note the useful distinction found in many areas of sports and the arts between the "degree of difficulty" and the "quality" of the performance. It implies that we *can* have high standards for *all* students, *assuming that the student is well placed.* Similarly, it implies that so-called criterion-referenced tests and the current attempt by NAEP to match items to standards confuses "input" standards with "output" standards: whether or not I get difficult but simplistic questions correct bears little relationship to whether my performances and products are consistently of high quality at that level.
- *Ultimate and milestone standards, not age-cohort expectations.* We may appropriately set a standard that *none* of our current students can be expected to meet. There are industry or professional standards whether or not our best students can meet them; there are exit-level twelfth-grade standards of excellence whether any of our eighth-graders can meet them. It follows that we can *justifiably* give a B to an eighth-grade student who receives a 3 out of 10 on a very difficult, standard-referenced writing assess-

ment, just as we now give high grades to fifth-grade students even though they do not come close to meeting twelfth-grade standards. It is vital to anchor a scoring scale with a genuine standard, even if no one can (at this point in time) meet it, to ensure that the assessment does not become a minimum-competency test and to ensure that the scoring criteria are derived from genuinely excellent performances, not merely the best of current (and possibly mediocre) performances.

- *Indicators and valid descriptors of acceptable performance, not arbitrary "cut scores."* A minimum standard should correspond to some valid, qualitative distinction "in the field" or serve as a valid predictor of future success. Asking someone to type seventy words per minute with fewer than two mistakes is not arbitrary; demanding a test score of sixty or sixty-five often is. *It is also arbitrary to say that getting 80 percent on any old test is equal to "mastery,"* as many schools committed to outcomes-based education are wont to do. Such "cut scores" are typically chosen on the basis of numerical habits and norms, not by careful analysis of the meaning or impact of borderline cases of performance.
- *Demanding quality work from everyone, not arbitrary quotas.* Though people do not think of grading on a curve as setting an arbitrary quota, it of course does so. If our standard is high, and it is one we wish all students to meet, grading on a curve undercuts our mission. (Lest teachers who give all A's are viewed as lowering standards, policies should be established to distinguish between outstanding teaching and corrupted grading.)

Accountability and Local Standards

As I noted above, Dewey suggested that educators are often insincere in their views about the impact of education: we testify to its power and importance, but we rarely take responsibility for its failures. Dewey wryly reported a comment made by a friend of his that the real measure of progress in education would be the possibility of "bringing suit at law to compel payment of damages by educators to educatees for malpractice."[23] We are not there yet, but the time is close.

At the very least, we should be able to do a better job of addressing the proactive question that the superintendent of the Jefferson County (Kentucky) schools posed to his teachers and administrators: "What are you willing to guarantee?" Until we are willing to ask, answer, and act on such questions, there can be no accountability.

One New York superintendent I know has tried to do just this. She argued that since her district professed that "all children can learn," it made sense to expect all students in her district to pass all the New York Regents exams in every course. This was greeted with howls of protest by the high school faculty, who pronounced it impossible. The superintendent then turned it right around: What *was* the faculty willing to set as a target percentage for the next year? After some harrumphing, discussion, and inquiry, the faculty set themselves the goal of a passing rate some 14 percent higher for the next year than had been achieved in preceding years— and proceeded to meet the target. South Carolina did the same when it quadrupled the number of students taking Advanced Placement courses and tests and successfully sought to keep the state passing rate constant.

Whether we term it "quality control" or "accountability," the process involves a public obligation by a faculty to a set of standards, criteria, and performance targets that seem out of reach but are reachable. What matters, then, is what the total quality management movement calls "continuous progress"—the tangible and public commitment to be consistently better, in reference to the most worthy indicators. If the faculty sets clear, public targets; if the parents have a clear and present voice; if the students, former students, and institutional customers have a voice—*then* we will have accountability that will improve schools.

Notes

1.   T. Peters, *Thriving on Chaos* (New York: HarperCollins, 1987), pp. 101–102. This does *not* imply that the schools are fodder for business! It implies that every level of schooling must judge the quality of its work by the success of students at the *succeeding* levels of education and in adulthood.

2. See, for example, the Gallup poll results on public attitudes toward the six national goals developed by the governors and endorsed by the Bush administration, in which test-score data rated far below such indicators as school discipline, size of classes, and caliber of staff. S. M. Elam, "The 22nd Annual Gallup Poll of the Public's Attitudes Toward the Public Schools," *Phi Delta Kappan* 72 (1990): 41–55.

3. A. Hirschman, *Exit, Voice, and Loyalty in Firms, Organizations, and States* (Cambridge, Mass.: Harvard University Press, 1970).

4. J. E. Chubb and T. M. Moe, *Politics, Markets, and America's Schools* (Washington, D.C.: The Brookings Institution, 1990).

5. Ibid., pp. 35, 32.

6. Hirschman, *Exit, Voice, and Loyalty in Firms, Organizations, and States*, pp. 33, 43 (emphasis in the original). In fact, Hirschman presciently warns explicitly that greater competition between public and private schools would likely lead to the decline of public schools, because only the most well-educated and socially secure people will exit the public schools when their voices are not heard (see pp. 44–46).

7. Ibid., p. 37.

8. Chubb and Moe, *Politics, Markets, and America's Schools*, p. 30ff.

9. See ibid., p. 71ff. Leaving aside the technical arguments that one might get into with Chubb and Moe about their gain index, one major problem with their argument in light of the issues of this book is their unsubstantiated claim that the simplistic multiple-choice tests they used to measure gains were adequate to the task.

10. A. W. Astin, *Assessment for Excellence: The Philosophy and Practice of Assessment and Evaluation in Higher Education* (New York: American Council on Education/Macmillan, 1991), p. 17.

11. P. Ewell, "To Capture the Ineffable: New Forms of Assessment in Higher Education," in G. Grant, ed., *Review of Research in Education* (Washington, D.C.: American Educational Research Association, 1991).

12. Ibid., p. 96.

13. S. Lightfoot, *The Good School: Portraits of Character and Culture* (New York: Basic Books, 1983), p. 26.

14. See R. Callahan, *Cult of Efficiency* (Chicago: University of Chicago Press, 1962). There is a spooky similarity to the simplistic schemes devised then and now. The problems were similar then too: among them, an influx of immigrants and a perceived threat to traditional standards and past high performance.

15. Wyoming, to my knowledge, is the only state that does this; Vermont's portfolio plan is certainly in the same spirit. New York's commissioner has proposed a bold new "compact" between the state and local officials to honor this idea as well.

16. J. Dewey, "Education as Religion," in J. A. Boydston, ed., *The Middle Works of John Dewey: 1899–1924* (Carbondale: Southern Illinois University Press, [1922a] 1983), p. 318.

17. B. Caldwell and J. Spinks, *The Self-Managing School* (New York: Falmer Press, 1988).

18. Callahan, *Cult of Efficiency*.

19. Edward Elliot of the University of Wisconsin, as quoted in ibid.

20. See G. Wiggins, "Standards, Not Standardization: Evoking Quality Student Work," *Educational Leadership* 48 (1991): 18–25.

21. J. Dewey, "Mediocrity and Individuality," in J. A. Boydston, ed., *The Middle Works of John Dewey: 1899–1924* (Carbondale: Southern Illinois University Press, [1922c] 1983), p. 291. This article is worth rereading in its entirety, because Dewey carefully and astutely argues that test scores are more like data from actuarial tables than "facts" about individuals: useful for broad-brush analysis of likely trends but inadequate for predictions about individuals.

22. J. Dewey, "Individuality, Equality, and Superiority," in J. A. Boydston, ed., *The Middle Works of John Dewey: 1899–1924* (Carbondale: Southern Illinois University Press, [1922b] 1983), p. 296.

23. Dewey, "Education as Religion," p. 317 in Boydston, *The Middle Works of John Dewey*.

BIBLIOGRAPHY

Alverno College Faculty. *Assessment at Alverno College.* (Rev. ed.) Milwaukee, Wis.: Alverno College, 1985.

American Council on the Teaching of Foreign Languages. *ACTFL Provisional Proficiency Guidelines.* Hastings-on-Hudson, N.Y.: ACTFL Materials Center, 1982.

American Psychological Association. "Standards for Educational and Psychological Testing." Washington, D.C.: American Psychological Association, 1985.

Anastasi, A. *Psychological Testing.* (1st ed., 4th ed., 6th ed.) New York: Macmillan, 1954, 1976, 1988.

Archbald, D., and Newmann, F. *Beyond Standardized Testing: Authentic Academic Achievement in the Secondary School.* Reston, Va.: NASSP Publications, 1988.

Aristotle. "Nichomachean Ethics." In J. Barnes (ed.), *The Complete Works of Aristotle.* Princeton, N.J.: Princeton University Press, 1984.

Astin, A. W. *Assessment for Excellence: The Philosophy and Practice of Assessment and Evaluation in Higher Education.* New York: American Council on Education/Macmillan, 1991.

Baker, E., Freeman, M., and Clayton, S. "Cognitive Assessment of History for Large-Scale Testing." In M. C. Wittrock and E. L. Baker (eds.), *Testing and Cognition.* Englewood Cliffs, N.J.: Prentice-Hall, 1991.

Baron, J., and Sternberg, R. (eds.) *Teaching Thinking Skills*. (New York: W. H. Freeman, 1987).

Barrett, W. *The Illusion of Technique*. New York: Anchor Books, 1978.

Berk, R. A. (ed.). *Performance Assessment Methods and Applications*. Baltimore, Md.: Johns Hopkins University Press, 1986.

Berlak, H., and others. *Toward a New Science of Educational Testing and Assessment*. New York: State University of New York Press, 1992.

Berryman, S. "Sending Clear Signals to Schools and Labor Markets." In J. L. Schwartz and K. A. Viator (eds.), *The Prices of Secrecy: The Social, Intellectual, and Psychological Costs of Current Assessment Practice*. A Report to the Ford Foundation. Cambridge, Mass.: Educational Technology Center, Harvard Graduate School of Education, 1990.

Binet, A., and Simon, T. "New Methods for the Diagnosis of the Intellectual Level of Subnormals," "The Development of Intelligence in the Child," and "New Investigation upon the Measure of the Intellectual Level Among School Children." In A. Binet and T. Simon, *The Development of Intelligence in Children*. Salem, N.H.: Ayer, 1983. (Originally published 1905, 1908, 1911.)

Bishop, J. "Why the Apathy in American High Schools?" *Educational Researcher*, 1989, *18*, 6–10.

Bloom, B. S. (ed.) *Taxonomy of Educational Objectives*. Vol. 1: *Cognitive Domain*. White Plains, N.Y.: Longman, 1956.

Bloom, B. S., Madaus, G. F., and Hastings, J. T. *Evaluation to Improve Learning*. New York: McGraw-Hill, 1981.

Bok, S. *Secrets: On the Ethics of Concealment and Revelation*. New York: Random House, 1983.

Bond, R. "Making Innovative Assessment Fair and Valid." In Educational Testing Service (ed.), *What We Can Learn from Performance Assessment for the Professions*. Proceedings of the 1992 ETS Invitational Conference. Princeton, N.J.: Educational Testing Service, 1993.

Brown, J. S., and Burton, R. R. "Diagnostic Models for Procedural Bugs in Basic Mathematical Skills." *Cognitive Science*, 1978, *2*, 155–192.

Brown, J. S., Collins, A., and Duguid, P. "Situated Cognition and the Culture of Learning." *Educational Researcher,* Jan./Feb. 1989, *18,* 32–42.

Bruner, J. *The Process of Education.* Cambridge, Mass.: Harvard University Press, 1960/1977.

Bunderson, C. V., Inouye, D., and Olsen, J. "The Four Generations of Computerized Educational Measurement." in R. L. Linn, (ed.), *Educational Measurement.* (3rd ed.) New York: American Council on Education/Macmillan, 1989.

Burke, P. *You Can Lead Adolescents to a Test But You Can't Make Them Try.* Washington, D.C.: U.S. Office of Technology Assessment, U.S. Department of Commerce/National Technical Information Service, 1991.

Caldwell, B., and Spinks, J. *The Self-Managing School.* New York: Falmer Press, 1988.

Callahan, R. *Cult of Efficiency.* Chicago: University of Chicago Press, 1962.

Center on Learning, Assessment, and School Structure (CLASS). *Standards, Not Standardization.* Vol. 3: *Rethinking Student Assessment.* Geneseo, N.Y.: Center on Learning, Assessment, and School Structure, 1993.

Chickering, A., and Claxton, C. "What Is Competence?" In R. Nickse and others (eds.), *Competency-Based Education.* New York: Teachers College Press, 1981.

Chubb, J. E., and Moe, T. M. *Politics, Markets, and America's Schools.* Washington, D.C.: The Brookings Institution, 1990.

Cizek, G. J. "Confusion Effusion: A Rejoinder to Wiggins," *Phi Delta Kappan,* 1991, *73,* 150–153.

College Board. "Evaluating the AP Portfolio in Studio Art" and "General Portfolio Guidelines." In College Board, *Advanced Placement in Art.* Princeton, N.J.: ETS/CEEB, 1986.

Collins, A., Brown, J. S., and Newman, S. E. "Cognitive Apprenticeship: Teaching the Crafts of Reading, Writing, and Mathematics." In L. B. Resnick (ed.), *Knowing, Learning, and Instruction: Essays in Honor of Robert Glaser.* Hillsdale, N.J.: Erlbaum, 1989.

Congressional Office of Technology Assessment. *Testing in American Schools: Asking the Right Questions.* OTA-SET-519. Washington, D.C.: U.S. Government Printing Office, 1992.

Cronbach, L. J. *Essentials of Psychological Testing.* (4th ed., 5th ed.) New York: HarperCollins, 1984, 1990.

Csikszentmihalyi, M., and Larson, R. *Being Adolescent: Conflict and Growth in the Teenage Years.* New York: Basic Books, 1984.

Department of Education. *Assessment for Better Learning: A Public Discussion Document.* Wellington, New Zealand: Department of Education, 1989.

Department of Education and Science, Assessment Performance Unit. *Mathematical Development, Secondary Survey Report 1.* London: Her Majesty's Stationery Office, 1980.

Department of Education and Science, Assessment Performance Unit. *Science in Schools.* Report no. 1. London: Her Majesty's Stationery Office, 1981.

Department of Education and Science. Assessment Performance Unit. *Task Group on Assessment and Testing (TGAT) Report.* London: Her Majesty's Stationery Office, 1988.

Department of Health, Education, and Welfare (ed.). *The American Revolution: Selections from Secondary History Books of Other Nations.* HEW Publication OE 76-19124. Washington, D.C.: U.S. Government Printing Office, 1976.

Department of Labor. *What Work Requires of Schools: A SCANS Report for America 2000.* Washington, D.C.: U.S. Government Printing Office, 1991.

Dewey, J. "Moral Principles in Education," "Current Tendencies in Education," "Education as Religion," "Individuality, Equality, and Superiority," and "Mediocrity and Individuality." In J. A. Boydston (ed.), *The Middle Works of John Dewey: 1899–1924.* 15 vols. Carbondale: Southern Illinois University Press, 1977, 1985, 1983, 1983, 1983. (Originally published 1909, 1917, 1922a, 1922b, 1922c.)

Dewey, J. *Democracy in Education.* New York: Macmillan, 1916.

Dewey, J. *How We Think: A Restatement of the Relation of Reflective Thinking to the Educative Process.* Lexington, Mass.: Heath, 1933.

Ebel, R. L. *Measuring Educational Achievement.* Englewood Cliffs, N.J.: Prentice-Hall, 1965.

Edgerton, R. "An Assessment of Assessment." In Educational Testing Service (ed.), *Assessing the Outcomes of Higher Education.*

Proceedings of the 1986 ETS Invitational Conference. Princeton, N.J.: Educational Testing Service, 1987.

Educational Testing Service (ed.). *The Redesign of Testing for the 21st Century.* Proceedings of the 1985 ETS Invitational Conference. Princeton, N.J.: Educational Testing Service, 1986.

Educational Testing Service (ed.). *Assessing the Outcomes of Higher Education.* Proceedings of the 1986 ETS Invitational Conference. Princeton, N.J.: Educational Testing Service, 1987.

Educational Testing Service (ed.). *Assessment in the Service of Learning.* Proceedings of the 1987 ETS Invitational Conference. Princeton, N.J.: Educational Testing Service, 1988.

Educational Testing Service (ed.). *The Uses of Standardized Tests in American Education.* Proceedings of the 1989 ETS Invitational Conference. Princeton, N.J.: Educational Testing Service, 1990.

Educational Testing Service (ed.). *What We Can Learn from Performance Assessment for the Professions.* Proceedings of the 1992 ETS Invitational Conference. Princeton, N.J.: Educational Testing Service, 1993.

Elam, S. M. "The 22nd Annual Gallup Poll of the Public's Attitudes Toward the Public Schools," *Phi Delta Kappan,* 1990, *72,* 41–55.

Elbow, P. *Writing with Power: Techniques for Mastering the Writing Process.* New York: Oxford University Press, 1981.

Elbow, P. *Embracing Contraries: Explorations in Learning and Teaching.* New York: Oxford University Press, 1986.

Ennis, R. H. "A Concept of Critical Thinking," *Harvard Education Review,* 1962, *32,* 81–111.

Ennis R. H. "Critical Thinking and the Curriculum." *National Forum,* 1985, *65,* 28–31.

Ennis, R. H. "A Taxonomy of Critical Thinking Dispositions and Abilities." In J. Baron and R. Sternberg (eds.), *Teaching Thinking Skills.* New York: W. H. Freeman, 1987.

Ewell, P. "To Capture the Ineffable: New Forms of Assessment in Higher Education." In G. Grant (ed.), *Review of Research in Education.* Washington, D.C.: American Educational Research Association, 1991.

Feuer, M. J., Fulton, K., and Morrison, P. "Better Tests and Testing

Practices: Options for Policy Makers." *Phi Delta Kappan,* 1993, *74,* 530–533.

Finch, F. L. (ed.). *Educational Performance Assessment.* Chicago: Riverside/Houghton Mifflin, 1991.

Fitzpatrick, R., and Morrison, E. J. "Performance and Product Evaluation." In R. L. Thorndike (ed.), *Educational Measurement.* (2nd ed.) New York: American Council on Education/ Macmillan, 1971. (Reprinted in F. L. Finch [ed.]. *Educational Performance Assessment.* Chicago: Riverside/Houghton Mifflin, 1991.)

Foucault, M. *Discipline and Punish.* New York: Vintage Books, 1977.

Frederiksen, N. "The Real Test Bias." *American Psychologist,* 1984, *39,* 193–202.

Fredriksen, J. R., and Collins, A. "A Systems Approach to Educational Testing." *Educational Researcher,* Dec. 1989, *18,* pp. 27–32.

Gadamer, H.-G. *Truth and Method.* New York: Crossroad, 1982.

Gagné, R. "Learning Outcomes and Their Effects: Useful Categories of Human Performance." *American Psychologist,* 1984, *39,* 377–385.

Gardner, H. "Assessment in Context: The Alternative to Standardized Testing." In *Report to the Commission on Testing and Public Policy.* B. Gifford (ed.), Boston: Kluwer Academic Press, 1989.

Gardner, H. *The Unschooled Mind: How Children Think and How Schools Should Teach.* New York: Basic Books, 1991.

Gentile, C. *Exploring New Methods for Collecting Students' School-Based Writing.* Washington, D.C.: U.S. Department of Education, 1991.

Gilbert, T. F. *Human Competence.* New York: McGraw-Hill, 1978.

Gilligan, C. *In a Different Voice: Psychological Theory and Women's Development.* Cambridge, Mass.: Harvard University Press, 1982.

Gilligan, C., and Wiggins, G. "The Origins of Morality in Early Childhood Relationships." In J. Kagan and S. Lamb (eds.), *The Emergence of Morality in Young Children.* Chicago: University of Chicago Press, 1987.

Glaser, R. "A Criterion-Referenced Test." In J. Popham (ed.), *Criterion-Referenced Measurement: An Introduction*. Englewood Cliffs, N.J.: Educational Technology Publications, 1971.

Glaser, R. "The Integration of Instruction and Testing." In Educational Testing Service (ed.), *The Redesign of Testing for the 21st Century*. Proceedings of the 1985 ETS Invitational Conference. Princeton, N.J.: Educational Testing Service, 1986.

Glaser, R. "Cognitive and Environmental Perspectives on Assessing Achievement." In Educational Testing Service (ed.), *Assessment in the Service of Learning*. Proceedings of the 1987 ETS Invitational Conference. Princeton, N.J.: Educational Testing Service, 1988.

Glaser, R. "Expertise and Assessment." In M. C. Wittrock and E. L. Baker (eds.), *Testing and Cognition*. Englewood Cliffs, N.J.: Prentice-Hall, 1991.

Goodlad, J. I. *A Place Called School: Prospects for the Future*. New York: McGraw-Hill, 1984.

Gould, S. J. *The Mismeasure of Man*. New York: W. W. Norton, 1981.

Gragg, C. "Because Wisdom Can't Be Told." in M. P. McNair and A. C. Hersum (eds.), *The Case Method at the Harvard Business School*. New York: McGraw-Hill, 1954. (Available as a reprint from the Harvard Business School Publishing Division, Boston, Mass. HBS Case 9-451-005.)

Grant, G. (ed.). *Review of Research in Education*. Washington, D.C.: American Educational Research Association, 1991.

Grant, G., and Associates. *On Competence: A Critical Analysis of Competence-Based Reforms in Higher Education*. San Francisco: Jossey-Bass, 1979.

Grant, G., and Kohli, W. "Assessing Student Performance." In G. Grant and Associates, *On Competence: A Critical Analysis of Competence-Based Reforms in Higher Education*. San Francisco: Jossey-Bass, 1979.

Hamlyn, D. W. "The Logical and Psychological Aspects of Learning." In R. S. Peters (ed.), *The Concept of Education*. New York: Routledge & Kegan Paul, 1967.

Haney, W. "Testing Reasoning and Reasoning About Testing." *Review of Educational Research*, 1984, *54*, 597–654.

Haney, W. "Making Testing More Educational." *Educational Leadership,* 1985, *43,* 4–13.

Haney, W. "We Must Take Care: Fitting Assessment to Functions." in V. Perrone (ed.), *Expanding Student Assessment for Supervision and Curriculum Development.* Alexandria, Va.: Association for Supervision and Curriculum Development, 1991.

Haney, W., and Madaus, G. "The Evolution of Ethical and Technical Standards for Testing." In R. K. Hambleton (ed.), *Advances in Educational and Psychological Testing: Theory and Applications.* Norwell, Mass.: Kluwer, 1991.

Haney, W., and Scott, L. "Talking with Children About Tests: An Exploratory Study of Test Item Ambiguity." In K. O. Freedle and R. P. Duran (eds.), *Cognitive and Linguistic Analyses of Test Performance.* Norwood, N.J.: Ablex, 1987.

Henderson, E. H. *Teaching Spelling.* (2nd ed.) Boston: Houghton Mifflin, 1990.

Highland, R. W. *A Guide for Use in Performance Testing in Air Force Technical Schools.* Lowry Air Force Base, Colo.: Armament Systems Personnel Research Laboratory, 1955.

Hippocrates. "Fractures," *Hippocratic Writings.* (G. E. R. Lloyd, ed., and J. Chadwick and M. N. Mann, trans.). New York: Viking Penguin, 1983.

Hirschman, A. *Exit, Voice, and Loyalty in Firms, Organizations, and States.* Cambridge, Mass.: Harvard University Press, 1970.

Hirst, P. H. "The Logical and Psychological Aspects of Teaching a Subject." In R. S. Peters (ed.), *The Concept of Education.* New York: Routledge & Kegan Paul, 1967.

International Baccalaureate Examination Office. *Extended Essay Guidelines.* Cardiff, Wales: International Baccalaureate Examination Office, 1991.

James, W. *Talks to Teachers.* New York: W. W. Norton, 1958. (Originally published 1899.)

Kandel, I., *Examinations and Their Substitutes in the United States* (reprinted from *American Education,* Men, Ideas and Institutions Series II). New York: Arno Press, (1936) 1971.

Kentucky General Assembly. *Kentucky Education Reform Act (KERA).* House Bill 940, 1990.

Kiddle, H., and Schem, A. J. (eds.). *The Cyclopaedia of Education.* New York: E. Steiger, 1877.

Kline, M. *Mathematics in Western Culture.* New York: Oxford University Press, 1953.

Kline, M. *Mathematics: The Loss of Certainty.* New York: Oxford University Press, 1980.

Kuhn, T. S. *The Structure of Scientific Revolutions.* (2nd ed.) Chicago: University of Chicago Press, 1970.

Lewis, N. (trans.). *Hans Andersen's Fairy Tales: A New Translation.* London: Puffin Books, 1981.

Lightfoot, S. *The Good School: Portraits of Character and Culture.* New York: Basic Books, 1983.

Linn, R. "Barriers to New Test Designs." In Educational Testing Service (ed.), *The Redesign of Testing for the 21st Century.* Proceedings of the 1985 ETS Invitational Conference. Princeton, N.J.: Educational Testing Service, 1986.

Linn, R. (ed.). *Educational Measurement.* (3rd ed.) New York: American Council on Education/Macmillan, 1989.

Linn, R. "Educational Assessment: Expanded Expectations and Challenges." *Educational Evaluation and Policy Analysis,* 1993, *15,* 1–16.

Linn, R., Baker, E., and Dunbar, S. "Complex, Performance-Based Assessment: Expectations and Validation Criteria." *Educational Researcher,* 1991, *20,*15–21.

Lowell, A. L. "The Art of Examination." *Atlantic Monthly,* 1926, *137,* 58–66.

McClelland, D. "Testing for Competence Rather Than for 'Intelligence.'" *American Psychologist,* 1973, *28,* 1–14.

McCloskey, M., Carramazza, A., and Green, B. "Curvilinear Motion in the Absence of External Forces." *Science,* 1980, *210,* 1139–1141.

Madaus, G., and others. *From Gatekeeper to Gateway: Transforming Testing in America.* Chestnut Hill, Mass.: National Commission on Testing and Public Policy, Boston College, 1990.

Messick, S. "Meaning and Values in Test Validation: The Science and Ethics of Assessment." *Educational Researcher,* 1989a, *18,* 5–11.

Messick, S. "Validity." In R. Linn, (ed.), *Educational Measurement.*

(3rd ed.) New York: American Council on Education/Macmillan, 1989b.

Millman, J., and Greene, J. "The Specification and Development of Tests of Achievement and Ability." In R. Linn (ed.), *Educational Measurement*. (3rd ed.) New York: American Council on Education/Macmillan, 1989.

Mitchell, R. *Testing for Learning*. New York: Free Press/Macmillan, 1992.

National Assessment of Educational Progress. *Learning by Doing: A Manual for Teaching and Assessing Higher-Order Thinking in Science and Mathematics*. Princeton, N.J.: Educational Testing Service, 1987.

The National Center for Research on Evaluation, Standards, and Student Testing (CRESST). *The CRESST Line* (quarterly publication of the University of California, Los Angeles, Graduate School of Education), Winter 1993.

Neumann, W. "Educational Responses to the Concern for Proficiency." In G. Grant and Associates (eds.), *On Competence: A Critical Analysis of Competence-Based Reforms in Higher Education*. San Francisco: Jossey-Bass, 1979.

Nickse, R., and others. *Competency-Based Education*. New York: Teachers College Press, 1981.

Nuland, S. B. "The Gentle Surgeon." In S. B. Nuland, *Doctors: The Biography of Medicine*. New York: Vintage Books, 1988.

Oakes, J. *Keeping Track: How Schools Structure Inequality*. New Haven, Conn.: Yale University Press, 1985.

Office of Strategic Services. *Assessment of Men: Selection of Personnel for the Office of Strategic Services*. Troy, Mo.: Holt, Rinehart & Winston, 1948.

Page, D. P. *Theory and Practice of Teaching: or The Motives and Methods of Good School-Keeping*. Savage, Md.: Barnes & Noble, 1953. (Originally published 1847.)

Passmore, J. *The Philosophy of Teaching*. Cambridge, Mass.: Harvard University Press, 1980.

Perry, W. G., Jr. *Forms of Intellectual and Ethical Development in the College Years*. (Rev. ed.) Troy, Mo.: Holt, Rinehart & Winston, 1970.

Peters, R. S. (ed.). *The Concept of Education*. New York: Routledge & Kegan Paul, 1967.

Peters, T. *Thriving on Chaos*. New York: HarperCollins, 1987.

Piaget, J. *The Child's Conception of the World*. (J. Tomlinson and A Tomlinson, trans.) Totowa, N.J.: Rowman & Allanheld, 1983. (Originally published 1929.)

Piaget, J. *The Language and Thought of the Child*. (M. Gabain, trans.) New York: New American Library, 1974. (Originally published 1932.)

Piaget, J. *The Moral Judgment of the Child*. New York: Macmillan, 1965. (Originally published 1932.)

Piaget, J. "Affective Unconscious and the Cognitive Unconscious." In J. Piaget, *The Child and Reality: Problems of Genetic Psychology*. New York: Grossman, 1973.

Raven, J. "A Model of Competence, Motivation, and Behavior, and a Paradigm for Assessment." In H. Berlak and others, *Toward a New Science of Educational Testing and Assessment*. New York: State University of New York Press, 1992.

Ravitch, D. R., and Finn, C. E., Jr., *What Do Our 17-year-Olds Know?* New York: HarperCollins, 1987.

Resnick, D. P., and Resnick, L. B. "Standards, Curriculum, and Performance: A Historical and Comparative Perspective." *Educational Researcher*, 1985, *14*, 5–21.

Resnick, L. B. *Education and Learning to Think*. Washington, D.C.: National Academy Press, 1987.

Resnick, L. B. "Tests as Standards of Achievement in School." In Educational Testing Service (ed.), *The Uses of Standardized Tests in American Education*. Proceedings of the 1989 ETS Invitational Conference. Princeton, N.J.: Educational Testing Services, 1990.

Riesman, D. "Society's Demands for Competence." In G. Grant and Associates, *On Competence: A Critical Analysis of Competence-Based Reforms in Higher Education*. San Francisco: Jossey-Bass, 1979.

Rogers, G. *Validating College Outcomes with Institutionally Developed Instruments: Issues in Maximizing Contextual Validity*. Milwaukee, Wis.: Office of Research and Evaluation, Alverno College, 1988.

Roid, G. H., and Haladyna, T. M. *A Technology for Test-Item Writing.* Orlando, Fla.: Harcourt Brace Jovanovich, 1982.

Ryle, G. *The Concept of Mind.* London: Hutchinson House, 1949.

Schwab, J. J. *Science, Curriculum, and Liberal Education.* Chicago: University of Chicago Press, 1978.

Schwartz, J. L., and Viator, K. A. (eds.). *The Prices of Secrecy: The Social, Intellectual, and Psychological Costs of Testing in America.* A Report to the Ford Foundation. Cambridge, Mass.: Educational Technology Center, Harvard Graduate School of Education, 1990.

Senge, P. M. *The Fifth Discipline: The Art and Practice of the Learning Organization.* New York: Doubleday, 1990.

Shanker, A. "A Good Job for Good Grades" (in his Where We Stand column). *New York Times,* March 5, 1989.

Shanker, A. "The Social and Educational Dilemmas of Test Use." In Educational Testing Service (ed.), *The Uses of Standardized Tests in American Education.* Proceedings of the 1989 ETS Invitational Conference. Princeton, N.J.: Educational Testing Service, 1990.

Shepard, L. "Why We Need Better Assessments." *Educational Leadership,* 1989, *46,* 4-9.

Shoenfeld, A. H. "Problem Solving in Context(s)." In R. Charles and E. Silver, (eds.), *The Teaching and Assessing of Mathematical Problem Solving.* Reston, Va.: National Council of Teachers of Mathematics/Erlbaum, 1988.

Sizer, T. R. *Horace's Compromise: The Dilemma of the American High School.* Boston: Houghton Mifflin, 1984.

Sizer, T. R. *Horace's School: Redesigning the American High School.* Boston: Houghton Mifflin, 1991.

Slavin, R. E. (ed.) *Using Student Team Learning.* (3rd ed.) Baltimore, Md.: Johns Hopkins University Press, 1986.

Smith, F. *Insult to Intelligence: The Bureaucratic Invasion of Our Classrooms.* Portsmouth, N.H.: Heinemann Educational Books, 1986.

Snow, R. E. "Progress in Measurement, Cognitive Science, and Technology That Can Change the Relation Between Instruction and Assessment." In Educational Testing Service (ed.), *Assessment in the Service of Learning.* Proceedings of the 1987 ETS

Invitational Conference. Princeton, N.J.: Educational Testing Service, 1988.

Stiggins, R. "Assessment Literacy." *Phi Delta Kappan,* 1991, *72,* 534–539.

Terenzini, P. "The Case for Unobtrusive Measures." In Educational Testing Service (ed.), *Assessing the Outcomes of Higher Education.* Proceedings of the 1986 ETS Invitational Conference. Princeton, N.J.: Educational Testing Service, 1987.

Thorndike, E. *Educational Psychology.* Vol. 1. New York: Teachers College Press, 1913.

Thorndike, R. L. and Hagan, E. P. *Measurement and Evaluation in Psychology and Education.* (4th ed.) New York: Wiley, 1955.

Van Manen, M. *The Tact of Teaching: The Meaning of Pedagogical Thoughtfulness.* New York: State University of New York Press, 1991.

Ward, W. C. "Measurement Research That Will Change Test Design for the Future." In Educational Testing Service (ed.), *Assessment in the Service of Learning.* Proceedings of the 1987 ETS Invitational Conference. Princeton, N.J.: Educational Testing Service, 1988.

Weaver, C. *Understanding Whole Language.* Portsmouth, N.H.: Heinemann Educational Books, 1990.

White, E. E. *Elements of Pedagogy.* New York: Van Antwerp, Bragg, 1886.

Wiggins, G. "Rational Numbers: Scoring and Grading that Helps Rather Than Hurts Learning." *American Educator,* Winter 1988, 20–48.

Wiggins, G. "A True Test: Toward More Authentic and Equitable Assessment." *Phi Delta Kappan,* 1989a, *70,* 703–713.

Wiggins, G. "Teaching to the (Authentic) Test." *Educational Leadership,* 1989b, *46,* 41–47.

Wiggins, G. "Secure Tests, Insecure Test Takers." In J. L. Schwartz and K. A.. Viator (eds.), *The Prices of Secrecy: The Social, Intellectual and Psychological Costs of Testing in America.* A Report to the Ford Foundation. Cambridge, Mass.: Educational Technology Center, Harvard Graduate School of Education, 1990.

Wiggins, G. "Standards, Not Standardization: Evoking Quality Student Work." *Educational Leadership,* 1991, *48,* 18–25.

Wiggins, G. "Creating Tests Worth Taking." *Educational Leadership,* 1992, *49,* 26–33.

Wittrock, M. C., and Baker, E. L. *Testing and Cognition.* Englewood Cliffs, N.J.: Prentice-Hall, 1991.

Wolf, D. "Opening Up Assessment." *Educational Leadership,* 1987/1988, *44,* 24–29.

Wolf, D. "Portfolio Assessment: Sampling Student Work." *Educational Leadership,* 1989, *46,* 35–39.

Wolf, D., Bixby, J., Glen, J., III, and Gardner, H. "To Use Their Minds Well: Investigating New Forms of Student Assessment." In G. Grant (ed.), *Review of Research in Education.* Washington, D.C.: American Educational Research Association, 1991.

Zacharias, J. "The People Should Get What They Want: An Optimistic View of What Tests Can Be." *National Elementary Principal,* 1979, *58,* 41–45.

INDEX

A

Accountability: aspects of, 15, 256–291; concept of, 257; and expectations, 285–288; fairness and equity in, 268; and local standards, 288–289; and meritocracy, 270–274; as responsiveness, 256–266; and school districts, 274–282; and secrecy, 86; and standards, 282–285; unit of, 264; and value added, 266–270, 280

Accreditation, and accountability, 270, 279–280

Addams, J., 131

Admissions, maximal qualification for, 167–168, 180

Admissions offices, as rejection offices, 107, 180

Advanced Placement (AP): and art portfolios, 54, 164, 197; and incentives, 154; and public tests, 97; and resources, 200, 235; scoring rubric for, 52–53, 70, 165; as standard, 46, 173, 282, 289

Albermarle Paper Co. v. *Moody*, 21

Alberta, Canada: accountability in, 266, 269, 273; writing assessment in, 57

Allen, S., 55

Alverno College: complex perfor-mances at, 17, 32; contextual validity at, 232; and self-assessment, 53–54

Amateur Athletic Union, 286

Ambiguity, morality of, 124–132

American Automobile Association (AAA), 184

American College Testing (ACT), 91, 167

American Council on Education, 227

American Council on the Teaching of Foreign Languages, 159, 238–239, 253

American Educational Research Association, 19

American Psychological Association (APA): Ethical Principles of, 19, 81, 94; Standards of, 20–21, 32, 81, 105, 119, 225

Anastasi, A., 243–244, 245, 255

Apple Computer, 277

Archbald, D., 71

Aristotle, 50, 125, 136

Artistry, concept of, 38

ARTS PROPEL, 64

Assessment: and accountability, 256–291; and aims of education, 34–37, 209, 216, 217, 247; aspects of, 1–33; and authenticity, 206–255; better forms of, 3–6; bill of